Arctic Homeland

Arctic Homeland

Kinship, Community and Development in Northwest Greenland

Mark Nuttall

University of Toronto Press
Toronto   Buffalo

First published in North America by University of Toronto Press 1992

Published in Britain by Belhaven Press 1992

ISBN 0–8020–2886–1 (cloth)
ISBN 0–8020–7391–3 (paper)

Canadian Cataloguing in Publication Data

Nuttall, Mark
    Arctic homeland

Includes index.
ISBN 0-8020-2886-1 (bound) ISBN 0-8020-7391-3 (pbk.)

1. Inuit - Greenland.* I. Title.

E99. E7N8 1992   998.2'004971   C92-093802-7

Printed and bound in Great Britain

Contents

Acknowledgements   vi

List of acronyms   vii

1. Introduction   1

2. Inuit communities, the Arctic frontier and the emergence of
    modern Greenland   12

3. Hunting and contemporary subsistence in northwest
    Greenland   24

4. Landscape and memoryscape   38

5. Becoming a person   59

6. Becoming kin   76

7. Strangers   101

8. Loss, loneliness and return   118

9. Sharing and the ideology of subsistence   136

10. Community and development   155

11. An Arctic homeland in the modern world   175

References   183

Select glossary   189

Index   191

Acknowledgements

My research in Northwest Greenland was made possible by an Economic and Social Research Council Competition Award, which included an additional twelve months of funding to enable me to get to grips with the Greenlandic language. This book is a revised version of my Ph.D thesis, which was undertaken at the Scott Polar Research Institute, Cambridge. Thanks go to many people there, including my supervisor Piers Vitebsky. During the process of writing, I also received help and advice from Jean Briggs, Charles Jedrej, Liz Cruwys, Beau Riffenburgh and Alan Barnard. They all read and commented on various parts of the draft, while David Riches and Leo Howe deserve special mention for the suggestions they made to the entire work. Thanks must go to Jayne Nuttall, who helped with typing much of the original manuscript.

Throughout the project I received much needed encouragement from my parents, John and Patricia Nuttall, and from Alix Kalim. It is impossible to do justice to their support with a simple acknowledgement such as this.

My fieldwork, however, would not have been possible without the kindness and hospitality of numerous people in Greenland. My thanks to Robert Petersen, Keld Hansen, Henrik de Renuard and Marie Holm who all gave advice in Nuuk. Henrik Bay made sure I caught the boat from Ilulissat, Upernavik Kommune provided me with accommodation while I made arrangements to leave for my chosen field site, John Spielman cheered me up with his enthusiasm for icebergs, and David and Lone Kristiansen kept a space on their floor where I could roll out a sleeping bag whenever I passed through Upernavik town. Hans Poulsen provided much needed room and endless supplies of tea whenever I needed to work on my notes, or to simply escape for an hour or two. Finn O. Kapel and Lars Reimers brought conversation and whisky during a short field visit, while Joanna and Ulrik Poulsen slowed down my re-entry home while I made a stopover in south Greenland.

Finally, while I have chosen to protect the anonymity of the people of Kangersuatsiaq, the fact that I do not mention any of them by name here does not mean that I carry any reservations about my experiences. Only I know what their hospitality and kindness has meant to me. Their acceptance of a stranger was unquestioning, and I feel privileged to have shared something of their way of life. I dedicate this book to them, but especially: *Johannsikkunnut. Qujanaq.*

List of acronyms

ANCSA	Alaskan Native Claims Settlement Act
GTO	Grønlandsk Teknisk Organisation/Greenland Technical Organization (now called Nuna-Tek)
ICC	Inuit Circumpolar Conference
KGH	Kongelige Grønlandsk Handelskompagni/ Royal Greenland Trade Company
KNI	Kalaallit Niuerfiat/Greenland Trade
KTU	Kalaallit Tunisassiorfiat (the processing division of the KNI)

1

Introduction

An Arctic homeland

During the 1960s and 1970s, social anthropological research in the Arctic devoted much energy to studying ethnic conflicts between indigenous Inuit and transient Whites, the latter being seen as representatives of colonialism. In Greenland differences between Inuit and Danes were founded upon an ideological, as well as ethnic, conflict that stemmed from two and a half centuries of Danish colonial and post-colonial rule. The introduction of Home Rule in Greenland in 1979 was the eventual outcome of this conflict.

Greenlandic Inuit were regarded as unique in that they were, and still are, the only population of Inuit origin to have attained a degree of independence. During the 1980s, however, there was a gradual shift from an initial Inuit ethnic identity to an identity now defined in political and national terms (Dahl 1988). As approximately one fifth of the total population of 55,000 is Danish, the Greenlandic Home Rule government (consisting entirely of native Inuit) now claims to represent the interests of both Inuit and Danes living in the country.

This transition to political identity is illustrated by Home Rule government aims and policies, known as 'Greenlandization' (*Grønlandisering*), which are concerned with increasing revenues from renewable and non-renewable resource exploitation as a way of achieving greater political and economic independence from Denmark. Most notably, throughout the 1980s, the ruling Siumut party concentrated on developing the fishing industry. While Greenlandization is an economic and political process, it is also ideological, stressing national identity. This is not only illustrated by economic policy, but by the social and political dominance of West Greenlandic (Kitaamiutut), the official and majority dialect of the Greenlandic Inuit language Kalaallisut.

The new emphasis on a national Greenlandic identity, however, together with policies of economic development, now comes into conflict

1

with emerging local level identities and interests. While the years leading to self-government emphasized an ethnic identity and sense of distinctiveness of Inuit *vis-á-vis* Danes, the years since Home Rule have seen a gradual expression of Inuit identities *vis-á-vis* other Inuit identities within Greenland. In the more peripheral areas of Greenland, most notably the hunting districts, the local concern is with the extent to which the development of a commercial inshore fishing industry is detrimental to the hunting way of life.

This book deals with a localized, as opposed to national, identity in Northwest Greenland by exploring a complex framework of shared values, norms and moral codes which provide a sense of continuity and of community. For the greater part of my fieldwork, totalling twenty months in 1987–8, I lived in Kangersuatsiaq (Map 3), a village in the southern part of Upernavik district (Map 2). Although I established friendships in the villages of Kullorsuaq and Nutaarmiut, which I visited several times, the material presented here either comes from Kangersuatsiaq, or is directly relevant to it.

My research interests were concerned with community (see below) and kinship. I was particularly interested in contemporary Inuit ideas of the person, the ideology of subsistence, and the importance of seal hunting for identity and a sense of place. This was necessary to understand in order to evaluate the potential compatibility of subsistence sealing with economic development. One of the most central features of community cognition is a person's name. It underpins a system of values that continues to be important to people as they find themselves part of an emerging Greenland in an increasingly complex world. The name pervades virtually every aspect of life in Kangersuatsiaq and this book tries to convey some idea of its importance. It is impossible to understand kinship in Upernavik district, for example, without recognizing how names influence the application of terminology for terms of address. Later chapters explore this, together with what meanings names and kinship have for different people.

While much has been written on Greenlandic society, mainly by Danes, I know of no contemporary social anthropological work dealing with the ethnography of the southern part of Upernavik district. The northernmost villages have been the subjects of eskimological and geographical investigation in the past (see Jørgensen et al 1978, LeMouel 1978, Haller 1986), but the district as a whole has escaped extensive anthropological scrutiny. Although feelings of intrusiveness never left me, my initial sense of unease about being an inquisitive outsider relaxed when I was adopted by a local family. What I learned about life in Northwest Greenland came from the family who took time to teach me and allowed me to become a member of their community. The difficulties arise now that I attempt to translate aspects of their culture in a social anthropological fashion.

This work does not set out to be an authoritative account of Inuit culture in Upernavik district. Like most ethnographies it deals with context, although anthropologists enjoy the privilege of using the ethnographic present and doubtless this work makes claims that 'people

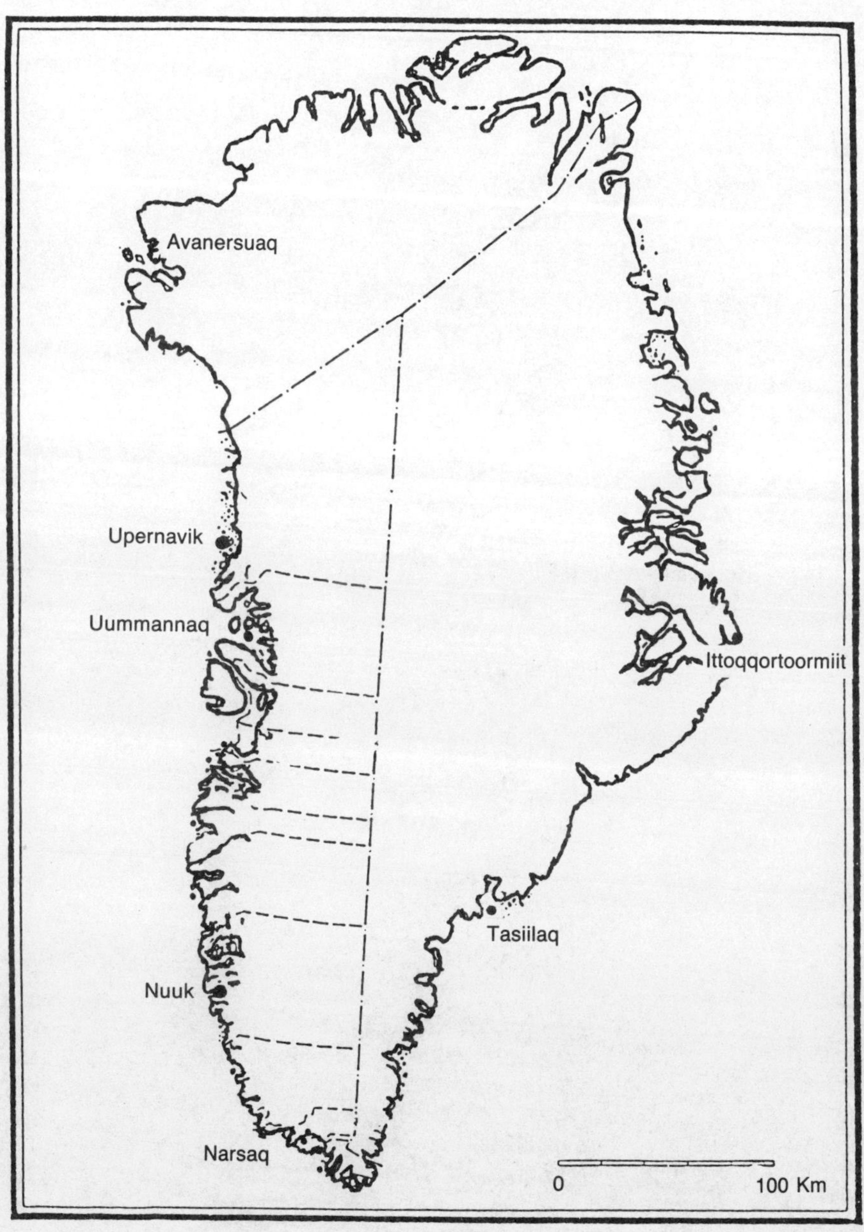

Map 1 Greenland

Map 2 Upernavik district

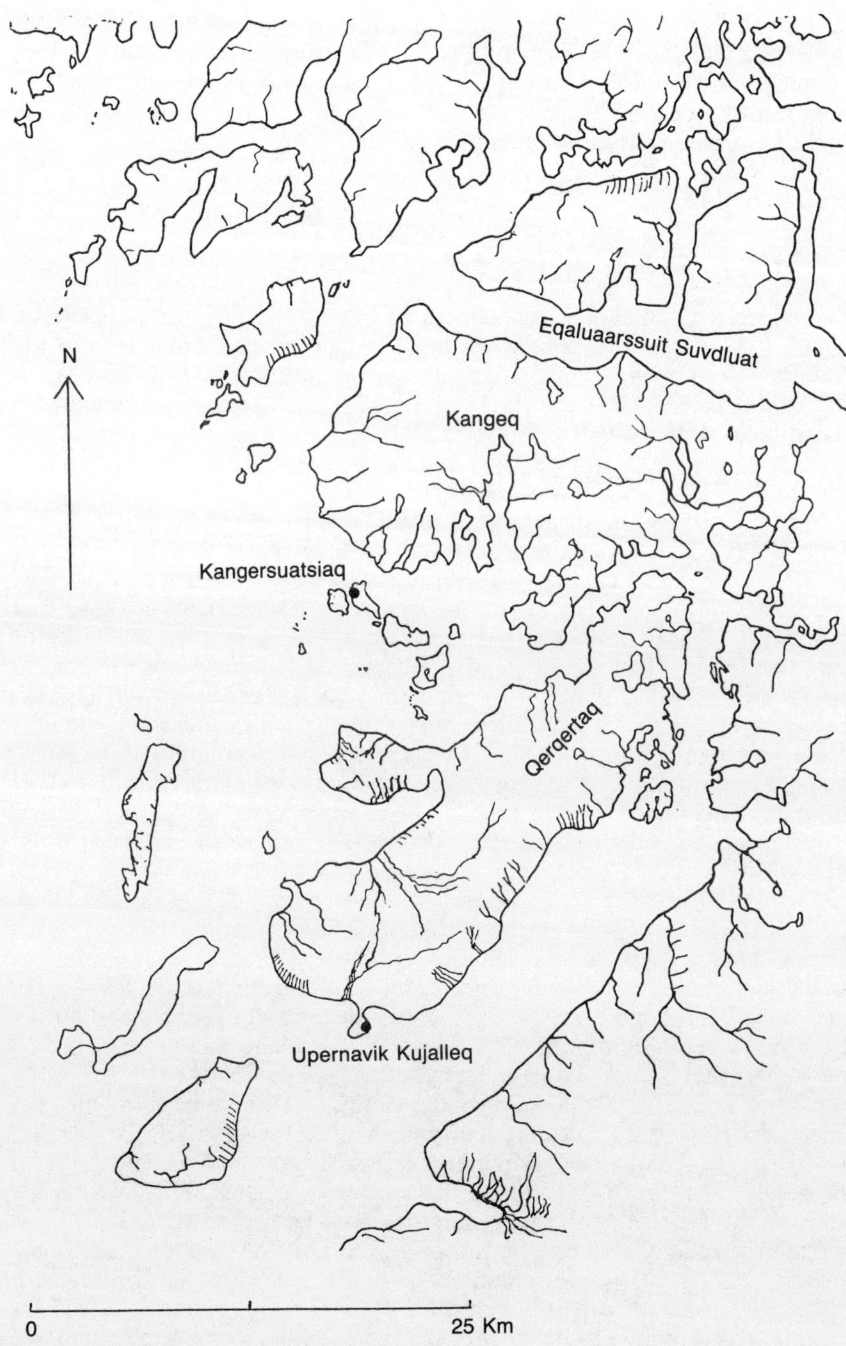

Map 3 Kangersuatsiaq and immediate area

do this' and 'people in Kangersuatsiaq think such and such'. On the basis of only a transitory journey through other people's lives, I am wary of attempts at definitive analysis. At best, any anthropological work can only hope to be provisional. Through ethnography and narrative I try to build up a picture that is illustrative of life in the southern part of Upernavik.

Dramatis personae – Josepi's family

Several characters appear throughout the text. They are the people with whom I developed the closest relationships and most are members of the family I lived with. I have changed their names but not, I hope, their essential qualities and warmth. I have chosen not to use a pseudonym for the village. Along with Upernavik Kujalleq, Kangersuatsiaq is one of two villages south of Upernavik town and this type of study would run into difficulties if I tried to conceal its location.

When I arrived in Kangersuatsiaq, I spent one week living in the schoolhouse. During this time, because of language difficulties, I found it difficult to make contact with the villagers. Later, many told me they were shy and reluctant to invite me into their homes. During those first few days, I began to despair of the seemingly linguistic impossibility of ever learning Greenlandic and 'succeeding' as an anthropological fieldworker. Then late one afternoon towards the end of my first week, David, a hunter in his late thirties, came to the schoolhouse and asked if I wanted to go fishing with him. Through a combination of sign language and the occasional Danish word, he explained it would be for the whole summer. We would live in tents at his family campsite to the east of Kangersuatsiaq. His idea was to hire me as a fisherman and what I did not know he would teach me.

David returned the following day to collect me and we set off in his boat with his wife, Aninnguaq, and their two young children. Upon arrival at the camp we were greeted by David's brother Eirik, some six years his junior. Eirik had returned from south Greenland the year before and was now living in his father's house. We erected our tents and before long we were enjoying mugs of steaming tea, while the children played down by the water's edge. Shortly after, we heard the whine of an outboard motor as it approached the camp. It became clear to me that it was Josepi, David's father, returning from a day's search for capelin. I had first heard of Josepi while in Upernavik town and was advised that he would be a useful informant. I watched as he was welcomed by his sons on the far side of the bay, close to where he had his tent. Josepi had already been in the camp for a month and his tent was surrounded by fishing gear, plastic boxes, supplies of benzine, various species of dried fish, rifles, piles of driftwood and an outboard motor. He took off his fishing overclothes, put on his flat cap and walked over to meet me. We attempted a conversation in faltering Danish while Aninnguaq cooked a pot of seal meat over the primus stove.

In the days that followed we were joined by Josepi's youngest son Juuna, a quiet man in his late twenties, and by his two daughters Lydia and Naja, and their children. A week later, two of Aninnguaq's sisters and their husbands also came to the camp from Nutaarmiut. Over the next few weeks, I learned to fish and even started to dream in Greenlandic. Camp life was only occasionally interrupted by visits to Kangersuatsiaq for food staples such as bread, sugar, tea and coffee, and for ammunition and benzine.

During this time I was trying to arrange accommodation in Kangersuatsiaq. There were no free houses available and word had been put around that I was looking for lodgings. There were several possibilities, yet no definite offers. Most families in Kangersuatsiaq are large and their houses small and I was a stranger, a *tuluk* (Englishman). While some people understood my reasons for wanting to stay, most, I learned later, believed I would remain for only a few weeks before returning home. Because I was away from Kangersuatsiaq living in the camp it was also unreasonable of me to expect that anyone would take me into their home on the basis of having had little or no interaction with me.

Towards the end of the summer, Josepi and Naja told me that I could be part of their family while I was in Greenland. Juuna had arranged for me to live in his house, as Josepi's home was overcrowded and Marie, his wife, was housebound and suffering from cancer. It was agreed that I should live as a family member, helping with simple household tasks as well as hunting and fishing activities. At the beginning of the autumn we moved back to the village and I found myself a corner in Juuna's one-room house.

When I first met him, Josepi was 63 and had a reputation as an *ilisimatooq*, a wise or learned man. Both he and his family were the first in Kangersuatsiaq to agree to help me in my work, the direction of which was influenced by my role as extended household member. My association with Josepi's family allowed me glimpses of how people think about others who are given the names of deceased relatives. Four months after my arrival, Josepi's wife died. One year later, Josepi himself died suddenly after a brief illness. The belief that the name is like a person's soul (see Chapter 5) means that people never simply die; they continue because the name remains on earth. This sense of continuity is central for an understanding of community. The continuity of the person allows for the continuity of personal relationships, social life and consciousness of community. It also helps to ameliorate social change (see Chapter 10). There are parallels between the human and animal worlds, in that people and seals have souls. Seal souls must be propitiated to ensure the continued return of the animals on whom people most depend. Names, kinship and community inform the ideology of subsistence (Chapter 9) which expresses a concern for others through sharing and sentiment.

While not setting out to describe the social structure of the village, this ethnography focuses on the way Kangersuatsiaq is expressed and thought about as a community by its members. It is therefore necessary to discuss what I mean by community, a concern of much anthropological debate and something that evades definition.

Symbolism and the idea of community

In the past, social anthropological and sociological discussion of community has tended to concentrate on social structure and society's various interlocking institutions. It has also brooded about how social change forces small-scale societies to undergo a process of fragmentation resulting in the acceptance of behaviour and values of the dominant society (e.g. Mair 1963, Wilson and Wilson 1954). More recently, however, the work of social anthropologists has shown that the old cultural repertoire may survive below the surface as 'subterranean' attitudes (see, e.g. for the Inuit, Briggs 1985: 1). Even when social change has undermined the former structural bases of a cultural group, ethnic identity often assumes a new expression in the form of conscious ethnicity (e.g. Epstein 1978).

In the Arctic, ethnic boundary maintenance has been a persistent theme for many researchers (e.g. Ben-Dor 1966, Kennedy 1982). In particular, Ben-Dor's study of Makkovik on the Labrador coast questioned the definition of community as a small-scale parochial social organisation with interaction based on well-established relationships. Instead, he argued that Inuit and Settlers, the two ethnic groups in Makkovik, lived in a 'multi-cellular' community. Both maintained their cultural identity and remained socially distant. Some ten years later, Kennedy's re-study of Makkovik explored the differences between Inuit and Settlers against a background of recent changes in lifestyle and the economy. The two groups still shared a similar territory and economy but idiosyncratic meaning was used in emphasizing difference. Despite a certain convergence in lifestyle, Kennedy is led to conclude that the 'contemporary process of symbolically demarcating separate domains suggests that, even today, both peoples are "holding the line"' (1982: 134).

This symbolic demarcation, the creation and maintenance of a boundary, is a theoretical perspective explored by Cohen in his concern with the symbolic construction of community (see Cohen 1985, 1986, 1987). Cohen's approach does not suggest a new definition of what is meant by community, but instead he concentrates his 'examination of the nature of community on the element which embodies . . . [a] sense of discrimination, namely, the boundary' (1985: 12). In placing the emphasis on what people have in common and how they use this to distinguish themselves from other groups, Cohen does not concentrate on social structure but on the symbolic aspect of the community boundary. By regarding symbolism as allowing a capacity to make meaning, in the sense of there being nothing inherent in a symbol that informs people how to act towards it, he sees community as a phenomenon that has a complexity of cultural symbols. Each symbol has a different meaning for every member of the community. 'The symbols of community are mental constructs: they provide people with the means to make meaning. In so doing, they also provide them with the means to express the particular meanings which the community has for them' (ibid: 19).

Cohen's study of Whalsay, in Shetland, shows how the community boundary is constituted symbolically. Despite recent social and economic change from a subsistence-based crofting society to a modern, capital-intensive commercial fishing economy, the people of Whalsay still maintain a profound sense of cultural identity. Whalsay islanders may share a similar lifestyle with people in mainland Britain, but this does not suggest that their sense of distinctiveness, of 'being Whalsa', cannot be sustained and expressed (Cohen 1987).

Kangersuatsiarmiit

In this book, 'community' refers to what continues to be important to the people of Kangersuatsiaq. The chapters which follow explore a sense of belonging, locality and continuity. Sentiment, kinship, friendship and fellowship are part of the system of values which are important for identity. Among Inuit groups this identity and sense of place is most immediately expressed with the suffix *-miut*, meaning 'people of'. The people of Kangersuatsiaq are no exception. While being Greenlanders (Kalaallit), at the same time they define themselves as Kangersuatsiarmiut, or more often in the vernacular Kangersuatsiarmiit (*-miut* becomes *-miit* in the Kangersuatsiaq dialect). In this way they express their attachment to their locality and distinguish themselves from the people of Upernavik (Upernavimmiut), from the people of Kullorsuaq (Kullorsuarmiut), and so on.

Over the past few years there have been changes in Upernavik district, most notably technological. However, this has not harmed the hunting culture to any great extent. Haller showed how 'the new implement can be "adapted" into the Greenlandic culture without a change in the Greenlander's spatial organisation within his surroundings' (1986: 139). Real threats to the subsistence lifestyle come from animal-rights groups and environmentalists and, as later chapters show, from Greenlanders themselves who occupy political positions and are ambitious for economic development.

For the Kangersuatsiarmiit a consciousness of belonging finds expression in the local environment (Chapter 4), in naming and kinship (Chapters 5 and 6), and in sharing (Chapter 9). There is also a consciousness of the encroachment of the outside world and this leads to some form of symbolic expression of belonging to Kangersuatsiaq (see ideas of being a 'genuine Greenlander' in Chapter 9, and Chapter 7 on strangers). So, as well as feelings of having something in common (such as sharing something of each other through the name), there is also a sense of being different from others. The rhetoric of a homogeneous Greenlandic community (Chapter 2) obscures the very diversity within Greenland itself. Chapter 11 suggests that this diversity can be sustained as communities symbolize their identities and absorb change through the transformation of new developments into an existing cultural framework.

Haller's (1986) study of Nuussuaq in northern Upernavik district is important in its concern with understanding the location of communities in relation to their hunting territories. In Chapter 4 I elaborate on Haller by exploring how the hunting territory of Kangersuatsiaq is thought about by those who live and travel there. Places become repositories of local memories and there is a sense in which the landscape, what I shall call a 'memoryscape' for the Kangersuatsiarmiit, defines the extent of community territory, as the physical expression of Kangersuatsiaq.

This book also explores different meanings held by the Kangersuatsiarmiit amongst themselves, concerning how they relate to landscape, kinship and personal names. These have a symbolic aspect in that they do not tell people how to act. There is nothing inherent in a kin term that informs people of its significance, for example. Similarly, an *atsiaq* (someone who is named after a dead person) means different things for different people, who each work out their own meanings. That the form of a cultural item is held in common does not mean a consensus as to how people orientate themselves in relation to it. This is the symbolic element of community (Cohen ibid).

Village and community – terminological usage

Throughout this book I use the words 'village' and 'community', but it should not be taken that they are interchangeable terms. They refer to spatial, social and moral entities. Community is used in the sense outlined above and it is hoped that the material presented illustrates this. Kangersuatsiaq as a village, however, is the physical and administrative place where people live. Its use does not refer to the complexity of social relationships and feelings of community and locality. Rather, it is a sense of continuity and community which can be said to make people feel they belong to Kangersuatsiaq village.

Administratively, Greenland is divided into eighteen districts which each have a municipal centre or 'town'. The capital is Nuuk, which has the largest population. Each district has a municipal council (*kommune*) which has a certain amount of autonomy in managing district affairs. The towns are the administrative centres which serve the villages of the district. There are some sixty villages in Greenland, which differ in size and population. For example, Ikerasaarsuk in Upernavik district has just three houses, while Alluitsup Paa (Syd Prøven) in the southerly district of Nanortalik has a population of over 600.

After Danish colonization, there was a progressive northward expansion and establishment of towns – originally called colonies. The larger villages (now called *bygd* in Danish and *nunaqarfiit* in Greenlandic) were established as *udsteder* (lit. 'outposts' or 'out places') by the Royal Greenland Trade Company. There was a store and trading post in these *udsteder* which also served the other smaller settlements, known as *boplads* ('dwelling places'). In 1906, Upernavik district had twenty-eight settlements but the closing down of many *boplads* has seen a dramatic decline to eleven inhabited places (including Upernavik town). Kangersuatsiaq was established as an *udsted* and originally served Ulua and

Ingiugdlissoq, two *boplads* which are now closed. The population of these places moved to Kangersuatsiaq in the late 1940s.

A note on Greenlanders and Inuit

Throughout this book I use both 'Greenlanders' and 'Inuit' as interchangeable terms. Inuit is the name for the Eskimo-speaking peoples who inhabit the Arctic from Siberia across North America to East Greenland. However, there are regional variations. It is now commonly accepted to talk about Alaskan Eskimos (who comprise two main linguistic groups: Inupiaq and Yup'ik), Canadian Inuit (Inuvialuit in the west, and Inuit in the eastern Arctic), and Greenlandic Inuit. The latter are split into three linguistic groups; Inuit/Kalaallit along the west coast, Inughuit in the far north, and Iit in the east and north east. Collectively, all are known as Kalaallit. They speak Kalaallisut (lit. 'in the way of a Greenlander'), which is related to other Inuit dialects. However, most dialects are mutually unintelligible. Although they are agglutinative and follow similar rules in the construction of words from roots and postbases, they differ in morphophonology. As the term Kalaallit (sing. Kalaaleq) is translated to mean both Greenlanders and Inuit, I follow the general use within the country.

2

Inuit communities, the Arctic frontier and the emergence of modern Greenland

The economic frontier

In Greenland and throughout the circumpolar north contemporary Inuit society bears the cultural scars of a long history of contact with other peoples and ideologies. From early barter with the first European explorers and whalers, through to dealings with traders, missionaries and colonists, the aboriginal inhabitants of the Arctic have been drawn into a situation of cultural dependency that has eroded traditional bases of social organization. This dependency continues today as Inuit are assimilated into mainstream economic, political and cultural life. Like all northern native peoples, Inuit face an uncertain future while their homelands become the focus of increasing worldwide attention.

The non-native history of the Arctic has been bound up with the economic exploitation of renewable and non-renewable natural resources. A frontier ideology that sees land as wilderness with an economic value continues to inform both the processes of development and the cultural images and perceptions held by outsiders, governments and industrialists. This ideology rests on a conviction that social and economic development is one necessary aspect of the inexorable material, scientific and intellectual progress of humankind. Within this evolutionary context, industrialization and economic development are seen as illustrating the transcendence of nature by civilization.

Western belief in the inexorability of progress can trace its origins to the development of rational scientific knowledge, and the rejection of religious mythology as the basis for understanding the workings of the universe. Newton's mathematical language systematized Descartes' dualistic theory of the rational ordering of the natural world, thereby establishing science as the dominant deterministic world-view. Until the development of quantum theory, the Cartesian split between subject and object continued to inform the atomistic outlook of all branches of science. This mechanistic understanding of the processes and workings of the natural order, together with the gradual diminishing of belief in a creator God as designer and operator of the universe, was accompanied by the growth of a capitalist economic system. Innovations in technology and economic progress fostered belief in the supremacy of industrialization and with the publication of Darwin's *Origin of Species* in 1859, the idea of social and economic progression was endorsed by evolutionary theory.

As a result of imperialism and colonial expansion, it is these Western views of development and modernization which have shaped the post-contact history of aboriginal peoples throughout the world. The resulting cultural devastation and ideological conflicts are nowhere more immediately apparent than in the contemporary Arctic.

The history of the Arctic as an economic frontier has its beginnings in the whaling industry in the Eastern Arctic and with the fur trade in Canada and Alaska. With its origins in Basque whaling, the European whale industry developed into the competitive 'Greenland fishery' for Right whales between the English and Dutch off the coast of Spitzbergen in the seventeenth century. Over-exploitation of the bays of Spitzbergen and the ice-filled Greenland Sea led to the seeking out and discovery of new waters in Davis Strait and Baffin Bay, where Right whales thrived in abundance. In pursuit of the Right whale, Scottish, English and Dutch whalers became regular visitors to the coasts of Baffin Island and Greenland, making contact and trading with the Inuit at their settlements and hunting camps. Evidence of the presence of these whalers is still to be found in the English and Dutch names given to harbours and other places along the west coast of Greenland.

Bartering took place on a significant scale between the whalers and Inuit. Knives, gun flints, gunpowder, woollen clothes, tea, sugar, pots, pans and kettles were among the most common items whalers traded in return for blubber, narwhal tusks, and for seal, caribou and fox skins. But while such material impact on the Native culture is difficult to assess, the whalers also brought diseases to which the Inuit had no immunity. Within a few years of the first and regular contacts with Europeans, entire Inuit communities were wiped out by influenza, measles, typhoid, smallpox and other epidemics.

As will be seen below, once the Danish government took over responsibility for trade in Greenland in the late eighteenth century, the development of the Greenlandic economy was guided by a paternalistic attitude that aimed to protect Inuit culture. In Canada and Alaska, however, trade was more immediately exploitative, informed and guided by the demands of Euro-American markets rather than inspired by any humanistic concern towards aboriginal peoples.

From the time it received its charter in 1670, until the early twentieth century, the Hudson's Bay Company dominated Canada's fur trade.

During this period the Inuit became dependent on trading posts, cultural values changed and the spiritual relationship between Inuit and the animals they hunted was disrupted. In the twentieth century, in addition to the continuation of the fur trade, there was a development of mining and forestry in the Canadian sub-Arctic. Following World War II, an expansion in mining activity together with the development of hydro-electric projects reinforced the southern vision of the Canadian North as a vast storehouse of potential wealth.

In recent years the industrial frontier of the Canadian Arctic has been bound up with oil and gas development. Oil had been produced at Norman Wells in the Northwest Territories since the 1920s, but in the 1960s drilling took place in the Beaufort Sea, and in the High Arctic at Melville Island and Resolute Bay. In 1967 Panarctic Oils, a consortium of oil companies, was formed to take an interest in Canadian Arctic exploration. Since the 1960s, major hydrocarbon developments have also taken place in the Mackenzie Delta and Beaufort Sea. In the 1970s, the Mackenzie Valley Pipeline Project was planned to transport Alaskan and Canadian gas from Prudhoe Bay and the Mackenzie Delta to southern Alberta. This brought enormous opposition from environmentalists and from Native peoples and resulted in an inquiry led by Judge Thomas Berger to evaluate the potential economic, environmental and social impacts of the pipeline. The inquiry provided a forum for Inuvialuit, Dene and Metis, the three Native groups through whose lands the pipeline would pass. Berger's findings recommended a ten-year moratorium on moving gas from the Mackenzie Delta by pipeline, this period being specified to allow negotiations between native organizations and the federal government regarding land claims agreements.

With the moratorium lifted, it is likely that increased industrial activity relating to the development of gas production in the Mackenzie Delta will occur throughout the 1990s. This results from Canadian government decisions in 1989 to grant licences for gas exports from the Mackenzie Delta to the United States, following the free trade agreement between the two countries. Construction of a pipeline is expected to begin in 1996. Considerable environmental, social and economic problems are anticipated from these new developments, especially as Berger's inquiry into the original project pointed out that high-level hydrocarbon development and the building of a pipeline would mean construction camps, access roads and an influx of large numbers of transient workers.

The effects of economic development on Canadian Inuit have already been considerable. The erosion of a subsistence hunting lifestyle was exacerbated by government resettlement policies which drew the Inuit into a position of greater dependency on the south. The presence in small settlements of large numbers of Whites who went North to work as administrators, trade managers, teachers, and construction workers also caused considerable ethnic conflict. But the prevailing attitude was one of incorporating the Inuit into the mainstream economic and cultural life of Canada. Through education, the aboriginal inhabitants of the Arctic were to be trained to take their place in the new period of frontier developments.

From its accredited European discovery by Vitus Bering in 1741, the development of Alaska, like that of Canada, has followed the exploitation of its natural resources. From the beginning, when Bering's expedition returned with sea otter furs, Alaska was prominent in both the Russian and British fur trades. Fur seals and sea otters, together with a number of fur bearing land animals, were exploited to near extinction over a period of 140 years. Whalers from New England hunted the bowhead whale in the waters of Bering Strait from 1847 and, from the 1880s, gold mining provided the foundation for the expansion of the Alaskan economy. With the discovery of vast reserves of oil and gas at Prudhoe Bay on the Arctic North Slope in 1968, the agenda for Alaska's future economic development was set.

The incorporation of Alaska's Inupiat and Yup'ik Eskimo people into mainstream American cultural and economic life has followed a pattern similar to the experiences of the Canadian Inuit. The colonial encounter meant disease, exploitation and dependency. Whalers and traders had already disrupted the indigenous Inupiat religion by the time the first Presbyterian missionaries arrived on the North Slope at the end of the nineteenth century. Catholic missionaries, however, who arrived in the Yup'ik area of south west Alaska around the same time, found that the Native people had been more resistant to outside influence, particularly to the Russian Orthodox Church (Fienup-Riordan 1983). In both the Inupiat and Yup'ik areas missionaries established boarding schools and assumed responsibility for religious and secular education until federal schools were established in the first half of the twentieth century. From this time, there were also improvements in health care and the Alaskan Eskimo population increased, more hunters and trappers moved to larger villages, customary subsistence activities declined and alternative employment opportunities became available both in the villages and in other parts of Alaska. While hunting and trapping remains an important and integral part of the Inupiat and Yup'ik economies, many people now find permanent and seasonal employment in commercial fishing, the oil industry and in urban centres such as Anchorage and Fairbanks.

Land claims and Inuit self-government

Throughout the circumpolar north, recent assertions of Native rights, and demands for self-government and the establishment of Inuit homelands have come about in response to the oil- and gas-based development strategies outlined above. The expansions in resource development in the 1960s and 1970s spurred the Inuit in Alaska, Canada and Greenland into making an ethnic and nationalistic response to the economic and environmental disturbance of their ancestral lands. Demands for self-government were accompanied by calls to protect both natural resources and the fragile Arctic environment of which Inuit culture is both an integral part and expression.

The Western rational economic understanding of the Arctic remains divergent from the views held by its indigenous peoples. The dualism between object and subject, and between mind and body that remains prevalent in Western thought, still shapes non-Native ideas and attitudes towards the landscape and its development. The separation of human consciousness from the natural world results in the loss of the subtle interplay between imagination and landscape that can only be realized through intuitive awareness. Some writers, such as Carl Jung and Joseph Campbell have pointed to the importance of myth, as an expression of the intuitive mind, in reconciling humanity with the environment. In the Arctic, myth is one way through which the relationship between Inuit and the land is expressed. As I shall show in Chapter 4, the dialectic between human nature and landscape is revealed in the resonance between experience, thought and intimacy, and provides a fundamental grounding for the continuity of Inuit culture.

It is the cultural, economic and spiritual relationship between Inuit and the land that economic development and industrial activity threatens to disrupt. In attempting to gain autonomy over their lives and some control over the level and extent of development, Inuit groups have managed to negotiate a number of treaties and settlements in recent years. In Alaska, the discovery of oil at Prudhoe Bay together with fears of other developments, resulted in the establishment in 1967 of the Alaska Federation of Natives (AFN). In 1971, following AFN demands for land claims, the Alaskan Native Claims Settlement Act (ANCSA) was passed by the United States Congress. While the Act did not recognize a claim to the whole of Alaska, it established twelve regional Native corporations, giving them control over one ninth of the state. Claims to the rest of Alaska were extinguished and $962.5 million was given in compensation. In effect, the Act, which excluded those born after 1971, made Alaska's Native people shareholders in corporate-owned land, alienating them further from their customary relationship with the land and shaping their future relationship with global economics (Chance 1990: 166). Furthermore, there are real possibilities that shares in the land now owned by Native corporations could be purchased by non-Native multi-national corporations in the future.

In Canada, in response to oil and gas development in the Mackenzie Delta, the Inuvialuit formed the Committee of Original People's Entitlement (COPE) in 1969, and in 1971 the Inuit Tapirisat of Canada (ITC) was founded in Ottawa as a voice for Inuit throughout Canada's North. In 1984 the Inuvialuit final agreement gave 35,000 square miles of the Northwest Territories to the Inuvialuit, together with financial compensation and other rights in return for their surrendering further territorial claims. But the Inuit of the Eastern Canadian Arctic are still pressing for their own land claims agreement and establishment of Nunavut ('our land'). In 1990 they signed an agreement in principle with the federal government, which anticipates a final agreement that will give Inuit the rights to oil, gas and coal in some 14,000 square miles of territory, the right to financial compensation, and the right to shares of government royalties from oil and gas development on crown land.

But for Inuit groups still fighting for a degree of self-determination, Greenland provides a model for which there is no precedent in the Arctic. As the only population of Inuit origin to have achieved Home Rule, Greenlanders have been pioneers in pushing forward towards the political frontier, where the riches are seen as autonomy over their own lives and future, together with the global recognition of a wider Inuit homeland as the only way to safeguard the Arctic environment.

The emergence of modern Greenland

Danish settlement in Greenland goes back to 1721 when the Lutheran missionary Hans Egede established a trading and mission station near present day Nuuk. Egede's original intention had been to search for the descendants of the Norse colony, established after Erik the Red's voyage to Greenland in the tenth century, and to convert them to Christianity. Egede, however, found no trace of the Norsemen, encountering instead nomadic Inuit hunters who already engaged in trade with whalers following Frobisher's voyage to Davis Strait in 1578. On arriving in Greenland, Egede initiated trade and missionary activities with the Inuit, but while the native population rejected their old religious beliefs and embraced Christianity, commercial activity did not prove to be such a successful proposition. Egede was able to undermine the authority and social position of the *angakkut* (shamans) but his failure as a merchant led the Danish government to assume responsibility for trade in 1726.

Throughout the eighteenth century unsuccessful attempts were made to create a viable trade network by transferring trading rights to independent companies. A Dane, Jacob Severin, was appointed as overseer for trade and missionary work in 1734, effectively stopping illegal trade between Greenlanders and Dutch whalers. In 1749 Det Almendelige Handelskompagni (Common Trading Company) took over Severin's responsibilities only to stumble continually until it was bought by the Danish state in 1774. This action resulted in the founding of the Kongelige Grønlandsk Handelskompagni, or KGH (Royal Greenland Trade Company) in 1776. This saw the establishment of a Danish Greenland trade monopoly which was to last until after the end of World War II.

The way this policy of positive isolation was to operate was laid down in the KGH's Order of 1782. The underlying tone was a paternalistic social philosophy inspired by a Rousseauesque conception of the Noble Savage that recognized implicitly the hunting culture of the Greenlanders: any trade had to benefit the indigenous population and the economic philosophy of the KGH was 'no profit, no loss'. To the Danes, the Greenlander was Rousseau's natural man living in a pure state of nature and thus able to satisfy easily his own physical wants. For Rousseau, the Noble Savage lived a free, healthy, happy life, but from the moment one man began to stand in need of the help of another, equality disappeared, leading to the ruin of humanity. The Greenlander, as the natural man, was to remain in an uncorrupted state by being kept isolated from European civilization.

17

Although the main objective of the KGH was 'to seek the best interest and advantage of the Royal Trade and Fishing with diligence and zeal – at all times and in all conditions' (Gad 1982: 20), the Greenlander was to be protected and dealt with in a 'reasonable and careful manner' (Gad ibid: 21). Social and sexual intercourse with Greenlanders was prohibited and Danes and Greenlanders were discouraged from visiting each other, except for business purposes.

However, the Greenlanders were involved in a trading economy, based mainly on whale blubber and sealskins, and became dependent on a number of trade goods to supplement their diet and technology. The paternalism of the Danes, although intended to preserve the indigenous hunting culture, in effect made the Greenlanders somewhat dependent on the wider world, despite being insulated from the instability of its markets. Jenness saw this closed economy as protecting the Greenlanders from the 'world beyond their borders', but not preparing them for the day when they would be exposed 'to civilization's perilous gusts' (1967: 32). The reality, according to Jenness, was that the Greenlanders were in a 'state of perpetual tutelage'. An example of this was an increase in sealskin prices in 1840 accompanied by a drop in the price of imported goods. In was on these items that the Greenlanders spent their extra cash. This mirrors the experiences of remote colonies throughout history. It was the same old story – luxuries became necessities. A greater dependence on store-bought goods effectively meant an increased dependence on the Danes. Despite their involvement in this Danish closed trade monopoly of their country, the Greenlanders did manage to continue their hunting way of life. The sea continued to be the main resource base, with the ringed seal (*Phoca hispida*) providing the mainstay of the local economy and its skin and blubber underpinning the trade network.

The period from the end of the nineteenth century until the 1920s saw a warming of Greenland's southern coastal waters, resulting in a migration of seals to plankton-rich colder waters along the northwest coast. Also, several species of fish, notably cod, appeared in the now warmer waters of the south. These climatic changes led to a profound revision of policy. A major transition from hunting to fishing was encouraged by the Danes, and many hunters in south and west Greenland had to change their attitude towards fishing, traditionally seen as a lowly pursuit, and abandon sealing and whaling activities. The fish were sold to the KGH and people were drawn from the inner fjords to the outer parts of the coast, where they could find jobs in the rapidly developing fishing industry. Traditional hunting camps were abandoned, the majority never to be reoccupied. By 1950 fish processing was capital intensive and industrialized.

Despite these changes, it was World War II that brought Greenland into the modern world. In 1941 the United States signed a treaty that recognized Danish sovereignty and allowed for the construction of military bases in the southwest. Together with the developing fishing industry, such contact ended Denmark's isolationist policies towards

Greenland. Colonial status was abolished in 1953, theoretically giving Greenlanders equal status to Danes.

Massive modernization of Greenland since this constitutional amendment has led to extensive changes in Greenlandic society. There have been improvements in health care, education and in housing, albeit improvements from a Danish, Northern European perspective. Development of the fishing industry was seen as the way to bring the benefits of civilization and a higher standard of living to the Greenlanders. Continued migration from rural areas was encouraged, and government policy stated that the fishing industry infrastructure was to be developed mainly in the ice-free west coast towns of Paamiut, Nuuk, Maniitsoq and Sisimiut. Furthermore, people were attracted to the towns by the withdrawal of investment from what were seen as 'unprofitable' villages. Schools and stores were closed as part of the centralization policy and investment re-channelled into the growing towns. Turning away from hunting, people found employment in fishing and in the shrimp processing plants and other subsidiary industries.

Rural–urban migration led to the fragmentation of kin-based groups that characterized village life. Incomers to the towns suffered from social and economic isolation, marginality and discrimination. Furthermore, the hunter was isolated from his means of subsistence production which he had previously owned and controlled. Faced with exclusion from urban opportunities, together with the unfamiliarity of town life as well as new values and ambitions, the migrants found themselves increasingly frustrated and despondent. Greenlanders also found themselves working alongside a population of mainly transient Danish workers, which resulted in an ideological and ethnic conflict.

Throughout the 1970s, Greenland experienced an emerging Inuit political awareness, generated by the Danish-speaking Greenlandic elite that had been educated in Greenland and Denmark during the 1950s and 1960s. Anti-imperialistic feelings led to the beginnings of nationalism and the formation of the left-wing Siumut (lit. 'forward') party, whose policies were given added voice by the *Sujumut* national newspaper.

In 1975 a Home Rule Commission was set up, to be followed by the Home Rule Act which was passed by the Danish government three years later. Greenlandic Home Rule came into force in 1979 after 79 per cent of the franchise had voted in a referendum held in January of that year. After its success in the first national election Siumut formed a majority government, with Atassut (lit. 'connection', a party favouring links with Denmark) in opposition. The other main political party, the leftist Inuit Ataqatigiit (Human Brotherhood) was to later hold the balance of power in support of Siumut after the 1983 election. Both ethnic Greenlanders and resident Danes have the right to vote and to be elected to the Landsting, the Greenlandic parliament which is based in Nuuk. However, to date there are no Danes in the Landsting.

When Home Rule was introduced, the Greenlandic Home Rule authorities inherited a post-colonial economy already characterized by a high standard of living and housing, and boasting a good system of social security. This economy was one that had been planned and developed by the Danes. Essentially, it had no sound internal basis to continue in any way that would prove viable under a national Greenlandic administration. As a people, Greenlanders are unique in being the only population of Inuit origin to have attained a degree of independence. However, Greenland is not a nation-state, but a partial structure (Dahl 1986: 321) in that it is still dependent on Denmark for economic support. Furthermore, the Danes retain control over defence and many public institutions. In the areas of education and health, for example, there are still very few qualified Greenlanders, ensuring a continuing supply of transient Danish teachers and doctors on short-term contracts.

Ethnic communities and the Inuit homeland

One of the interesting aspects of the road to self-government during the 1970s was the emphasis on ethnic identity and the emerging self-awareness that Greenlanders have common links with other circumpolar peoples. There was also a feeling of common origin, culture, history and future within Greenland. This is expressed in the official name for Greenland since Home Rule: *Kalaallit Nunaat* ('the Greenlanders' Land'), in Greenlandic popular music, in literature and in poetry. All this helped to nurture feelings of *kalaaliussuseq*; identity as a Greenlander. Home Rule emphasized the idea of the Greenlandic 'community', together with promoting a sense of Greenlanders working together towards the development of their country. National unity became a theme to elaborate and play upon:

> The main goal [of Siumut] . . . is to create a homogeneous, active and vigorous society which through responsible utilization of the country's own resources plus the necessary imports would manage to decide its own destiny [*Atuagagdliutit/Grønlandsposten* February 3rd 1977]

Writing about the Greenlandic community, the politician Lars Emil Johanssen emphasized

> that it has never before been as necessary for us Greenlanders to stick together as it is now. Therefore, I beg my fellow countrymen to be aware of our situation at this time so critical for our future and to stop the primitive quarrelling each one of us is guilty of every now and then. Instead we must learn to talk with each other – not only about each other – to find the solutions of our land [*Atuagagdliutit/Grønlandsposten* January 6th 1977]

A feeling of Inuit solidarity was consolidated in the late 1970s with the founding of the Inuit Circumpolar Conference (ICC), an organization established to give a voice to the Eskimo-speaking people in Siberia, Alaska, Canada and Greenland. Talk of unity and of a Greenlandic community *vis-á-vis* the Danes fostered a sense of togetherness. Emphasis was on the rediscovery of the Inuit 'soul', awareness of which became a theme of theatre and music. Young Greenlandic rock bands sang songs with titles such as 'I Greenlander' (*Kalaaliuvunga*), with lyrics that asked radical questions about modern Greenlandic society and the future of its people and culture. Owing to the centralization policy of the 1960s, most people were now living in fast-growing towns along the west coast. The villages were now seen as the last outposts of 'real' Greenlandic culture and were used as referents for the definition of Greenlandic identity.

The formation of the Inuit Circumpolar Conference, demands for the creation of Nunavut as an Inuit homeland in the Canadian East Arctic, and the achievement of Home Rule in Greenland are all examples of how politicized Inuit had become in the 1970s. The emphasis on ethnic distinctiveness as a reaction to external control over Inuit lives generated a new found sense of community, and even nationalism, that had no precedent in the histories of Inuit groups.

As a response to social, political and economic change, the young, emerging Native elites looked beyond a purely localized identity and sense of place towards wider national identities that championed the cause of Inuit as a people, rather than as diverse groups in space and time. Burch makes the point that traditional Alaskan Eskimo societies did not have distinct names. Individuals and groups were referred to by geographical location rather than other characteristics such as social organization (Burch 1975: 13). This persists in contemporary times, where individuals are identified with specific localities. This is also true for the rest of the Inuit area.

In Greenland a person is still identified by his home town or village. For example, a person from Kangersuatsiaq is a Kangersuatsiarmeeq (*-meeq* being the dialect version of *-mioq*, the singular form of *-miut/-miit*) and, as I have previously mentioned, all the members of the community are known as Kangersuatsiarmiit. In this way, they identify themselves and are identified by others with a particular place, and are thereby distinguished from the inhabitants of other places within Greenland.

However despite these local groupings, the use of more specific ethnic terms such as Kalaallit, Inuit and Inuvialuit are now common parlance. The use of these terms, however, has the potential to obscure the diversity within the Inuit area. Just as the European use of the term 'Eskimo' created the stereotype of a seal hunting, snow house dweller living on the pack ice, the use of broader ethnic terms has its own imagery which acts to misrepresent identity.

The term Kalaallit, used in Greenland to refer to Greenlandic Inuit as an ethnic group *vis-á-vis* Danes, is an example of how the importance of geographical location for identity definition can be made obsolete. The three distinct ethnic groups within Greenland of west coast Kalaallit, Inughuit in Avanersuaq district and Iit on the east coast are all subsumed under the general term Kalaallit (sing. Kalaaleq).

In Greenland the rhetoric of nationalism, both before and since the achievement of Home Rule, plays on the idea of a common culture, past heritage, and present and future identity. But the emphasis on a unified Greenlandic identity ignores the heterogeneous nature of contemporary Greenlandic society, which is made up of different organizations and occupational groups, and is characterized by greater mobility, differences in lifestyle and the emergence of a class structure. As distinct ethnic groups, Inuit in Avanersuaq, Tasiilaq and Ittoqqortoormiit distinguish themselves from West Greenlanders by dialect, mode of production and history.

In addition, even in West Greenland there are considerable differences in dialect, making people aware of a separate identity. For example, in Upernavik district the dialect diverges from standard West Greenlandic and is similar in structure and vocabulary to East Greenlandic, from which it originates. Even locally such differences are used and played upon in effective identity boundary maintenance. It is the aim of this book to demonstrate the importance of locality and sense of belonging to a particular community that persists despite the emergence of nationalism in Greenland. This is not to argue that the Kangersuatsiarmiit regard themselves as any more or less Greenlandic than people in Nuuk or elsewhere, it is simply that people work out different meanings about Greenlandic identity based on individual experience and allegiance to their local community.

Dahl (1988) argues that the political development of Greenland throughout the 1970s and 1980s was a process of nation-building. But the development of the nation-state is often accompanied by the invention of a tradition that cannot always be taken as dispassionate history (e.g. see Hobsbawm and Ranger 1983). Following on from this, Dahl regards the present Inuit ethnic groups throughout the Arctic as imagined communities of recent ideological construction.

In Greenland it is the current process of industrialization that is providing the occasion for the growth of nationalism, rather than the other way around. The idea of a Greenlandic Inuit community arose because of its relationship to the Danes. However, Greenlandic identity is no longer phrased within the context of ethnicity, as it was in the 1960s and 1970s, but in political and national terms. Gellner (1983) has argued that there are socio-economic and socio-psychological reasons for industrialized states to be organized in terms of nationality. The instrumental rationality and division of labour of industrializing territories demands a sense of cultural commonality and well-defined central economy. But specialization and the division of labour gives rise to individualism, with its potential for social and psychological isolation and disorientation. This is negated, Gellner argues, by the sense of identity the nation-state gives to the individual, who regards it, through personal identification, as an object of worship and veneration.

As will be shown, within a context of economic development in modern Greenland, the hunting and subsistence way of life in Upernavik is defined by politicians and developers as 'traditional', which in this sense means anachronistic. It is regarded as contributing to the lack of a unified Greenlandic identity and the persistence of a non-integrated economy. Cultural uniformity, therefore, is seen as a prerequisite for state-orientated economic success (Gellner ibid.).

National identity leaves no room for locality, possibly because of the intellectual tendency to regard society as an abstract object of thought. As a result, society as an entity is juxtaposed with other entities, all regarded as mutually exclusive; we see nationality and locality, society and individual, society and economy, primitive and modern, urban and rural, culture and nature. Such entities are regarded as incompatible rather than complementary opposites. As the following chapters illustrate, the emphasis on a national Greenlandic identity blinds us to the significance of the features of community life that make up the defining components of a local identity.

3

Hunting and contemporary subsistence in northwest Greenland

Hunting in modern Greenland

For the last four and a half thousand years Greenland has been inhabited by hunters. Archaeological research has determined that the first Paleo-Eskimo ancestors of the present Inuit population arrived in the north of the country sometime around 2120 BC (Knuth 1967). These people were coastal nomads, hunting seals, walrus and musk-ox. Although there were variations in subsistence patterns, successive waves of migrants from the Canadian Arctic continued to harvest the sea, subsisting mainly on seals and other renewable marine resources.

Despite the rapid modernization of most of Greenland and the decline of hunting as the mainstay of Inuit culture, the districts in the northwest and on the east coast have managed to retain a distinctive hunting lifestyle, and have avoided the rather severe infrastructural changes that have transformed the rest of the country beyond recognition.

The hunting of sea mammals is the principal occupation in the districts of Uummannaq (pop. 2,581), Upernavik (pop. 2,281), Avanersuaq (pop. 823), Tasiilaq (pop. 2,836), and Ittoqqortoormiit (pop. 545). The total Greenlandic Inuit population of these districts is 8,269, with 4,455 people living in villages (Statsministeriet 1988). These figures represent the Greenlandic Inuit population at the time of my fieldwork and exclude the fluctuating population of mainly transient Danes. Only in the districts of Upernavik and Tasiilaq does the rural population exceed the number of people living in the towns.

The population of these districts depends entirely on hunting as the basis for subsistence and represents about one fifth of the Greenlandic Inuit population (44,592). Hunting households remain units of both production and consumption. Seal hunting has a commercial element in the sense that sealskins are sold to the KNI, but it is more truly subsistence hunting as it drives the household economy. Seals are hunted to provide both food and a source of cash. Also, producing goods from seals is a small-scale activity, vulnerable to outside forces, particularly the international sealskin market and environmental pressure groups.

Hunting also remains important for some people residing in districts other than the five mentioned above; the Greenlandic municipal lists show a total of 8,455 Green (full-time) hunting licences issued as of January 1989. These licences are only issued to those who are engaged in occupational hunting.

Many studies of Inuit seal hunting have been concerned with describing more pragmatic aspects, such as environmental adaptation, predatory behaviour and the interaction between a population and its resource base. Research has concentrated on traditional and modern subsistence hunting techniques, with emphasis on an ecological approach rather than a concern with modes of subsistence, cultural factors and social relations. Such studies leave out the person of the hunter as a conscious being interacting with elements of the natural world. As will be made clear throughout this ethnography, hunting is not predation shaped by environmental determinism. As a form of social action, hunting involves human purpose and intention just as much as it involves skill and technique.

The externalization of nature and animals in Western consciousness informs a purely urban-focused misunderstanding of the world's remaining hunting and gathering peoples. The fundamental aspects of hunting are difficult for an urban mind, removed from a localized and personal relationship with the environment, to grasp. Ethnocentric Western attitudes, the inexorable encroachment of 'civilization', the politics of industrial capitalism and the animal-rights movement have ensured that, historically as well as in the present, 'the hunting societies of the world have been condemned to death' (Brody 1983: xi). A discussion of hunting in purely materialistic terms ignores ideological aspects of a world-view that regards the human and animal worlds as interwoven. The hunter is a producer of his means of subsistence, but the hunt is not mere economic pursuit of game; it is an expression of the intimacy between the social and natural worlds.

As later chapters discuss, hunting in Kangersuatsiaq and throughout Upernavik district entails an ideological and ritual responsibility to both animals and the environment. Rather than being an impulsive mechanistic response to immediate needs, hunting is directed by purposive action and the consciousness of the hunter. Furthermore, if the balance between the hunter and the natural world is to continue then it is incumbent on human beings to follow a code of morality and ensure the propitiation of animals and animal spirits. By his actions the hunter is accountable to the natural world and responsible for ensuring the stability of a multiplicity of sacred relationships.

Dependence on marine mammals for food is reflected in community hunting regulations and in the attitude of hunters towards the animals they hunt. The hunting household utilizes the meat, fat, and skin of the seal, and complex local rules exist which determine the sharing and distribution of the catch. A woman who throws away the kidneys of a seal while flensing it will say 'thank you' or 'let there be more', because failure to recognize that the seal has given itself up to the hunter willingly may result in a period of lean hunting for that hunter in the future.

The cultural expression of respect for animals is also manifest in first catch celebrations. A boy who catches his first seal will distribute gifts of meat to every household in his community and people are invited to his parents' home for coffee and cake. The first catch celebration is a recognition of the boy's development as a hunter and of the relationship he begins to nurture with his environment. Furthermore, it is an implicit statement of the vitality and continuity of the hunting way of life.

Throughout the Arctic, development and acculturation has meant an erosion of hunting skills and the gradual intrusion of a wage economy. The ideology of hunting has also undergone a high degree of secularization, especially in urban Greenland where rapid social and economic development alienated hunters from their means of subsistence. The spiritual interchange between the human and animal worlds no longer underpins the cultural vitality of many Inuit communities. Outside of the true Greenlandic hunting districts, most hunting is undertaken by wage-earners, quite often at weekends or during holidays. In addition there is a developing commercial hunting industry in the main towns.

Occupational hunters, in places such as Nuuk, Sisimiut and Paamiut, hunt primarily for cash. Throughout the year it is possible for town dwellers to buy hunting products, such as seal meat and caribou meat, seabirds such as guillemots, or fish such as halibut and salmon. Much of this produce is sold in open air markets known as *kalaaliminerniarfiit*, or *kalaaliaraq*. Some hunters do not set up stalls, but sell their produce from the boots of their cars, or lay the meat on pieces of cardboard and stand outside the main supermarkets. There is a healthy demand for fresh Greenlandic food from an urban population that is only a generation or two removed from a subsistence lifestyle.

Greenlandic hunting products also find their way into supermarket freezers. The majority of urban hunters, and an increasing number of hunters living in settlements, sell their produce to the KNI. Sales of hunting products by the KNI within Greenland include seal meat and seal blubber, frozen *mattak* (whale skin), frozen whale meat, *nikkut* (dried whale meat), and guillemots and eider ducks.

Even in those districts where hunting remains the dominant mode of livelihood, however, money now plays an integral part in the subsistence economy. Unlike commercial hunting in the towns, this has resulted in an integrated economy which is not necessarily harmful to traditional modes of subsistence. That a monetary economy is not inconsistent with an existing network of values is due to the fact that the mode of subsistence has incorporated money into its range of subsistence techniques.

In Upernavik district seal hunting has not escaped from the influence of modern technology, with increasing use of speedboats, rifles and seal nets. Over the past fifteen years or so there has been a dramatic decline in the use of the kayak, and very few hunters in the district now use one for open water seal hunting during the summer. For example, as of 1988, only one man in the settlement of Nutaarmiut (pop. 66) was still using a kayak for hunting purposes. Although many hunters still use kayaks in the spring for narwhal hunting and for retrieving seals shot from the ice-edge, fibreglass dinghies fitted with outboard motors are now the dominant means of transportation for hunting and travelling.

While these technological innovations may have found a place in the traditional mode of subsistence production, they have led to further dependency on a monetary economy. Hunters now need outboard motors, fuel, firearms and ammunition. A hunter can easily use up to twenty litres of benzine (at a cost of 100 Danish kroner in 1988) and 100 Dkr worth of ammunition during one hunting trip, yet possibly be unsuccessful.

The sale of sealskins can no longer be relied on as the main source of cash to cover the costs of hunting, or to provide income for store-bought goods that supplement a diet based on seal meat. Sealskin prices are dependent on an erratic market and average prices during my fieldwork were between 85 and 350 Dkr for nine categories of skin according to size and quality. Low prices have resulted in part from the anti-sealing protests that led to an EEC ban, from 1983, on the import of sealskins into Europe. In 1989 this ban was extended indefinitely.

Although directed originally towards the harvesting of harp and hooded seal pups off Atlantic Canada, the animal-rights campaign was extended in the late 1970s to include aboriginal seal hunting in the Arctic. The animal-rights argument is that the adoption of modern Western technology has actually removed Inuit subsistence activities away from any traditional context. While the skins of adult seals hunted in Greenland are exempt from the EEC ban, and despite the Home Rule government's subsidy of the domestic sealskin trade, the effects of the ban have intensified the marginal role of seal hunting in Greenland and hunters now find it increasingly difficult to continue their customary subsistence way of life.

Animal-rights groups stress the relationship of humans and animals by placing great emphasis on anthropomorphism and presenting a view of the world as an interconnected community of biological harmony. The Noble Savage is used as a powerful symbol of an idealized past. Images are evoked to show a spiritual and moral harmony with the natural world, a harmony which is already an inherent part of Inuit cosmology. But according to this view, as interpreted by the animal-rights movement, Inuit are now involved in a capitalist mode of production. They are no longer 'real' or 'traditional' primitive people and they hunt in order to sell skins to overseas markets. Animal-rights groups have depended on public support for their anti-sealing campaigns but little sympathy has gone the way of the people for whom such opposition has precipitated cultural disintegration.

Other observers have assumed that, because of the trade and cash elements, aboriginal hunting has undergone a process of commoditization. This perspective regards money as going hand in hand with development and modernization in the Arctic, and as previously having no part to play in traditional hunting societies. As a result, definitions of subsistence and tradition are imposed on those who have never before felt the need to define themselves.

Since Aristotle, and no doubt even earlier, many have commented on the depersonalizing aspects of money. Jesus taught that 'It is easier for a camel to pass through the eye of a needle than for a rich man to enter the Kingdom of God' (Mark 10: 25) and Christian dogma has often raged against greed. The Protestant ethic legitimized the earning of money but did not endorse the accruing of wealth for money's sake. In more recent times, anthropologists have often taken the view that money is indicative of a modern society and that there is no place for cash in pre-capitalist economies.

The negative reaction to materialism that seems rooted in much socio-logical and anthropological literature can be traced back to nineteenth century perspectives, including what Marx had to say about alienation and the labour theory of value. Put simply, Marx argued that people no longer see themselves in their products, which they now think produce them. Marx's concept of alienation can be traced back to Fichte, who began with Kant's epistemological premise that reality is a man-made construction. Creators become alienated from their creations which assume an independent existence. Hegel developed Fichte's ideas and saw alienation as inherent in the nature of spiritual creation, but stated that the self-alienation of human consciousness could be overcome through the process of knowledge and the recognition of the spirit as its own creation.

For Marx, individual alienation also meant alienation from other men with the result that human relationships and social bonds dissolved into selfish interests. But this had a profound effect on relationships between men precisely because such relationships were the realization of the rela-tionship of man to himself. Alienation ensured that man's essential self as a social being was no longer expressed in the creative activity of work. For Marx, instead of work being an expression of man, labour had become externalized and now had a value. This value was the proportion in which one commodity was exchanged for another and defined a parti-cular type of society where commodities are produced for exchange, rather than production for self-consumption. In a sense it was labour time being exchanged for labour time and this was reflected in money.

Because of the separation between the producer and the product owing to a transaction, the view is that money results in personal and anonymous relations. This is in keeping with the writings of Tönnies and Durkheim on the effects that progressive modernization has on *Gemein-schaft* and mechanical solidarity. Modernization and money, it is assumed, erode social solidarity and kinship relations. As Parry and Bloch put it, money is seen as 'a kind of acid which inexorably dissolves cherished cultural discriminations, eats away at qualitative differences and reduces personal relations to impersonality' (1989: 6). The negative and disruptive aspects of money are regarded as resulting in the fragmentation of close and personal relationships, together with a broader social associa-tion with people in the wider society.

But in northwest Greenland, as will be made clearer when the development of an inshore commercial halibut fishery is discussed in Chapter 10, as a supplement to subsistence hunting money is part of a symbolically constructed framework that emphasizes social and economic continuity rather than being based on large-scale profit. The image of the hunting community is one of a social and spiritual order rather than that of a wider economic system. It is only confused Western ideas and stereotypes of traditional and modern life that make it difficult for us to accept the survival of Inuit society in a context of modernity, where we see money as an undesirable element.

The incorporation of money into a customary mode of subsistence demonstrates the vitality of Inuit culture. The cash economy is only one part of a continuous process of adaptation and transformation that has characterized Greenlandic society ever since the first contacts with European explorers and colonists. In the past, for example, Inuit culture has absorbed an imported Christian religious tradition into an elaborate indigenous cosmology. Greenlanders have also met the challenges of colonialism together with technological innovations that have threatened to undermine the subsistence economy.

Today there are more social and economic changes to deal with, although it should not be taken that this will result in cultural disintegration and social dislocation. One of the most outstanding aspects of Inuit life, which I convey throughout this ethnography, is the emphasis on continuity rather than finality. As a way of beginning, I shall sketch the contemporary subsistence practices of the Kangersuatsiarmiit, with particular reference to the localized and seasonal availability of resources. The concentration on ecology and subsistence techniques is necessary for locating later discussion of subsistence ideology in an environmental context.

Upernavik district

Upernavik is the most northerly district in West Greenland, extending from Svartenhuk at 71° 28′ N up to Melville Bay at 75° N. The Greenlandic population of the district is 2,149 with 1,350 living in ten settlements served by the administrative centre of Upernavik town, which was founded as a colony in 1772. In addition there are 132 Danes in the district, residing mainly in Upernavik town (Statsministeriet 1988). Compared with the other districts, the population is predominantly rural.

Geographically, Upernavik district is really a pattern of islands with several peninsulas jutting out from the inland ice. The settlements are spatially organized to give easy access to their respective annual resource areas (Haller 1986). The southern part of the district has fjords which cut deep into an ice-free landscape extending some 120 km from the inland ice. The hinterland includes J.P. Koch's Land and most of Svartenhuk, and boasts table mountains and other peaks which rise to a height of over 1,600 m. Towards the coast the height of the land falls to some

600–700 m. The northern part of the district is characterized by the absence of the long fjords found in the south. Instead, there are several tidewater glaciers which calve continually into icefjords such as the Upernavik and Gieseckes Isfjords. A maze of islands predominate, with Nuussuaq the only notable peninsula (65 km long). Inland ice covers the Melville Bay coastal area, which also marks the boundary between Upernavik and Avanersuaq districts.

Kangersuatsiaq

Kangersuatsiaq lies some 60 km south of Upernavik town, and 25 km north of Upernavik Kujalleq, its closest neighbour and the most southerly village in the district. Approached by boat, Kangersuatsiaq comes into view as a cluster of houses precariously perched on a small, low-lying island situated about three-quarters of a kilometer off the mainland, named Kangeq (meaning 'headland' or 'promontory'). The name of the village is made up of the root *kangeq* and the postbase *+ (r)suatsiaq*, meaning 'especially big', thus translating as 'an (or 'situated near an') especially big headland/promontory'. The village is more commonly known throughout Greenland by its Danish name, Prøven, meaning 'tried'.

Throughout the 1770s attempts were made to establish the successful netting of beluga as an economic activity at the site of present day Kangersuatsiaq. But it was not until 1800 that an approved experiment was set up (Gad 1982: 256), and it is from this date that the history of Kangersuatsiaq is said to start. Although beluga whaling was important during the nineteenth century, the Inuit population has subsisted mainly by the harvesting of seals.

Many ships on whaling and exploratory expeditions also stopped off in Kangersuatsiaq. In 1875 H.M.S. Alert (of the British Arctic Expedition) called between 19–21st July. The ship's commander, Albert Markham, called it the 'quaintest of quaint little settlements. It consists of a neat little church, the Governor's residence, the storehouse, boiling down establishment, smithy, about two other wooden habitations, and some igdlus, or Eskimo huts' (1894: 38). Today, even seen from afar, the church and KNI manager's house stand aloof, overlooking the forty-five single-family wooden houses. At the time of fieldwork the village had a resident population of about 200, some seventy of whom were children.

The KNI store and warehouses are situated along the pier and this constitutes the village's main activity area. For the children, it is a play area and a small crowd is always present to greet any boat arriving from Upernavik town or another village. During summer, fibreglass dinghies equipped with outboard motors of varying horsepower are usually tied to the wooden landing stage or are out at their moorings and crowd the harbour. Men are continually in and out of their boats, either leaving or returning from hunting and fishing expeditions, and the noise of outboard motors reverberates throughout the day.

From nine o'clock in the morning, a small wooden rowing boat commutes regularly between the pier and the nearest iceberg. There is no fresh water supply on the island and the municipal council is responsible for employing two men to fetch freshwater ice to meet this need. At the first glimpse of the returning boat a large crowd assembles down at the landing stage, complete with brightly coloured buckets and plastic tubs. There is a little gentle pushing and employment of elbows needed if one is to stand a chance of filling one's bucket with the largest and cleanest pieces of ice. Several people are always left standing empty handed and must wait on the pier for the ice boat to go out and come in again.

Fetching ice always provides gossip and furnishes complaint: 'Really, that one had four tubs full!', 'I was *waiting* here, its so tiring!' While people carry their loads between the ice boat and their water tanks, others trudge between the store and their houses several times a day. These shopping expeditions are either for staples to supplement their diet or more commonly for soda pop and confectionery.

The walk up from the store area passes the fish racks which are full of dried cod and tom cod, giving off a smell a little reminiscent of freshly mown grass. At the top of a small slope leading into the centre of the village is the old meeting house. It was at the side of this small yellow building that, shortly after my arrival, I found a place where I could learn both a little of the language and something of village life.

At the side of the old meeting house a group of men is always to be seen. Indeed, there is rarely a time when no one is to be seen standing there. The side of the old meeting house is a good vantage point from which to observe the comings and goings of daily village life. From here the men can see the pier, the harbour, the store, the school, the church, the workshop and most houses. In other words, one can see almost everything going on in the village; boats leaving and arriving, people going to the shop and walking from the harbour area back to their houses.

This spot is the place where the men can gather information and news about what is going on in the village. One can see how many seals a hunter has caught, or how many fish he has. One joins the group, no matter how small it is, because there is always something interesting which can be seen or heard. It is a place to hear anecdotes and to tell stories. It is also the arena for the returning hunter to tell of his inevitable adventures to a ready and attentive audience.

In the early 1980s a new community hall was built on the northern edge of the village. This provides the main centre of activity outside of the home during the evenings. On various nights, the community hall acts as a venue for meetings of the Hunter's Association and the community council, for bingo evenings, for table tennis and for dances and discos. It is also used occasionally for showing films and for meetings of the temperance society.

Religion remains important for the Kangersuatsiarmiit and church services are held every Sunday. The district priest is a Greenlander who lives in Upernavik and services in Kangersuatsiaq are conducted by the catechist or his assistant, who are both local men.

While Christianity is not a source of ideological conflict, education sits uneasily within a network of customary values. The school takes children from the age of seven up to fifteen, when some children go on to the boarding school in Upernavik. My own experiences as a teacher in the school gave me an insight into a system that allows Danish teachers to teach Greenlandic children an imported Danish curriculum in the Danish language. Many parents feel their children are no longer given the opportunity to learn the skills necessary for continuing the hunting way of life. It becomes difficult for boys to join their fathers on hunting and fishing trips, except at weekends and during holidays, while girls do not acquire the basic skills associated with the processing of the catch. These problems will be discussed in more detail in Chapter 10.

Seasonal round

For the Kangersuatsiarmiit, the sea (*imaq*) remains the primary physical feature affecting life. The land is not as important a resource base and people continue to depend upon marine resources. Hunters rely on catching the ringed seal (*Phoca hispida*) during winter and spring and, to a lesser extent, in summer. The harp seal (*Pagophilus groenlandicus*) and hooded seal (*Cystophora cristata*) are more important in late summer and autumn.

Unlike Canadian Inuit settlements, which are not in close proximity to prime hunting areas owing to government centralization policies, Kangersuatsiaq enjoys a localization of resources. As discussed in the next chapter, hunters have a detailed knowledge of their local area. While this involves a conceptualization of the natural environment as something deeper than a mere empirical understanding, there are pragmatic aspects of interaction between hunters and their local resource base. The annual subsistence cycle responds to seasonal change and is organized accordingly. I have not chosen to divide the subsistence year into four seasons as a matter of convenience, the Kangersuatsiarmiit understand the year as comprising summer (*aasaq*), autumn (*ukiaq*), winter (*ukioq*) and spring (*upernaaq*).

Summer

The end of May and beginning of June sees the break up of the fast sea ice which forms in winter and continues throughout the spring. The dogsledging season is over, outboard motors are brought out of storage and boats are put back in the water. Hunters engage in open water seal hunting and inshore halibut fishing. There is a dramatic decrease in the number of ringed seals, however, in the coastal hunting area because they migrate to the inner fjords. The icebergs that calve off the tidewater glaciers, into such areas as the Upernavik Isfjord, desalinate the waters, attracting vast numbers of fish, notably cod, which thrive off the abundant plankton. This provides excellent fishing for the seals and so fewer are taken by hunters in the offshore areas. Certainly, during the summers of 1987 and 1988 there was less time invested in seal hunting compared to other seasons.

Summer provides an opportunity for hunters to diversify and to concentrate on long-line fishing for Greenland halibut (*Reinhardtius hippoglossoides*). This is significantly different to other forms of subsistence activity because halibut are seen exclusively as a resource primarily to be sold for cash. As mentioned, although the Home Rule government subsidizes the sealskin trade, thus helping to ameliorate the EEC ban, hunters in Upernavik district now have great difficulty in continuing a way of life based entirely on seal hunting. Fishing for Greenland halibut is seen as one way to compensate for the decline of sealskin prices.

A small-scale inshore commercial fishery was beginning to develop at the time of my fieldwork. An ambitious plan to develop Upernavik district, based on the halibut fishery, has been laid down by the municipal authorities. A rather radical structural upheaval is envisaged including the construction of fish and shrimp processing plants, new housing, an airport and the development of tourism. This plan, together with the ideological conflict it entails, will be looked at in greater detail in Chapter 10.

Greenland halibut are Arctic flat-fish which can weigh up to 10kg. In the recent past, the most important Greenland halibut fishing areas were Ilulissat and Uummannaq districts (Mattox 1973). Inuit once prized the fat of the fish for use as lamp oil. The present development of the Greenland halibut fishery in Upernavik district consolidates its historical and cultural significance at the local level, but it is difficult to say what future role it will play in the fishing industry of Greenland as a whole.

The fishery takes place in the nearby fjords to the east of Kangersuatsiaq. Many hunters take their families out of the village to spend the summer in fishing camps. The use of these summer camps is based on the allocation of rights by the community to individual families, rights which recognize criteria of ownership as regular occupation, maintenance of the sites and storage of equipment. From my own experiences in these camps, fishing provided the opportunity for an important social occasion as much as it did for earning money.

The camps are scenes of intense social activity as kin and friends meet, often for the first time in many months. Life becomes one constant round of going from one tent to another to eat fresh seal meat, fish and sea birds. Regular breaks are taken from setting long-lines and gutting halibut to travel in large groups to various points in the landscape for picnics or capelin fishing, or to simply walk in the summer sunshine. Children fish for tom cod, women and men sit in tents and talk of events and catch up with news from other villages.

While Greenland halibut are caught and prepared for sale to the KNI, other species of fish, sea birds and the occasional seal are harvested for sharing and consumption in the camps themselves. Working in the halibut fishery is an exclusively male occupation, with the women in the camps playing no part in the processing of the catch. The fish are taken back to the village and sold to the processing plant or to one of the two KNI factory ships which anchor in the vicinity of the main fishing areas during July, August and early September.

While some families are giving up subsistence activities for several months of the year and are diversifying, investing money and energy in fishing, many hunters tend to regard the halibut fishery as money gathering. The crucial difference between seal hunting and halibut fishing is that, while sealing entails a minor commercial element, halibut are regarded only as a source of income. This is also different from subsistence fishing for Arctic char and salmon. Meat, char and salmon are shared and consumed locally, while halibut are seen as 'money in the water', important as a supplement to seal hunting.

While the municipal and Home Rule authorities regard the halibut fishery as more economically desirable than non-profit-making subsistence hunting, this view conflicts with the way the Kangersuatsiarmiit define themselves in relation to seal hunting, which continues to have profound social, ideological and spiritual importance. Once the summer Greenland halibut fishery ends in early autumn, people revert to seal hunting.

Autumn

In the middle of August the sun dips below the horizon for the first time in three months. For many, the Greenland halibut fishery has drawn to a close and attention reverts to seal hunting. At this time, however, Arctic char (*Salvelinus alpinus*) return to the fjords, rivers and streams east of Kangersuatsiaq, in particular to Eqaluit and Eqaluaarsuit Sulluat. Arctic char are prized as a delicacy, especially when salted, so people begin to work on their nets. They place these at the river mouths to catch the fish as they swim upstream. Sometimes camps are set up, as char fishing expeditions can last from one day to up to a week.

Most of the char catch is kept for consumption within the household, although a little is sold or given to others in the village. Some families preserve the fish by salting it for winter storage. Salted char is a welcome change in January and February, when seal meat is often the only other type of food available.

There is also some jigging for tom cod (*Boreogadus saida*) around Sioraq and a few older men continue to fish for Greenland halibut in the area around Kangerlussuaq. Much of what they catch is sold to the KNI. Until recently, the tom cod fishery provided jobs for women and young people who were employed to gut and dry the fish for export. When it was eventually realized that the market was non-existent, the KNI stopped buying tom cod and in the summer of 1988 most of the fish drying racks were pulled down. Some men continued to fish for tom cod to use for dog food.

Kangersuatsiaq is the most northerly place along the west coast of Greenland where Atlantic salmon can be found (*Salmo salar*), although numbers vary from year to year and the annual catch is not particularly high. For this reason, very few people engage in salmon fishing and during the autumn of 1988 only eight men in the village maintained nets. Salmon are usually caught for personal consumption, although when a fisherman lands a large fish he may choose to sell it. The checking of salmon nets has to be carried out every day, especially when a man has several nets in different places. Travel by speedboat allows a large area to be checked in a few hours, although quite often the nets remain empty. Fishing for salmon involves considerable time and expense, in terms of nets and benzine, yet yields comparatively little.

More importantly, however, autumn brings an increase in the number of ringed seals, and the majority of hunters now spend their time taking these until thousands of migrating harp seals pass Kangersuatsiaq on their way to the whelping grounds off Newfoundland. The harp seals migrate in large groups called *amisut*, and there is a considerable increase in hunting efficiency, not only because of the large numbers of seals, but because they have accumulated a thicker layer of blubber. This means that most seals which are shot tend to remain afloat. During the summer a large proportion sink before the hunter has a chance to retrieve them.

In October some hunters set beluga nets near Kangeq in the hope of a catch as the occasional whale passes near the village. Older hunters remember the time when thousands of beluga whales (*Delphinapterus leucas*) would migrate annually through the narrow strait between Kangersuatsiaq and the nearby island of Sioraq. This was the highlight of the hunting year and everyone in the village would participate in the catch. Nets were set at both entrances to the strait and trapped hundreds of whales at a time. The beluga were then shot from shore or from small dories. The hunt was an important community occasion, with meat shared by all and providing an important store of food that lasted throughout the winter.

The beluga migration routes are now further offshore and people explain this change as happening when the number of motor boats increased. Together with the vibrations and noise of the generator, the sound of outboard engines is generally believed to have scared the whales away. Today, the only reminders of the beluga hunt, apart from stories told by older people, are the net winches on either side of the strait and several iron pots that stand on Sioraq. These pots were used for boiling blubber for sale to the Royal Greenland Trade Company.

Nowadays most hunters head north to the villages of Nuussuaq and Kullorsuaq and join others from all over the district as the beluga migrate south from Melville Bay. If successful, the hunters return to the village with huge supplies of fresh whale meat and *mattak* (the skin, which is eaten raw and frozen). They will have already sold a considerable amount of both meat and *mattak* to the KNI, but the hunters keep enough for local consumption, distribution and sale. As will be seen in Chapter 9, the sale of *mattak* and whale meat has severe implications for the customary ideology of subsistence in Kangersuatsiaq.

Winter

Late autumn is the time for the hunting household to accumulate and prepare a large winter store of seal meat, both for human consumption and for dog food. Most of this meat is preserved as frozen meat known as *quaq*. The first ice of the winter forms in the fjords and along the coast and, from the middle of November, the sun disappears below the horizon, bringing darkness until the beginning of February. By this time the men have already brought their boats up out of the water and removed the outboard motors.

For up to two or three weeks, darkness and the unstable new sea ice can confine people to the village. The last KNI supply boat from Upernavik town drops off mail and some essential winter stores, and people withdraw into their homes where indoor activity intensifies. Among other things, the women involve themselves in the repairing and preparation of skin clothing, while the men are busy working on seal nets, dog harnesses, sledges and other equipment necessary for winter hunting.

Once the newly-formed fast ice is stable enough, the men walk out to set their seal nets under the ice near small islands, icebergs or along the coast where tidal movements create cracks in the ice, used as breathing holes by ringed seals. The ringed seal is the only non-migratory species of Arctic seal and spends the winter under the ice. When the ice is faster, more stable and covered with snow, travel by dog sledge between the village and the netting sites increases the size of the area a hunter can cover. Seal nets must be checked every day as the skins of the seal are soon eaten into by amphipods, making the skin, and often some of the meat, useless.

Seal netting continues into early spring and remains the most important activity during winter, although fishing for Greenland halibut with long-lines through holes in the ice is carried out at selected localities. But the halibut fishery is hampered by winter ice conditions that determine whether the fishing grounds can be reached by dog sledge.

Spring

From late winter into early spring (March–April), the ringed seals begin to moult. Crawling out of their breathing holes, they bask on the ice as there is now plenty of sunshine. The basking seal, known as *uuttoq*, is stalked by the hunter who uses a white canvas blind attached to a small sledge. The hunter mounts his rifle upon the sledge which he then pushes slowly along the ice, crawling behind it until he is some 100m from the seal. Hunting *uuttoq* is a highly efficient form of subsistence activity and many seals are caught this way. However, the moulting skin is usually useless and is either thrown away or fed to the dogs. During May the fast sea ice begins to break up, and much seal hunting takes place from the ice edge. Boats are put onto the sledges and taken from the village to the nearest area of open water. The hunters then sit or stand in wait, in a silence only occasionally broken by gentle conversation and the hiss of primus stoves as water is boiled for tea.

At this time, seabirds begin to arrive in the area after their long migration north. Many species are harvested, in particular the guillemot (*Uria lomvia*), kittiwake (*Rissa tridactyla*), eider duck (*Somateria mollisima*), and several types of seagull. Sea birds are either caught in separate hunting expeditions, or while the hunters are at the ice edge waiting for seals. The break up of the fast ice completes the annual subsistence cycle.

This brief description of the annual subsistence cycle has outlined the main hunting and fishing activities carried out. But while subsistence activities revolve around the pattern of seasonal variation, the hunter moves through a changing environment that cannot simply be described in empirical terms. While the hunter acquires knowledge of sea mammals and their movements, together with the necessary skill and techniques to pursue and capture them, he must also be knowledgeable about the behaviour of the natural world. Hunting involves an interaction with the natural world and the hunter is engaged in a dialogue with elements of it. The next chapter focuses on the environment in which subsistence activity takes place as a way of introducing the sense of locality, belonging and community this book takes as its theme.

4

Landscape and memoryscape

The role of landscape in culture: some general remarks

In Kangersuatsiaq, the way people think and talk about landscape reveals a complex and rich repository of local knowledge used in the cultural construction of community. As this book is not concerned with the study of a community in social structural terms, but in the sense of continuity and meanings held by its members, this chapter explores the importance of landscape as the physical expression of Kangersuatsiaq. By doing so, it is my intention to use this as a starting point for later discussions about how community is expressed and culturally constructed in other ways. These all illustrate a sense of continuity and feeling of place. In focusing on landscape and the area commonly held to be the hunting place (*piniarfik*), this chapter outlines notions of locality and community boundary.

In Upernavik district, as in all areas of the world where landscape plays an important role in culture, the conceptual ordering of experience derives from encounters and interactions with the physical environment. Social anthropologists have shown how northern hunting peoples are inextricably linked with the natural environment both socially and psychologically (for example Nelson 1969, 1983). This is also a noted feature of hunting and gathering societies worldwide.

Such intimacy is often of a spiritual nature, which has led some writers to see the absence of this in Western consciousness as characteristic of modernity (Carmody 1981). Secular attitudes to landscape are often abhorrent to those peoples for whom the natural environment has deep religious significance (e.g. Toelke 1976). For hunting peoples such as the Koyukon of the Alaskan boreal forest, elements of the natural world permeate religious ideology. Because the Koyukon environment is vested with spiritual power '. . . human existence depends on a morally based relationship with the overarching powers of nature' (Nelson 1983: 240). The continuity of such a relationship requires the propitiation of the spirit powers associated with the forest, together with a respect and reverence towards natural entities. Survival is often dependent on correct, conscious and careful human action to maintain the balance between the human and natural worlds.

In Western thought, from the late eighteenth century, perceptions of the natural world were re-shaped in response to the effects of technology and economic development on the landscape. Concern about the ravages of civilization on man's essential inner self led some writers to idealise rural life. Lopez, writing of the close association of human and landscape, sees it as an 'archaic affinity' that is 'an antidote to the loneliness that in our own culture we associate with individual estrangement and despair' (Lopez 1986: 266). But even when Western attitudes towards landscape see it as something other than a commodity in economic terms, there is a difference between perceptions influenced by, for example, the Romantic poets and those who point out the inherent savagery of nature (e.g. Dillard 1974).

Some anthropologists have been concerned with the analysis of landscape as wilderness and the way that the dichotomy of village and wild places are central features of cosmology. The structuralist emphasis on culture:nature has also gone some way, in its concern with the externalization of the environment, in showing how landscape stands apart from the warm secure human world. Myth and fairytale often exemplify this in their treatment of nature as enchanted and a place to fear.

Recently, landscape has received more attention from those interested in its symbolic significance. Besson (1979) has shown how the institution of family land among Jamaican peasantries has a symbolic, rather than practical use. Local authorities and those concerned with rural development regard family land as uneconomic and underproductive. Besson argues that this is a negative ethnocentric perspective. Family land tenure is not inefficient, but symbolizes permanence and the continuity of kin groups. Cohen (1987) sees features of a Shetland landscape such as place names, crofting land and peatbanks as elements of a cultural past that act as reference points for orientation in the present. They are features of social identity, and the croft 'condenses the past through the landscape itself, and through its associations with the natural calendar; with community; with an earlier mode of subsistence and the ideal of self-sufficiency' (Cohen 1987: 109).

As was seen in Chapter 2, for Inuit groups the land (*nuna*) has become the focus of identity and political aspiration although, since Home Rule, the latter is no longer the case in Greenland. My concern in this chapter is with landscape as a memoryscape. This will be elaborated upon later, but by way of brief definition, memoryscape is constructed with people's mental images of the environment, with particular emphasis on places as remembered places. The area utilized by an individual hunter is part of the community hunting area and, by virtue of belonging to the community, the places a hunter frequents are stamped with the indelible marks of community. These marks are not visible, but are manifest in place names, memories of hunting and of past events. All give a sense of a bounded locality distinct from the memoryscape of neighbouring communities. To borrow the often used Lévi-Strauss phrase, places are 'good to think with' and nurture a feeling of belonging.

As I mentioned in the previous chapter, however, it is the sea (*imaq*), in all its forms, that is the primary physical feature affecting life in Upernavik district. The population of Kangersuatsiaq and the southern part of the district has been concerned with sea-use, as opposed to land-use, though, there has been a small, but significant, exploitation of inland valleys when caribou were hunted. There was caribou hunting in Kangeq between 1850 and 1922 and in J.P. Koch's Land until the mid-1960s. This is based on informants' information and little exists in the literature which mentions use of the land (except Bryder *et al*. 1921: 430–516, Haller 1986: 97). Today there is no caribou hunting because the caribou population has probably disappeared from the hinterland east of Kangersuatsiaq. In the northern part of West Greenland, caribou are now found only in the southern part of Svartenhuk. I agree with Haller that the land 'cannot be considered a resource base' (ibid: 97), although sledging routes sometimes involve long detours over the land, usually when the fast sea ice is unstable making winter and spring travel dangerous. I would elaborate upon Haller's observation by arguing that, in the southern part of Upernavik, the land was important in the past and still plays an important role in the cognition of Kangersuatsiaq.

The physical environment is important as the place where a hunter secures the means for his family's existence; in Haller's study he uses the term action space (ibid: 43). As will become clear, it is also thought space. Before discussing the idea of landscape as memoryscape, it is necessary to outline how the Kangersuatsiaq area is perceived and most immediately expressed as community territory.

The physical environment: local perceptions

The physical environment is perceived by the senses and through the interaction of experience, thought and language it is modified, ordered and conceptualized. The Kangersuatsiarmiit talk about the seascape and ice-scape in the same way as landscape. All three are contoured and the mind, through language, recognizes and expresses shape and form.

Seascape

As Kangersuatsiaq is an island, people's lives are dominated by the sight and sound of water. Along with the sky, its many moods provide the subject matter for much casual daily comment, always within the context of talk about the weather. Early in the morning, groups of men gather by the old meeting house to watch and discuss the weather. It is usually the first topic of conversation and continual observations are made throughout the day, with occasional attempts at forecasting the outlook for the following few days. The Greenlandic for weather is *sila*. A more detailed consideration of this concept will follow in the next chapter, but for this discussion it is sufficient to say that in its broadest sense it refers to 'that which is outside', 'the air' and 'the weather'.

People look to the sea for their very existence. From it come seals (*puisit*), which give themselves up to the hunter to be converted into meat (*neqi*), fish (*aalisakkat*) and other marine creatures. Dependency involves knowing when and where to hunt. When men discuss the weather, they remark upon the subtle changes in the mood of the sky and the corresponding reactions in the sea. Sila 'moves' and Greenlanders say '*uagut naluarput*'; 'we do not know it'. *Sila* interacts with, and influences the sea and makes it a calm sea (*imarippoq*) or a strong one (*maliallerpoq*), or brings the wind (*anori*) which causes waves (*malit*) and a rising sea (*qaffiavoq*). People come to recognize when a large wave (*maliarsuk*) is about to become a swelling wave (*ingiulik*), thus placing a hunting trip in a difficult position because of a probable storm (*anorersuaq*), or when it will pass, leaving nothing but a ripple (*minittorneq*).

Sila, by bringing the wind and by changing the sky, ensures the seascape is in constant flux. However, there are permanent and recurring features, such as eddies (*qalaliatut*; 'things which bubble and boil under the water'), or places where one can see the land casting shadows on the water (*qoqaat*). Just as *qoqaat* can darken the sea, the water can also reflect light (*qillaaluttoq*) in certain places and in different seasons. The sea then, is not seen as a featureless expanse of 'broad water' (*imartuneq*); its surface (*immap qaa*) contours twist and change. Wind and tide bring icepans (*kassut*), icebergs (*iluliat*) and movement discernible to an observing eye.

Ice-scape

Sea ice dominates the environment of the Kangersuatsiarmiit from October through to June. With a dog team, travel on sea ice is possible from the end of December until late May. Because the sea ice is forever changing and unpredictable, the hunter requires a comprehensive understanding of its behaviour and movement. This knowledge finds expression in an elaborate vocabulary that refers to formation and type of ice.

The Greenlandic language differentiates between sea ice (*siku*) and freshwater ice (*nilak*). During summer and early autumn the sea is *sikueruppoq*; 'ice-free', or 'has no ice'. The formation of sea ice in autumn is eagerly anticipated and in early October thin ice (*sikuaq*) forms in the inner fjords. Towards the end of October the harp seal hunting season is over and most hunters have taken their boats out of the water. By the middle of November the ice (*siku*) has spread out beyond the bays until the sea is frozen over (*sikuvoq*).

There is a period of two or three weeks just before Christmas when winter darkness and the brittle condition of the new ice make dogsledging impossible. During this time the hunters make final preparations to their sledges and seal netting equipment. Some hunters walk on to the ice to hunt ringed seals at their breathing holes (*allu*), which the seal makes by pushing its head through the new ice. In darkness these breathing holes are difficult to find and are quite often snow covered. Breathing hole hunting has declined over the last several years and today only a few older hunters practise it. Most hunters prefer to set seal nets under the ice rather than wait for several hours for a seal to come up for air. Compared to breathing hole hunting, which may result in a kill of only one or two seals during a wait of several hours, seal netting involves less time spent on the ice and may yield up to four seals in one net. In addition many younger hunters talk of the danger involved in walking on new ice to look for breathing holes, as this type of hunting takes place when the ice is only two or three inches thick.

New ice (*sikuliaq*) can be unsafe in parts, with dark patches revealing the sea underneath. For the hunter, knowledge of where to set foot on fast ice is vital for survival. Just as the seascape is in motion, the sea ice is not immutable. Wind and sea currents ensure the instability of the ice-scape. Icebergs locked into the ice can become almost permanent features for several months, but tidal movements can disrupt them. A smooth flat stretch of ice (*manerak*), which is ideal for sledging on one day, may 'become open water' (*imarorpoq*) on another and is not to be taken for granted. As the winter progresses the ice-scape changes and eventually becomes broken (*manillat*) and a floating pack (*sikorsuit*) during late spring, leaving only fast shore ice (*qaanngoq*) which is safe to travel along. By June seals are being hunted by boat once more.

Landscape and community boundary

In Greenland, compared with more nomadic northern hunting peoples, Inuit society has been characterized by fixed settlements for several centuries. This has meant that groups of people have remained in the same areas, instead of traversing larger parts of the country according to season. The regular return of families to the same campsites during spring and summer, and the constant use of particular hunting areas means each community has its own recognized territory. For the people of Kanger-suatsiaq, as for the inhabitants of all other Greenlandic settlements, their hunting and fishing grounds lie within the immediate neighbourhood.

In the literature on the appropriation of the natural environment, anthropologists have long debated the distinction between territoriality and land tenure. Hunter-gatherers have generally been regarded as having territory while agricultural societies are characterized by a land tenure system. Ingold (1986) has argued that this distinction is founded on an evolutionist tendency to regard land tenure as demonstrating a human transcendence over nature, while regarding hunter-gatherers as victims of environmental determinism. From this perspective it is inappropriate to talk of hunting societies as having tenure precisely because they are seen to have no mastery over their environment. Agricultural societies, on the other hand, have evolved along the continuum from primitive to modern thereby freeing themselves from the constraints of nature.

This idea of territoriality is reductionist in tone because it restricts any analysis of hunting and gathering societies to an understanding derived only in terms of materialism. Ignoring any possibility of behaviourism, social relations and consciousness the concern is with adaptive strategies and optimal foraging, with co-operation and interaction, and with the relation of a population to its environmental resource base. The scene is one of '. . . hunters and collectors, wandering about in small hordes in their tribal territories seeking game, roots, fruits, grubs, and so forth' (Evans-Pritchard 1965: 58). But as Chapter 3 showed, hunting cannot be viewed simply as an aspect of material relations. It must be seen as an aspect of relations between people, between people and places, and between people and animals. Chapter 9 will elaborate further on this, but for the moment I am concerned with the emphasis on the distinction between territory and tenure.

Tenure implies ownership in agricultural societies, while hunting peoples are generally regarded as being owned by the land. Again this denies sociality, human intention and purpose. Another problem lies with the tendency to regard hunter-gatherers as nomadic, with a high degree of mobility within large territories determined by the seasonal round. Any notion of tenure does not fit easily into analyses that stress such an ecological fit between a hunting band and its environmental niche.

Anthropologists have a tendency to categorize, to simplify and pass judgement on another culture that quite often does not correspond with the ways of seeing and understanding within that culture. So, in an anthropological world-view people have either territoriality or they have tenure. To have both only confuses the anthropologist's analysis of social structure. But for hunter-gatherers the opposition between territoriality and tenure is not mutually exclusive but complementary. The Kangersuat-siarmiit are not nomadic yet they exploit a wide territory. They also have land tenure but they are not agriculturalists, nor do they say that they own the land.

It is useful to follow Ingold here, who says that tenure '. . . is an aspect of that system of relations which *constitutes* persons as productive agents and directs their purposes, territoriality is an aspect of the means through which these purposes are put into effect under given environmental circumstances' (1986: 130–131). In one sense, a bounded territory is a way of marking off the resource allocation of a particular group, in another, territoriality can be seen as a symbolic demarcation of the environment. Tenure is the use of places and sites within the group's territory. But it is important to recognize that use does not necessarily imply ownership. In Kangersuatsiaq tenure involves allocation to sites and recognition of use by certain individuals, as will be explained below.

The literature on Greenlandic Inuit hunting patterns usually emphasizes two conflicting issues (see Brøsted 1986, Petersen 1963, 1965). These are as follows.

1. Greenlandic society is characterized by the freedom of the individual, and combined with this is the recognition that no one owns the animals Inuit hunt. Therefore every individual has the right to use the land and to hunt and fish wherever he wants.
2. The right to exploit hunting territory is regulated by the community, since it is the local community that controls these areas. Membership of the community is a prerequisite for use of its resource areas. But this is not to exclude others. Strangers and outsiders can hunt in another community's area provided they are staying there.

In practice, this second aspect provides the foundation for use. The community both controls and allows access to its hunting territory. Individuals have rights over certain areas owing to community allocation which recognizes they have exclusive use. Examples here include netting sites for seals, salmon and beluga, campsites and storage sites. I shall now outline how this works in the Kangersuatsiaq area.

Netting sites

Compiled by me from interviews and regular participation in hunting and fishing trips, Map 4.1 shows the places where hunters have rights to set nets for seals, salmon and beluga whales. Each hunter has his own netting sites which cannot be used by others, except under certain circumstances, as will be seen below. Sons usually inherit the right to use such sites from their fathers. Individual netting sites are found only near the mainland or around small islands, since there are no community regulations restricting rights to set nets around icebergs, where individuals have free access.

Campsites and storage sites

To the east of Kangersuatsiaq in the area around Qerqertaq, there are numerous campsites. These are usually only occupied during late spring, summer and early autumn, are used by individual families and have quite often been established for several generations. Tents tend to be erected on the same spots, with areas set aside for other relatives and visitors. In the summer of 1987, when I arrived at Josepi's family campsite near Qerqertaq, I was allotted a place where I could pitch my tent. The following year, when we returned to fish for the summer, I retained my rights to the same site. There was nothing particularly significant about the site in the sense of it being a good or bad site, except that the family I was with had prescriptive rights to it.

At certain points in the landscape, hunters maintain storage sites used for equipment or as meat caches. Hunting equipment may be kept close to netting sites, seal meat is stored for use as dog food when hunters are away for several days, and extra supplies of benzine are taken out to places near the main summer fishing camps. By maintaining storage sites

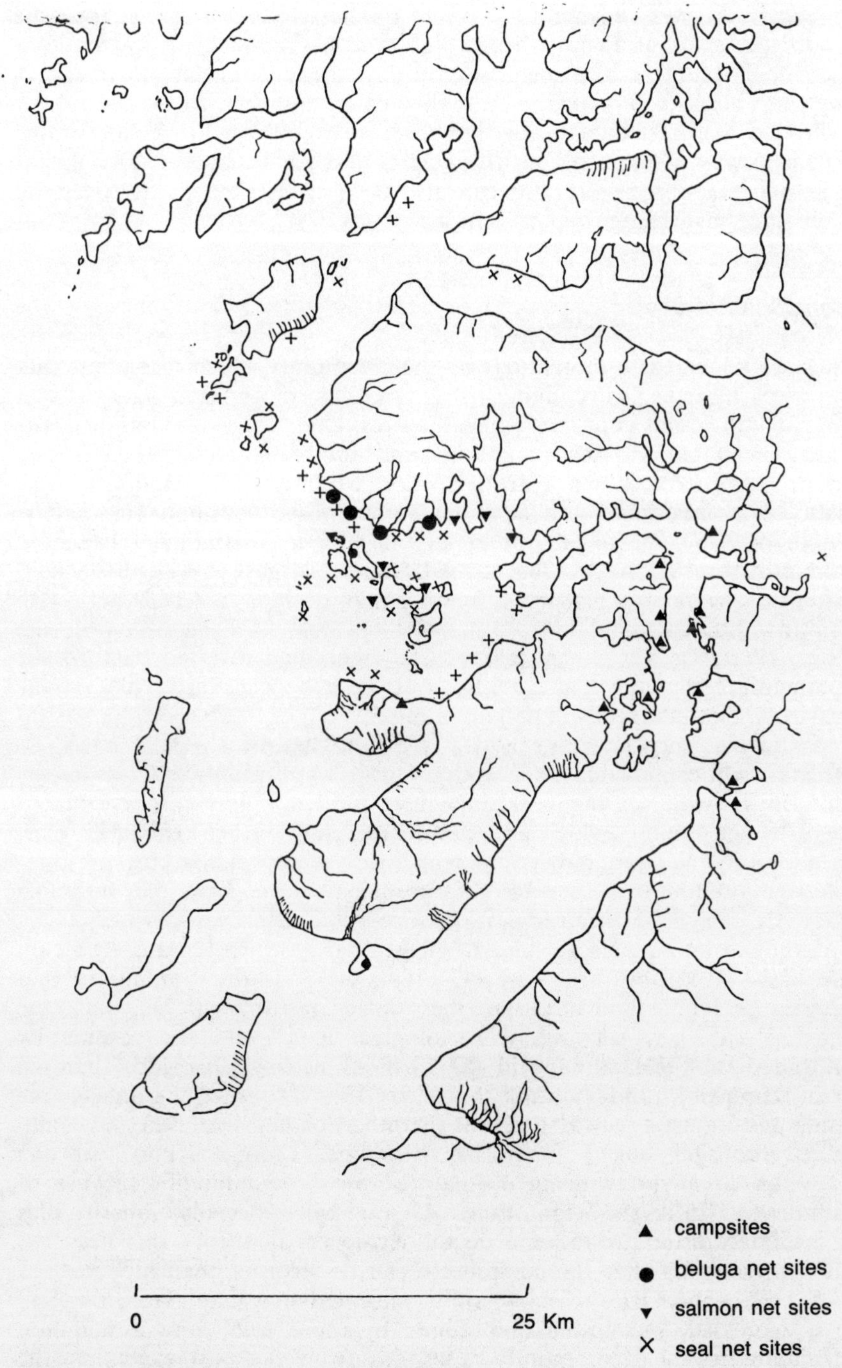

Map 4.1 Netting sites

in winter, hunters ensure they have supplies dispersed throughout the landscape, enabling them to travel light and never too far from food for their dogs. Hunters who spend several days away from the village checking seal nets usually skin the seals they catch and then cache several for collection at a later date. Some families have even started to build hunting huts as a way of marking out their claim to a particular site. This means a permanent storage site that can also be used as shelter. However, all such sites have recognized conditions of use.

Conditions of use

Sites are allocated to individuals by the community which recognizes that the users have exclusive rights to tenure. This recognition only lasts as long as individuals continue to use the sites. Once use is discontinued, the rights revert back to the community and another hunter is then free to take the site over. When a death occurs, a hunter's son relinquishes the rights to an inherited site if he chooses not to use it within a 'reasonable' length of time. As an example, an old hunter discontinued use of a salmon netting site at Avalleq, a small island just next to Kangersuatsiaq. After he surrendered his rights, another man decided to set his net there. The first hunter complained to me that the new user had stolen his site ('*Karl tillipaa*'). But others insisted the rights had reverted back to the community, allowing another hunter to take over exclusive use on the basis of his affiliation to the community.

As long as such sites are used and maintained on a regular basis, no other person can establish a claim. Campsites are usually marked out by tent rings, while netting sites may have particular large stones, placed there by the hunter, which are used in securing the net year after year. In addition, the storage of equipment is also a way of marking prescriptive rights. Quite often storage sites are personal and inherited, although there are many that are temporary, such as food caches.

Although individuals do have privilege of use, which is transferable on the basis of kinship and descent, ultimately it is the community that decides on tenure and access to the hunting territory. In this way, the geographical area becomes a sociological area, with the community imprinted on the landscape in the form of netting sites, local hunting area, campsites and hunting huts. In the case of inheritance, the community must acknowledge that the inheritor has also used and maintained the sites during his father's lifetime. I do not know of any examples of anybody being disinherited by the community because of failure to fulfil this condition. A son will normally inherit sites immediately after his father's death. However, in theory this may not happen, showing that the community can be stronger than blood.

As this chapter tries to show, subsistence activities take place in a local area expressed, recognized and shared by those who enjoy a common affiliation to their community. Episodes from the past exemplify the importance of locality. For example, people were often killed if they ventured into the hunting area of another community (e.g. Rink 1866: 214). In contemporary Greenland, such extreme treatment of outsiders has now been reduced to silent complaint and joking (see Chapter 9), though strangers are still regarded as people to fear (see Chapter 7). In the following pages, I shall elaborate on this sense of locality. In particular, the significance of places, names and stories (or memories) show how landscape is constituted in relation to the inhabitants of Kangersuatsiaq.

Talking about maps

I had been involved with Josepi's family for some three and a half months when I asked if he could show me, on maps, some of the places where he used to hunt for caribou. My growing confidence in the language was the determining factor in deciding to pursue my interest in mapping areas of the past utilization of land and sea by the older hunters in the village. Because of the decline of caribou hunting and the introduction of new technology, hunting methods are changing. Many parts of the Kangersuatsiaq hinterland are no longer visited, caribou hunting campsites have been abandoned and very few people now have knowledge of certain areas and previously significant points in the landscape. All the other hunters agreed that if anyone knew anything about the old days (*itsaq*) it would be Josepi.

Josepi immediately showed enthusiasm at my request and said we could start the following day. It was the end of October and the days were growing shorter. Darkness was beginning to confine Josepi to the village and he now used his time making seal nets in preparation for the winter season. When I arrived, carrying my 1:250,000 scale maps of Kangersuatsiaq and the southern part of Upernavik district, I found Josepi had his own maps ready. He said he was glad I had brought maps which covered such a wide area, as his hunting routes extended from J.P. Koch's Land in the north, to the southern part of Svartenhuk, bordering Uummannaq district, a distance of some 120 km.

I handed the maps to Josepi who, unfolding them, sat forward and sank into silence. I occupied myself with studying the topographic details on Josepi's maps, while he seemed lost in the contours of the land and the myriad fjords before him. Finally, he put down the map, rolled himself a cigarette, and poured a cup of coffee from the flask he kept under his small table. I went into the kitchen and, taking a mug from the cupboard, helped myself to coffee from the large flask reserved for the rest of the family.

Josepi's enthusiasm was immediately infectious as he then talked at length of the places he would hunt for caribou, first with his father and later with David. His reminiscences went back as far as 1932 when he first joined his father at the age of nine on a journey to J.P. Koch's Land. Such journeys, undertaken by kayak and *umiak* (skin boat), would take an average of twenty-two days, he told me. I watched as he traced his numerous expeditions with his finger, weaving in and out of fjords, pointing to places he would stop *en route* to eat, to hunt, to rest and to camp. He showed me the mountains he wandered among and the rivers he crossed. He told me to mark the places where he had hunted caribou and I noted the dates and campsites. I felt I was gaining access to a past which contained a different view from contemporary attitudes and responses to the land, particularly those held by younger hunters.

After some two hours of conversation, we were disturbed by Josepi's grandchildren coming home from school. His attention was drawn to other things, to talk of the arrival of the supply boat and of activity down on the pier. Josepi said he wanted to see if any visitors had arrived with the boat. His grandchildren told me the first of the winter's supplies were being unloaded. I folded my map and went down to watch.

The following day I visited Josepi again. Being so closely associated with his family, hardly a day went by without my spending some time in his house. He asked me if I had brought my map. I said I would go and fetch it, expecting to be told of more hunting expeditions and campsites. Once more, Josepi took the map and spread it on his table. Pointing to part of a small ice-cap close to the inland ice, he said 'This map is wrong. There is no ice here, these are two ice-caps, not one.' I marked off the part of the map which showed ice. 'This, here, is land and there is no ice,' he reaffirmed.

Josepi paused, poured himself some coffee, and then returned to the map. Pointing to a spot just to the west of the smallest of the two ice-caps, he told me he had seen a woman's grave there, first in the 1940s and then on later trips. He said her name was Gertuluk and that it was written on a wooden cross. He knew no more about her, but he did remember that the grave was surrounded by wild flowers and that berries grew in abundance. He had first seen it after walking east on one occasion from Ujarqat Qaqortut ('the white rocks') towards the inland ice, in search of caribou. He told me that he could remember that the area was beautiful (*alianaak*) but that he found no trace of caribou.

Josepi spoke with authority, rolling a cigarette when he seemed satisfied that he could remember no more about Gertuluk. He had told me the cartographers were wrong, his comments made with the confidence of knowing the land, of having traversed it in search of meat. I accepted his version of the map because it had come from his memory. I wondered later whether he had simply been looking at my map in comparison, to check the finer details of his mental map.

An individual hunter's image of the environment evolves in relation to his experience of it. The landscape becomes something which is constituted in relation to each individual. Memory is singularly important because individual ideas are personal and through knowledge and memory hunters 'negotiate images and understandings of the land' (Basso 1984: 22).

Josepi enjoyed reading maps. It was like looking back over a lifetime, with each experience and every hunting trip made familiar. But maps, as Josepi showed me, are profoundly inaccurate compared with a hunter's memory of the places they chart. Most older hunters I interviewed had difficulty relating to sheet maps. Place names are often wrong and informants tend to understand oblique aerial photographs far better. I found that sheet maps were useful as a reference to which a hunter could 'add his own layers of detailed information' (Brody 1983: 47).

Josepi said he would like to teach me the place names of the surrounding area, the names which could not be found on the map, but that we could start another day. Talking to him started me thinking about the land in another way. It did not seem enough just to record land use sites, there were additional layers of meaning to understand.

Later, I studied my maps in Juuna's house, marking in his father's routes. I began a conversation with Juuna and he showed me some of the places he had travelled to with Josepi. Pointing to a place, Juuna would say it was 'dark' (*taaq*), or 'frightening' (*ersinaq*) or 'beautiful' (*alianaak*). He showed me the route of a journey he once made to Umiiarfik (a fjord in the Svartenhuk area) and I asked him if it was beautiful there. Juuna replied that it was an 'evil' (*ajortoq*) place because he had dreamt of ghosts and strange people living under the earth while camped there.

This led me to attempt to elucidate patterns of thought focused on landscape. What is of interest is how these thought patterns reveal a hidden landscape. The way individuals are predisposed to regard and think about their environment can only be seen with reference to the variables of memory, personality and emotions. I have already sketched out how the environment is immediately perceived by the senses, in terms of knowledge and experience underlying and informing this perception. I now want to build on this a little by considering the above-mentioned subjective variables. A useful starting point is to examine place names.

Naming places

Whenever I travelled with people from the village, either in the immediate vicinity of Kangersuatsiaq or on extended trips throughout the district, I would always mark our routes on 1:250,000 scale maps produced by the Danish Geodetic Institute. To start with, I also found these maps useful for learning about local place names and geographical features. As I have shown though, local knowledge and Danish maps do not always share similar features, especially when different experiences of distances are taken into account. Also, as mentioned above, I began to use local perceptions of landscape as material to fill in the blanks on the 'official maps' and to correct what were seen as mistakes. In addition, careful study of both local land and sea use and the Danish maps reveals three perceptual layers that have been imposed on landscape and environment in Upernavik district. These are the perceptions of colonists and explorers, whalers, and the indigenous Inuit.

These three perceptual layers manifest themselves in place names and it is their study, known as onomastics, that provides a framework within which to work. Onomastics require both an interpretation of place names and a consideration of how closely they conform to geography. In addition, their etymology involves a discovery of analogy, description and hidden meaning, revealed in memory and in storytelling.

The colonial habit of place-naming reduces the landscape to an impersonal piece of territory, previously thought to be devoid of life. For the explorers and colonists, the land was there awaiting 'discovery' and to be claimed for the country they represented. The landscape was seen as empty and claiming by naming 'differed little from dogs pissing on street corners in strange neighbourhoods' (Cooke 1981: 58).

In Upernavik district examples include J.P. Koch's Land, Holm Island, J.A.D. Jensen Islands, and Sanderson's Hope. These are names of explorers, prominent figures and sponsors. Sanderson's Hope at 72° 46′N was named by the Elizabethan explorer John Davis after William Sanderson, one of the sponsors of his 1587 expedition to discover the Northwest Passage. He is said to have named it Sanderson's Hope for the Passage (Lopez 1986: 330). It is a 1,042m high mountain just to the south of Upernavik town and in Greenlandic it is called 'big rock'.

Throughout northern Greenland there are places named after kings, queens, explorers and even societies (e.g. Geographical Society Island at 73° N on the northeast coast). Names can be seen as being possessive in that they indicate ownership by a person or group. More importantly, they establish power and territorial claim and historically they tell how 'men of action created names for themselves as they lived' (Robinson 1973: 323). As for the practice of naming places after royalty, one polar scholar, exemplifying the attitude of the exploring fraternity, suggested that critics '. . . should ask themselves whom else but royalty they would choose if they set out to do honour to the highest in their land' (Debenham 1942: 544).

Throughout the eighteenth and nineteenth centuries, Scottish and English whalers systematically exploited the waters in Upernavik district and are responsible for several place names, such as Sugar Loaf, Dark Head and Horse Head. The whalers, as indeed the explorers, took their own cognitive stereotypes with them into the Arctic. Their expectations were informed by those who went before them and the Arctic was seen as an unforgiving wilderness. Much of this was expressed in song and ballad:

> Now Greenland is a horrid place
> Where our fisher lads have to go
> Where the rose and the lily never
> bloom in spring
> And there's only ice and snow
> ['The Greenland Whale Fishery',
> nineteenth century traditional
> whaling song].

Successive waves of whalers, explorers and travellers ventured into the Arctic and specific images emerged based on their accounts. Subjective impressions were allowed to colour published journals of whaling voyages and of exploration and this led to an image others internalized and upon which they based their own ideas. Writing was influenced by immediate impressions and by the author's situation, such as the hardships endured, cold, inadequate equipment, homesickness, starvation and the death of fellow crew members. Image and geographical reality occasionally overlapped when it came to place naming, for example Devil's Thumb in the north of Upernavik district.

All this points to the importance of memory, personality and emotion as variables in the perception of landscape and the environment. For the purpose of this discussion I am interested in how these variables inform us of the Inuit relationship with the environment and it is this to which I now turn.

Memoryscape

Greenlandic place names in the Kangersuatsiaq area and in the rest of Upernavik district differ from the Danish names given to the same localities. This also holds for the rest of Greenland. Greenlandic names do not necessarily conform to geography, but they are multi-dimensional. This means they contain a physical, mythical, factual and historical meaning (Robinson 1973).

Each of these meanings overlap and converge. There are places which refer specifically to physical features such as Kangeq, Kangersuatsiaq, Sioraq ('sand island'), Qerqertaq ('island'), Kangerlussuaq ('big fjord'), Singarnaq ('yellowish grey'), Ikerasaq ('sound' or 'channel'), Saatoq ('thin, flat stone island') and Majuariaq ('hill').

Other names reflect analogy. Such places require a more powerful toponymical designation because they serve to remind people of other realms of experience and culture which transcend geography. Examples in the Kangersuatsiaq area include Iviangernat ('twin peaks resembling a woman's breasts'), Maniitsoq (an island resembling 'hummocky ice'), Toornaarsutoq ('little spirit'), Salleq ('the island in front of the inhabited place'), Qallunaaq ('Dane') and Anaana ('mother').

The majority of place names inform us of land and sea use, both in the present and in the past. Map 4.2 reveals a landscape named not because of features immediately apparent, but due to the importance of these places in subsistence activities, human activity and fellowship. The places I have marked on the map include:

Qammavik	– This sea cave means 'a place where hunters lie in wait for sea mammals'.
Ukalersalik	– 'A place where one finds Arctic hares' (*ukaleq*)
Arfeq	– 'Walrus'
Qasigiaqarfiup Kuua	– 'River which belongs to the place of the spotted seal'.

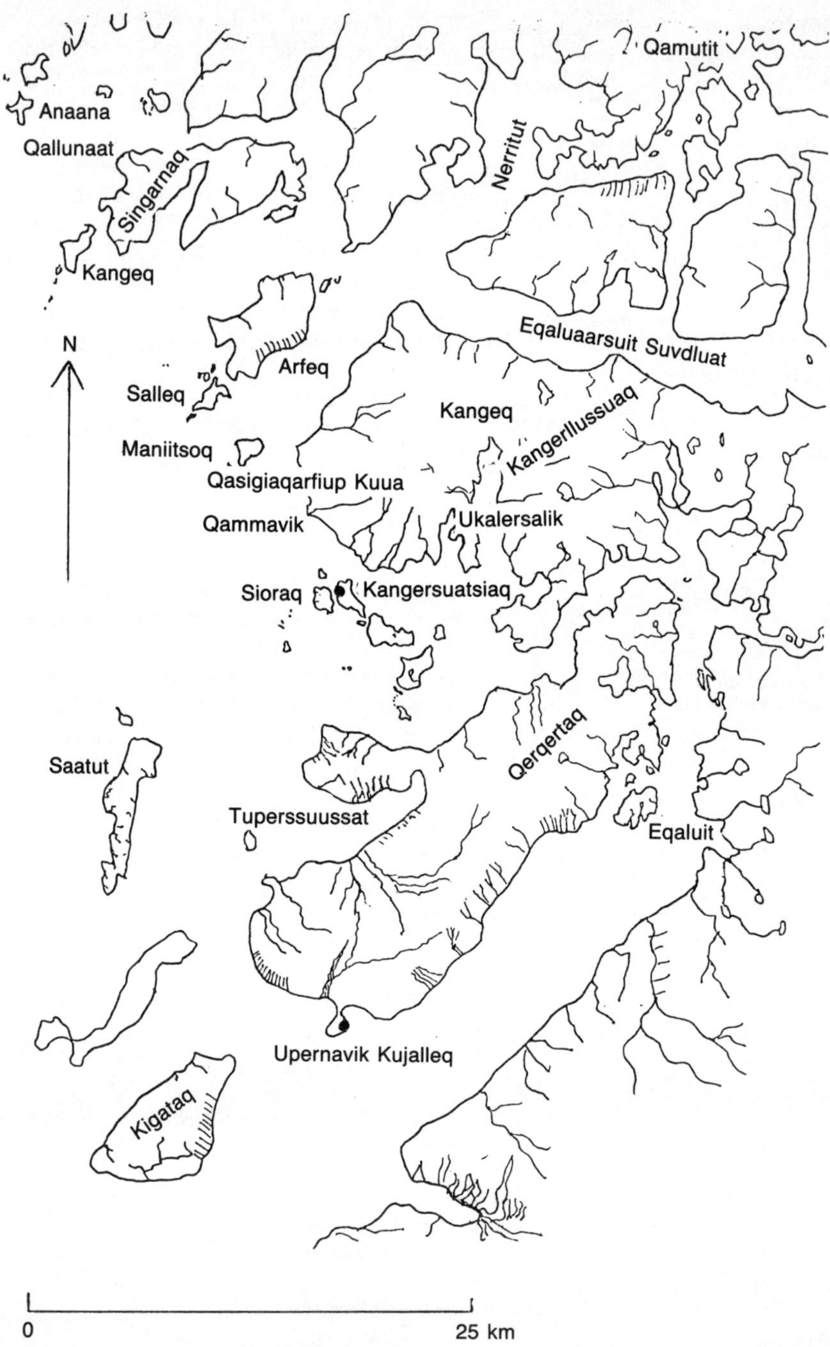

Map 4.2 Place names in the Kangersuatsiaq area

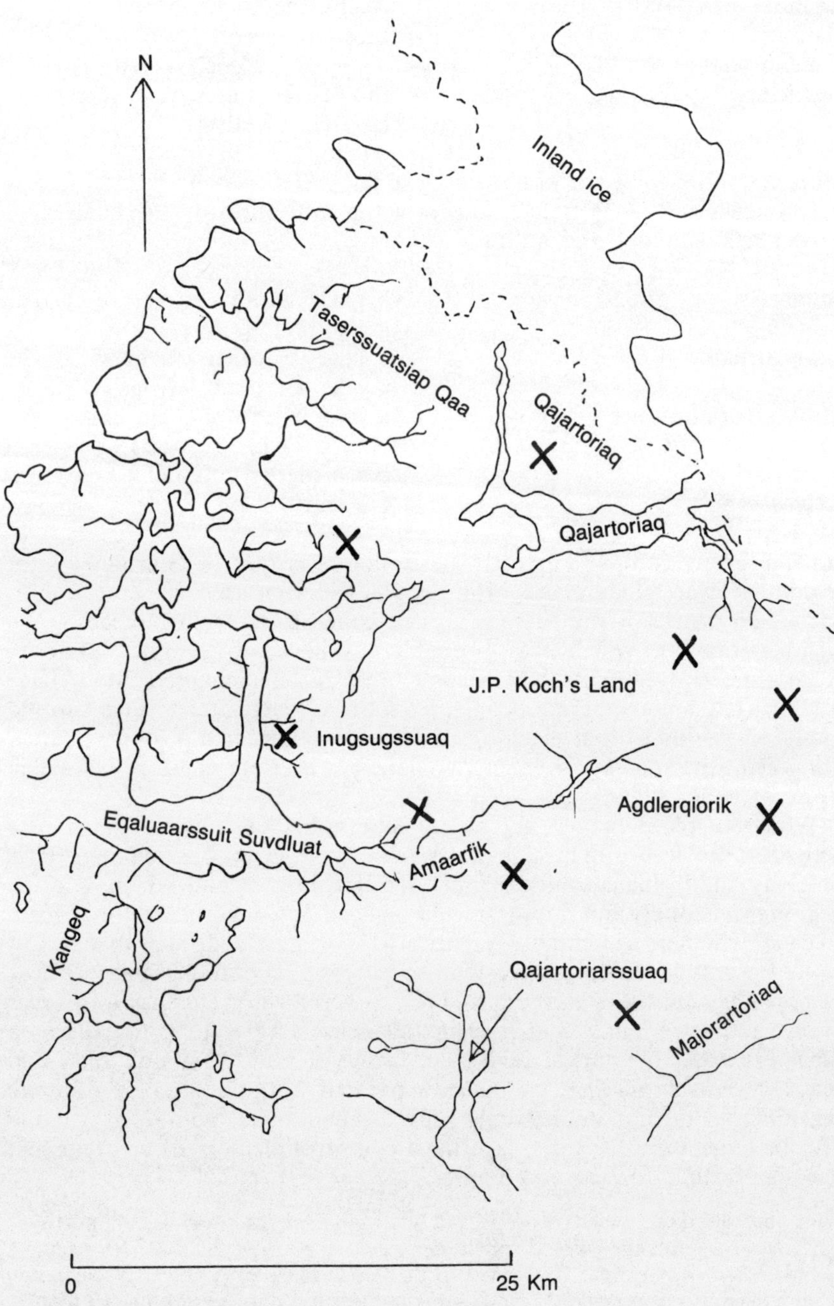

Map 4.3 J.P. Koch's Land. Place names and caribou hunting sites

Eqaluit	– 'Arctic char'
Qamutit	– 'Sled'
Tuperssussat	– 'a camping place'
Nerrittut	– 'the eaters', i.e. a place where 'they eat together'

Map 4.3 shows past caribou hunting areas in J.P. Koch's Land. Again, the Greenlandic place names illustrate the utilization of the landscape, particularly summer and autumn activities:

Amaarfik	– 'a place where kayaks are carried up from'
Qajartoriaq	– 'a lake (or other place) where kayaks are used'
Majorartoriaq	– 'a river where one can climb up' (with a boat or kayak)
Allerqiorfik	– 'place of the long-tailed duck'
Inugsussuaq	– 'big cairn'

An interesting comparison with the explorers is that in Greenland Inuit seldom, if ever, name places after people. Petersen notes an exception in Maniitsoq district where there is a place called Kamillakkut (meaning the Kamilla family), which was probably a kin based summer campsite (Petersen 1963: 276). As will become clear in later chapters, Inuit have other ways of remembering people. To name a place after a person would imply possession of that place. Inuit do refer to land in a possessive sense, but when a person says *nunaga* ('my land') it is in the sense of belonging to a particular place.

Whatever place names say about geography, analogy or subsistence activities, however, many have an additional layer of meaning. It is precisely that which is hidden and invisible in the land which is often neglected. Stories and myth unfold against a geographical backdrop. Events, whether contemporary, historical or mythical, that happen at certain points in the local area tend to become integral elements of those places. They are thought about and remembered with reference to specific events and experiences and it is in this sense I refer to landscape as a memoryscape. Memories take the form of stories about real and remembered things. They cannot be separated from the land even though place names do not immediately reflect such stories. Some place names may be mnemonic devices, triggering a collective memory of an event that has significance for the community:

In the old days, when people lived on Maniitsoq [a small island north of Kangersuatsiaq], they would sometimes travel to Kangersuatsiaq. There came a time when people were frightened to do this because of a powerful *angakkoq* who lived at Qammavik. At first, some hunters did not return home to Maniit-soq in their kayaks. It was thought they had capsized at Kinnguvik ['the place where one capsizes', *kinnguvoq*; capsizes]. Then more hunters disappeared, until one returned to tell of the *angakkoq*. The *angakkoq* was evil [*ajortoq*] and jealous of other hunters (*sangiarpoq*). He would lie in wait in his kayak at Qammavik until a hunter passed by with a seal. He would paddle his kayak behind the hunter until he was close enough to kill him and steal his seal. Some say the hunters went together and killed the *angakkoq*, but others say he saw them coming and flew away from Qammavik in his kayak over Kangeq to the mountains. [Transcript of several versions of a story told about Qammavik].

Other places contain within them stories that have a more individual memory about isolated events:

I will tell a story about Arfeq. I remember a man who once made a beautiful harpoon head [*tuukkaq*]. The first time he went out hunting with it he spotted a walrus on an ice floe. He paddled his kayak very carefully until he was close enough to throw his harpoon. He took aim and threw it, but the walrus dived. Pulling in his harpoon, he noticed the harpoon head had disappeared, but the shaft [*unaaq*] and the bladder float [*avataq*] were still there. He looked around but could not see the walrus. Feeling depressed at the disappearance of the walrus and the loss of the harpoon head he returned home. Later, during the evening, he went to visit his friend who was a big hunter. Still in low spirits, he told his friend of the day's events and of the loss of the beautiful harpoon head. However, his friend laughed and, reaching into his pocket, he said: 'Today I was out in my kayak and you thought *I* was a walrus! Here is your harpoon head!'

When I was a child I used to hear a story about Aappilattoq. It was dark and a ship was sailing towards the village. The children were very afraid because they thought some Qallunaat [Danes or Europeans] were coming to make war with the Inuit. They began screaming and crying and nobody could calm them. An old woman, who was a sorceress [*ilisiitsoq*], told the people to put out all the lights. She then went down to the water's edge and let down her hair. She dipped her hair in the water and told the ship to go away, because it was making the children afraid. She pulled her hair out of the water and the lights in the ship went out. The people saw that now instead of the ship there was an iceberg. Sometimes I think of the things that happened in my country, in the past. [Both stories told by Matheus L., aged 78]

Place names are important in story-telling because they are 'situating devices, as conventionalized instruments for locating narrated events in the physical settings where the events have occurred' (Basso 1984: 32). Such individual recollection becomes part of the community repertoire and gives access to a past that provides a direct link to the present. Taken from my field notes, the story that follows is a version of four corresponding accounts told to me by the actors involved.

In January 1986, two of Eirik's dogs disappeared from the village. They had been chained up outside Josepi's house and nobody in the village had seen them escape. Several days later, Eirik, Josepi and David set off to set their nets in the Salleq area. They planned to spend the night in the hunter's hut on the island where they would be joined by Peter and Abeli, two brothers from Kangersuatsiaq. All five men arrived at Salleq together and were the first hunters to use the hut that winter. Climbing up to the hut, they noticed footprints in the snow leading towards the hut and another set leading away up into the mountains. On entering, the men found Eirik's two dogs lying dead on the floor. Along the window sills, several candles had burned the length of their wicks, leaving pools of hard melted wax.

For the purposes of this discussion, I am not concerned with an interpretation of such stories, but rather to show how places become remembered places. This particular story points to something that is feared in the landscape. It was generally assumed that the dogs had been taken by a *qivittoq* (a mountain wanderer – see Chapter 7) but whatever the explanation, the story is recorded here to illustrate how a place such as Salleq becomes known as 'the place where Eirik's dogs were found dead', just as other places are ingrained in individual and collective memory as 'where I killed a walrus last autumn', or 'my father used to have seal nets over there'. For example, in August 1988, Josepi took Juuna to J.P. Koch's Land, a place he had last visited in 1966. On this latest trip, the two men had hoped to find caribou. They were unsuccessful and found nothing except Josepi's footprints at the site of his last camp. For Josepi this discovery was significant in having personal and family meaning but in the wider setting of the environment of the Kangersuatsiarmiit, one person's imprint on the landscape is interwoven with those of others to give a sense of continuity.

For the anthropologist, curious to discover a rich variety of myth, there is a tendency to attempt to unravel underlying structures of thought when people tell stories about real or imagined past events. The anthropological exercise becomes one of decoding the structural and psychological grammar. What does the storyteller mean when he says a man turned into a walrus? What kind of magic did the *ilisiitsoq* use? What does the story of the *angakkoq* tell us? But in conversation, for the Kangersuatsiarmiit themselves there is no explanation of events, no analysis of stories told (such as why Eirik's dogs were found dead at Salleq). As mnemonic devices, such stories serve to remind; Qammavik is the place where the *angakkoq* used to live, Aappilattoq is the place where the *ilisiitsoq* turned a ship into an iceberg, and so on. The imagery is one of associations, of connections between past and present that serve to give meaning to the everyday world, rather than examples of an unconscious archaic pysche.

Because hunting activity is 'carried out within certain *de facto* environmental boundaries' (Haller 1986: 146), knowledge does not usually extend to other community hunting areas. A change in place names indicating differences in dialect, or suffixed with *-kassak* ('bad', 'poor' i.e. 'of no significance for hunting') usually denotes a boundary at which subsistence activity stops. Within their own area, hunters have no difficulty in finding their way about, quite often in bad weather and fog. Landmarks are important indicators of direction and in winter survival may depend on a hunter's ability to memorize features of the ice-scape. Navigation becomes more difficult, however, when a hunter has little or no knowledge of a landscape. On several occasions I travelled with people in areas other than Kangersuatsiaq. Unfamiliarity with places, sudden storms and white-outs sometimes resulted in us getting lost. On one occasion, in bad weather, I spent three days camping on the ice with a hunter who said he could not 'think' his way home. We had to wait for the weather to clear before we could continue.

Once, I was travelling in late winter with a friend. We were heading north by dogsledge through Upernavik district. It took us five days to reach Kullorsuaq, the northernmost village in the district. Each night we had stopped at places *en route*; at Innaarsuit and Nutaarmiut, and for two nights at Nuussuaq. My companion had once lived in Kullorsuaq and had kin and friends there. He also had knowledge and experience of hunting in the local area. But our plans were to venture into Melville Bay to look for polar bear and to continue to Savissivik in Avanersuaq district. In good weather, and with fit dogs, Melville Bay usually takes five days to traverse. There are no sledge tracks to follow; few make the journey. It is possible to head far out on the sea ice, but the traveller must keep an eye on a few prominent headlands along the coast. If the ice is bad the coastline must be hugged and the journey can then take nine or ten days.

What set this journey apart from others I had made was not the length of time to be spent out on the sea ice, it was that we needed to use a map and compass and it was our shared responsibility to navigate. I remember the uncertainty in deciding on our route and the difficulty in distinguishing icebergs from land owing to the brightness of the sun's light. Distances were deceptive, there were no recognizable landmarks and we were once caught out in a storm because we had misjudged the time it would take to reach a particular headland.

For my companion Melville Bay was a memory-desert where 'each little place with its name and legend produced a vivid pause in the imagination' (Gunn 1969: 34). An area, while familiar to those who hunt and live there, none the less becomes unknown territory to those who have no knowledge or memory of it. Memory is a way of articulating the relationship between community and landscape, or between the landscape and an individual. Traces of memory are left in the immediate area, ensuring the writing of subsistence and other activities on the landscape.

Geography is extended to include an 'existentialist realm' (Tuan 1971: 183) and necessitates a consideration of meaning. In the Kangersuatsiaq area, the organization of geographical space involves a contemplative process whereby experience and memory are important considerations when trying to understand the locality. There is a fusion of spatial and cognitive symmetry. The environment is perceived in a particular way and people are involved in a dialogue with a landscape suffused with memory and highly charged with human energy.

Tuan sees the ordering of space as the result of 'man's need to discern order' (ibid: 184). Building on this, I consider what I have termed memoryscape as illustrating how the landscape is modified and culturally constructed. Through land and sea use, myth and historical events, an image of the community is reflected in the landscape. The community boundaries are extended into abstract space which then becomes an integral part of the community. Places in this area resonate with community consciousness. Such places are reference points, or what Robinson calls archives when he talks about 'the elusive identity hidden in the archives of the named cultural items, as well as people, that distinguish the landscape' (1973: 333).

In a contemporary hunting community such as Kangersuatsiaq, a hunter who daily criss-crosses the local area is aware of and involved with land, sea and ice. Each hunter has his own indelible personal memories, his own version of Josepi's footprints, as it were, that invest the landscape with personal and family significance. A person's relationship with the environment is informed by these memories, for 'without memory or the sense of historic continuity the man–land relationship remains overly economic; without economic control the relationship remains only spatial' (Burghardt 1973: 244).

There are stories, place names and individual experiences far too numerous to record. But every such event contributes to the creation of a landscape which is alive with recollection. For the people of Kangersuatsiaq, their local environment is a living place. Some areas may be good hunting territory, or notable char runs, or places to fear, or the scene of some great personal adventure. A picture emerges of a totality, a landscape that belongs to the community precisely because it is continually constructed during a continuous process of modification. The landscape and local environment is revealed in contours on the cognitive map used by individuals to orientate themselves; and their sense of community in relation to it.

Memories, names, and land and sea use are existential responses to what is originally abstract and unfamiliar. To interpret the Kangersuatsiaq hinterland as a sociological area one must be aware of ideology and personal as well as collective meaning. The Inuit relationship with the landscape involves an affinity that, in a Wordsworthian sense, is 'far more deeply interfused' precisely because it transcends mere economic exploitation of natural resources. The structuralist notion of a culture: nature dichotomy is far too simple because both realms overlap. Each encompasses and informs the other.

5

Becoming a person

The concept of the person

The previous chapter introduced the idea of landscape as an enduring memoryscape. Through the interplay of experience, memory and imagination the landscape becomes the physical expression of community, giving a sense of locality and cultural continuity. This chapter develops this further by exploring how a sense of continuity is given through the return and naming of people. As will become clear, children are returned deceased kin and community members, making the social landscape of Kangersuatsiaq a memoryscape of persons. How adults respond to children is determined, in part, by this.

In dealing with the idea of the Greenlandic person (*inuk*) as held by the Kangersuatsiarmiit, I am not so much concerned with an individual's conceptualization of self but with the identity of the person as having social significance. While this is in keeping with an anthropological interest in the social construction of the person (e.g. Carrithers *et al*. 1985), I do not write in ignorance of recent concerns about a conceptual definition of the person by others that is external to a person's self-concept (Cohen 1990). Cohen has complained that 'a great and obvious lacuna in the literature on naming is ethnography which deals substantially and descriptively with people's experience of being named and with the meanings they impute to their names as symbols or icons of themselves' (ibid: 10). But while it is important to be aware of experiential aspects of naming, this is obviously a difficult area for ethnographers as people may not always express how they feel about naming for both the social and individual construction of identity. In Chapter 8 I touch on the complexity of personal meaning and how this can lead to a situation of contested identities. For the purposes of this chapter, however, I restrict myself to a somewhat anachronistic concern with classification.

Anthropological discussion of the concept of the person usually takes as its precedent the essay by Mauss (1985) on the person as a category of

the human mind. A distinction between individual and person was made
by Radcliffe-Brown, who regarded the individual as a biological organism
to be studied by physiologists and psychologists, while the person 'is a
complex of social relationships . . . As a person the human being is the
object of study for social anthropologists' (1940: 194). Fortes elaborated
on this and viewed the person as social representation (La Fontaine 1985:
125). In recent years, ethnography from different parts of the world has
disputed Mauss's theory that concepts of the person are not found in non-
Western societies.

In Kangersuatsiaq, the person is seen as both a material and non-
material being. Non-material aspects, such as the name, give the person
a unique identity as well as locating him/her in a complex web of social
relationships that encompass both the living and the dead. This allows an
understanding of themes to be discussed in later chapters, such as kinship
and sharing, and provides a foundation for evaluating the social and
economic changes taking place in Kangersuatsiaq. The latter will be
discussed in Chapter 10.

For the Kangersuatsiamiit, the person is an expression of the continuity
of social life. Individualism, in the Western sense of achievement through
competition, has no place in the Greenlandic subsistence economy (see
Chapters 9 and 10). Rather, it is the person who, in sharing something of
others through the name, creates relationships of equality (see Chapter 6).
A person has the name souls of several deceased people, so there is a sense
in which one person combines aspects of several persons. Similarly, one
dead person's name soul is shared between several children who, despite
being themselves, are also one person. One significance of the person is
in 'conferring moral worth . . . on the social form, which includes as a
vital element the maintenance of continuity' (La Fontaine ibid: 132).
Before discussing the contemporary idea of the person in Kangersuatsiaq,
it is necessary to consider the religious background which informs it.

Lutheranism and pre-contact Inuit religion

Contemporary Christian Greenland is a blend of pre-contact Inuit religion
and Lutheran theology. Some aspects of the existing traditional
cosmology, such as name beliefs and religious attitudes to animals, still
lie beneath the surface, having been glossed over with the veneer of European Christianity. During the time of the early missionaries the two belief
systems probably existed side by side for some considerable time (Gad
1973). The success of the Lutheran mission was due to the translation of
abstract Christian doctrine and alien theological concepts into existing
elements of the Greenlanders' cosmology. Added to this is the Lutheran
doctrine of the 'Two Kingdoms' with the dichotomy of the spiritual and
temporal analogous to Inuit ideas of spirit and body. The translation of
Inuit cosmology into Lutheran thought, with some changes, has resulted
in the acceptance of Christian dogma. What follows is a consideration of
Lutheran theology and pre-Christian Inuit ideas of the person.

60

The arrival of European missionaries in the early part of the eighteenth century saw the gradual replacement of indigenous Inuit cosmology with new religious ideas. As well as the Lutheran catechism preached by Egede and his successors, the Moravian Brethren established a ministry at Ny Herrnhut near Nuuk in the early 1730s. Compared to the Lutherans, the Moravians had little knowledge of the Greenlandic language and were prevented initially from teaching their doctrines in a way which could be understood by the native population. According to Gad, the Brethren placed emphasis on revivalism and evangelicalism by preaching 'simple stories about the incarnation, a life of righteousness, and the passion and death of Jesus' (1973: 254). Moravian revivalism involved baptism followed by the learning of the catechism – the complete opposite of the Lutheran practice of firstly learning the catechism followed by declaration of faith and baptism.

The influence of the Moravians must not be underestimated. They kept a tight hold on the individual and promoted the idea of community. Close-knit family and communal networks were emphasized as the ideal of human life. This was incorporated easily into the existing West Greenlandic conflict between the individual and community. Lutheranism, as the state religion however, had more far reaching doctrinal success and very little of the syncretism between Christianity and Inuit religion can be traced to the Moravians.

Luther and the framework of Lutheran theology

Luther's doctrines represent an extreme reaction to what he saw as the capitalistic exploitation of mankind. By rejecting Rome's authority over the Church, he has been seen as an 'individualist who preached the supremacy of the individual conscience' (Storr 1988: 79). For Luther, God could be found in the heart and soul of the individual believer. His attack on the notion of the clergy and sacraments of the Church as the intermediaries between man and God pointed an accusing finger at the religious hierarchy. Luther's theology underpinned his later political ideas, particularly those which called for a return to an uncorrupt state where the peasantry were no longer exploited by authority.

Luther's doctrine of justification by faith emphasized that individuals can attain salvation once they have accepted Christ as their saviour. Faith in Christ was all that was needed for God's grace to be given. The religious hierarchy as intermediary between man and God was evidence of how society had become a degenerate civilization, taken over by a 'conscienceless money power' (Tawney 1972). Luther saw a division between the external world of evil, darkness and matter, and the good and light life of the spirit. By focusing on spiritual experience and through belief in God, the corruption of the world could be transcended.

The most important part of Luther's theology is his doctrine of the 'Two Kingdoms'. Central to this is the notion that God has created and presides over a spiritual order, which is concerned with salvation, and a temporal order which is concerned with mankind's existence in the material world and the experience of man as a social being.

Inherent in these Two Kingdoms is Luther's conception of man having two persons – again, spiritual and temporal. As a spiritual person, man exists only in relation to God, his soul must find its way to salvation through faith and by the grace of God. As a temporal person, the individual is not concerned with salvation and the state of his soul, but is involved in the external material world. Both kingdoms and both persons have been created by God and find themselves in juxtaposition as well as in conflict. The spiritual and the temporal are also opposed to each other as the Kingdom of God and that of the Devil (of which the temporal world is a manifestation). The Devil/temporal world wrestles with God for people's hearts and souls and only the right government of the spiritual kingdom can bring eternal life.

Pre-contact Greenland Inuit religion: the 'soul'

There is very little in the literature to go on in attempting to build up a picture of pre-Christian ideas of person and soul. Much early work was done by missionaries, both Lutheran and Moravian, and their writing shows their Christian ethnocentricism in their dismissal of the Greenlanders' belief system as superstition. Hans Egede denounced 'the Greenlanders' ignorance of a Creator' (1818: 183), while Crantz saw them as having:

> . . . in fact no apparent worship, either religious or idolatrous, nor any ceremonies which might be construed into the service of the Deity. There is, indeed, no word in their language for the Divine Being, from whence the first missionaries were led to imagine that they had no conception whatever of a divinity [Crantz 1820: 182]

Crantz thought that the extreme ignorance of the Greenlanders could be challenged because:

> It is only their natural slowness, stupidity and thoughtlessness, which prevent them from digesting their dark notions into a regular system . . . [ibid: 183]

The early missionaries set out to translate the doctrines of Christianity into the terminology of what they saw as Inuit 'dark notions' and formulate a coherent belief system, which they supposed to be lacking in Greenland. From the beginning, the Lutherans were motivated in learning the language of the Inuit. All religious instruction was in Greenlandic and by 1744 all four Gospels had been translated. By 1766 the entire New Testament was available in Greenlandic (Kleivan 1979: 176).

From the missionary accounts it seems that the idea of God as a supreme being and creator of the universe was difficult for the Greenlanders to grasp. Egede's successors, including his son Poul, concentrated on teaching about sin and grace, the day of judgement, purgatory, salvation and eternal life. Denunciation of the *angakkut* as liars (Egede 1818) was accompanied by the identification of *toornaarsuk*, their helping, oracular and initiator spirit, with the Devil (Sonne 1986: 200). From the literature we learn that Greenlanders viewed the person as consisting of body, name and soul and that they believed in the immortality of souls (Egede ibid, Rink 1875). Again Crantz tells us that:

> There are indeed some who believe, that their soul is not immortal or different from the living principle in other animals; but these are of the most stupid sort . . . [ibid: 184]

According to Rink, after death souls either travelled to an underworld of abundance or to an upper world where there was only starvation and cold (1875). What is important here is the belief in the immortality of some part of the person. The Lutherans took it to be the soul in the Christian sense. That the Greenlanders saw it as independent from the body helped the missionaries in their concern with its salvation.

Early ethnographers and travellers among the Greenlanders devoted some space to religious belief and cosmology in what were more general accounts of hunting and material culture. Like the missionaries, most wrote that the original belief was that the person consists of body, name and soul. Birket-Smith noted that, after death, there was a belief that the soul continued and could cause evil in the living as a ghost (1924: 443). Nansen, like Birket-Smith and others, mentions that the Greenlanders have a conception of two souls, namely 'breath' and 'shadow' (1894). For Nansen, the Eskimo belief in a soul arose from the existence of a 'shadow' self and the departure of breath at the time of death.

Birket-Smith and Nansen were writing at a time when the Inuit of West Greenland had already had considerable exposure to Christianity. The literature is influenced heavily by evolutionary theory and explains the belief in two souls in materialistic terms, with the shadow able to leave the body at night in order to hunt, fish, visit and dance. The idea of multiple souls will be discussed below, but although earlier theoretical perspectives may not stand up to rigorous anthropological criticism the idea of soul as shadow is significant. The contemporary idea of the person is informed by Christianity, as is each person component. In the next section, I follow on from this and start by examining the idea of 'becoming a person'.

From foetus to person

Naartuneq is Greenlandic for 'being in a state of pregnancy'. It is made up of the root *naartu-* ('foetus') and the postbase *-neq* ('the act or state of'). In the infinitive, the verb naartuvoq means 'to be/is pregnant', and a pregnant woman is called a *naartusoq*, 'one who is pregnant'. As will become clear later, children are the centre of attention in a Greenlandic household, but there is a certain ambivalence as to what constitutes a child. A woman who is pregnant, depending on her personal circumstances, will make her own decision as to whether she will keep the child or have the foetus aborted. During the period of fieldwork, several young unmarried women who found themselves pregnant decided to go to town for an abortion. Usually no attempt is made to conceal an abortion from family or community; an unmarried pregnant woman does not bring dishonour upon herself or her family. Often, unmarried mothers who decide to give birth may arrange to have their child adopted by a close relative. Similarly, abortion is a matter for individual women and is sanctioned neither negatively nor positively because it does not seem to present a moral or ethical issue.

The process of separation from the womb (*illiaq*) is one in which the baby (*naalungiarsuk*) is brought to a 'state of life' (*inuuneq*; life, or literally 'the state of being a person'). There is a powerful imagery and linguistic link between the womb (*illiaq*) and a house (*illu*). A pregnant woman is said to be *ilumippoq*; 'she has it within herself'. A man gets a woman pregnant by 'filling her' (*ilumiulerpaa*), in the same semantic sense as one inspires someone with a thought, or enters a house or loads a boat with camping equipment. An *illiaq* houses the *illaaq*, another word for foetus, just as an *illu* houses a person. The verb *inunngorpoq* refers to the parturition process. While it is appropriate to talk about a baby being born, an important linguistic clue is missed by merely translating *inunngorpoq* as 'is born'. *Inunngorpoq* comprises the root *inuk* (person) and the postbase *-nngorpoq* (becomes). Thus *inunngorpoq* means 'becomes a person'. The postbase *-nngorpoq* is used when talking about altered states, for example as follows:

nakorsanngorpoq	– becomes a doctor (*nakorsak*; doctor)
arnanngorpoq	– becomes a woman (*arnaq*; woman)
ataasinngorpoq	– becomes one, i.e. one o'clock (*ataaseq*; one)
palasinngorpoq	– becomes a priest (*palasi*; priest)

It is only in one sense that childbirth marks the beginning of life, the foetus being already alive in another sense. Informants told me that the unborn child was simply 'waiting to become a person' (*inunngormut utaqqippaa*). Only when the parturition process is complete is the child open to influences that are responsible for its development as a person. This seems to be an idea that is widespread across the Inuit area. For the Netsilik, Balikci observes that birth alone is not enough to ensure the baby is accorded the status of a social person (1970: 148). To become a social person the child must be named and Balikci says that infanticide could not take place once this had been done. Guemple reports that Inuit never regard the foetus as a person because it is not 'alive' until after it is born (1979a: 39–51). The child then receives a name from a namegiver and throughout life both address one another with *saunik* ('bone'). The sharing of a name with another integrates the child in 'a constellation of relations' who all become part of a *saunik* system (Guemple 1965: 326).

Similarly, for Greenlandic Inuit, a child does not become a full or proper person until it has received a name. A name is not only important for self-perception and perception by others, it also carries certain images that are necessary for social, psychological and cosmological renewal and integration. This importance of the name will become clearer in later chapters. Here it is introduced as a component of the person, or a spiritual concept applied in the social and individual construction of identity. As each differentiated individual is distinguished by a name, so it integrates him/her in an extended network of social relationships.

Components of the person

– *tarneq*: the personal soul
– *anersaaq*: the breath soul
– *ateq*: the name soul

A person's body (*timi*) is ephemeral and houses the spiritual components of *ateq*, *tarneq* and *anersaaq*. *Timi*, being the material and temporal part of the person is subject to disease and decay. *Timi* has a physical exterior substance and character, while the spiritual components are ambiguous in substance, character and appearance. All three can be seen as being a kind of soul in the sense that they are non-material parts of the body, belonging instead to the spiritual person. Thus, the Kangersuatsiarmiit conceptualize the person as comprising of three 'souls' as follows.

Tarneq: the personal soul

The meaning of *tarneq* was reshaped by the missionaries and has now become synonymous with the Christian 'soul'. Originally, there was probably a semantic link with *tarraq*, meaning 'shadow/reflection', and *taarneq*, meaning 'darkness'. Occasional stories are still told about *tarrajarssuk*, a mythical figure whose shadow alone can be seen. *Tarneq* is a reflection of the person, but is more accurately understood in Christian terms as '. . . a moralised and spiritualised self-consciousness of each separate individual in relation to a personalised God' (Leinhardt 1985: 147).

Here, Leinhardt is talking about the Sudanese Dinka concept of *weei* (breath), translated by missionaries to mean soul. It illustrates the parallels with the many other societies that have experienced changes in religious ideology as a result of contact with Christianity. This is not to say that Christianity has extinguished indigenous meaning. The idea of multiple souls fits comfortably within the framework of Lutheran theology in terms of an individual's experience and understanding. Yet *tarneq*, *anersaaq* and *ateq* are as different from one another as they are similar.

Tarneq is said to be present in latent form in the body at birth. It is something that will be nurtured as the child grows, with emphasis on a religious development. People talk of *tarnit* (souls) being dark and heavy when life, a personal relationship or the weather is said to be unpleasant (*tujorminaq*). After a church service, having heard the catechist talk about God, one's *tarneq* and heart (*uummat*) are 'light' (*qaamasut*), freed from darkness (*taaq*). Upon death, *tarneq* leaves the body and goes to God. As a component of the spiritual person it finds its way to salvation. The state of a person's *tarneq* is an indication of their character and development. A teenage girl, commenting on the growth of intelligence in her three year old brother, told me:

> He really is clever, watch him. His *anersaaq* is big now, but it's a pity his *tarneq* is so small. When he starts going to church [*qaqugu naalagiartaleruni*] his *tarneq* will get bigger. He has to learn about God.

As conceptualized by the Kangersuatsiamiit, *tarneq* is both personal and free, a person's life force that ultimately finds its way to God by way of lineal progression.

Anersaaq: the breath soul

Throughout my stay in the village, numerous informants identified *tarneq* with *anersaaq*. Both have been explained to me as breath or God's breath, or 'the breath God put into Adam'. More accurately, *anersaaq* translates as 'spirit' or ghost. In the Greenlandic catechism, *anersaaq iluartoq* is the Holy Ghost, *anersaapiluk* means an evil spirit, and *anersaakkoorneq* is a religious meeting. Again, there is a strong semantic link between *anersaaq*, *anerneq* (breath/spirit), and *anersaarpoq* (breathes/breathes in).

Tarneq and *anersaaq* are at once the same, but separate. *Tarneq* is passive and its exact location unknown, while *anersaaq* contains aspects of mind (the young girl quoted above associated the concept with intelligence) and is slightly more autonomous during a person's life. While it is acknowledged that *tarneq* leaves the body upon death, *anersaaq* is shadowy and independent, able to leave a person's body during life. Like *tarneq*, it is autonomous and personal, but upon death it remains in the land of the living as a spirit or ghost, as a reflection or memory of the dead.

Ateq (pl. atit): name and name soul

Ateq will be referred to throughout as both name and name soul, (the Kangersuatsiarmiit say 'my name is like my soul': '*atera soorlu tarniga*'). The name is independent and idiosyncratic, a person's life stream through which flows strength and character. Identity is more closely associated with the name. As will become clear later, identities continue when children are given the name of a deceased person, or the names of several dead people. As an indivisible entity, a person's *ateq* is a link in a wide network of social and spiritual relationships. While *tarneq*, as the personal soul, goes to God, *ateq* remains on earth, as does *anersaaq*. It is a form of active, dynamic and continuing social reincarnation, although the generational progression of name souls is not concerned with achieving merit and cannot be seen in terms of an ethical metempsychosis, or moral progression.

The name contains properties of the deceased which are ineradicable and, to some extent, naming determines a child's developmental path. Once named, a new born child is both him/herself and the person(s) whose names s/he receives. Acquisition of a dead person's name embellishes, or even creates, a living person's genealogical and social identity. Kin relationships are extended beyond biological kin to encompass a wider network of people related both biologically and socially to the deceased. Obligation and level of involvement vary but are seldom ignored. I shall return to this and similar themes later, when I hope to show how the name, despite being a common and central feature of cognition, acquires an elusiveness because people work out different interpretations of meaning. People may not always express what they ascribe to naming as a phenomenon. Seen in terms of the person as a social as well as spiritual construction, *ateq* is also a cultural item in the community repertoire, an item to which individuals are not passively orientated.

Just as place names are also images and memories inherent in the landscape, so a personal name is not only life, it is an image and a memory of persons. Names (*atit*) are reference points in a complex network of interpersonal relationships. People 'think with' personal names in a similar way to when they use place names to think themselves around the physical environment. With the rebirth of names, various types of relationship are continued as well as new ones made. A person's self-perception is influenced by the image and memory others have of the dead person after whom s/he is named, and by the position s/he occupies in the social and spiritual order.

Naming

Upon death a person's name soul leaves the body and remains homeless until it is recalled to reside in the body of a new-born child. A person who is named after a dead person is called an *atsiaq* (pl. *atsiat*). As this includes all people, then Greenlandic communities are made up entirely of *atsiat*. A dead person can have more than one *atsiaq*. The first child to be born after the death of another person is usually the most important and is called that person's *ateqqaataa*. The dead person is the *atsiaq*'s *aqqa*. Throughout Upernavik district an *atsiaq* is also called *aqqa*, although more commonly the dyadic relationship is referred to as *aqqa: atsiaq*. An *atsiaq* also is usually known as a dead person's *atiia*, in the possessive form.

Until the baptism, a child has no name until the catechist performs the naming ceremony. Throughout many parts of the Inuit area, the name is not tied to either sex and discussion in the literature is influenced by this striking feature. The name soul can be called back to take up residence in a child of either sex (e.g. Gessain 1980). However, this is not the case in West Greenland. By the end of the nineteenth century all of West Greenland had been influenced by Christianity. Baptism meant that the Greenlanders took Danish names and soon most traditional Inuit names were no longer in common usage. Today, personal names are often 'Greenlandicized', e.g. Daaveeraq ('little David'), and Susaat (Susan). Patronymic names were also taken in the Danish fashion by using the personal name of the head of the family, e.g. Kristiansen, Jensen, Immanuelsen, and Poulsen.

In West Greenland, all personal names are gender specific and a child can be named only after a person of the same sex. The *ateqqaataa* does not necessarily have to be born into the deceased's community. The whole of Upernavik district is characterized by close kinship and other social relationships and the first same-sex child to be born, in any village, will receive the name of a recently deceased person. Thus it is quite common to find *atsiat* in Upernavik town or Kullorsuaq named after dead people from Nuussuaq or Kangersuatsiaq. Such demographic spread means the name soul will not have to be 'cold', 'lonely' and 'homeless' for very long, as it would if naming was confined within the dead person's village. The name soul would then have to wait for a child to be born.

Once a death has occurred, the naming of the next new child is predetermined. Strictly speaking then, this is not reincarnation of a fully differentiated individual, but of whatever qualities and aspects are held to be contained in the name soul. A person's *tarneq* and *anersaaq* are not reincarnated. Furthermore, a dead person can have several *atsiat* and several dead people can share the same *atsiaq*. In the latter case, one person can have three or more name souls and it is usually the child's grandmother who decides on the other names of the child. There were several elderly informants who held that the child would cry if it was given the wrong names. The names are spoken to the child as a way of seeing what other name souls are reincarnated, despite the fact that they may already have an *ateqqaataa* or *atsiaq* elsewhere. As will be shown, multiple name souls in one *atsiaq* has more to do with diffusion of imagery and memory of a person.

As an *atsiaq*, the child enters into various relationships with the surviving relatives of its *aqqa*, who all address the *atsiaq* by the kin term applied to the dead relative. Corresponding terms of address are reciprocated by the *atsiaq*. A detailed consideration of kinship terms follows in the next chapter, but briefly, a dead man's *atsiaq* will be called 'father' by that man's children, and 'husband' by his wife. In addition to his *aqqa's* father calling him 'son', he will be called son by his genitor.

The baptism of the new child is important for the deceased's family. A relationship is established between the *ateqqaataa* and the family. More significantly, it is a re-establishment of a bond between deceased and bereaved. The dead person is said to have 'come home' (*angerlarpoq*) to the bereaved. There is a sense in that people are not naming/baptizing a new person, but are welcoming back a member of family and community. A child does not take a new name, thus becoming altogether another person in the cosmos, but re-enters an existing order of being, of which his name at least is already a part.

'Are you out of your mind?' – Raising children

As an *atsiaq* then, a child is a returned person. In some ways, this accounts for styles of childrearing and certainly cannot be ignored in any discussion of this. In Kangersuatsiaq the absence of any punishment of children by adults is notable. Instead children are generally free to learn by exploration, play, and the encouragement of adults. A child's development is nurtured by way of exploratory forays into dangerous situations, by mapping and understanding various networks of interpersonal relationships and by developing an awareness of negotiating strategies of interaction. The role of significant others in this nurturance process can be either passive or active, as the examples below show. Intelligence/consciousness (*sila*) and reason (*isuma*) are believed to be inherent in the child, and to some extent are said to be present in the name a child is given. Because of this, adults will refrain from excessive influence.

A child's development is seen as the development of *sila* and *isuma*. *Sila*, as I showed in the previous chapter, is most often expressed as weather, the elements, or air. But *sila* is understood as the fundamental principle underlying the natural world and is manifest in each and every individual. It is an all-pervading, life-giving spirit related to *tarneq* and *ateq*. *Sila* is the natural order, a universal consciousness and breath soul that contains within it all individual breath souls (see also Williamson 1988). It would be difficult to draw parallels with other religious traditions in order to understand fully the significance of *sila* for balance between the individual and the natural world. A person's *tarneq*, *ateq* and *anersaaq* are all elements of *sila* as an eternal unitary principle. *Sila* connects a person with the rhythms of the universe, enlarging and integrating the self with the natural world. Explaining *sila* and its significance for the individual, a thirty two year old man told me:

> You must never forget to breathe. Breath connects us to all things, to the spirit. I am a Christian, I believe in Jesus Christ, but the spirit is the same in all things.

Sila links the individual self and the environment, the personal and the universal. As the universal Mind, *sila* is the ground for the existence of every individual sub-mind present in each person. A person who lacks *sila* is said to be separated from an essential relationship with the environment that is necessary for social and pyschological well-being. In the sense used here, *sila* refers to a person's consciousness, intelligence and reasonable and sensible behaviour. The verb *silatuvoq* means 'is intelligent', or 'has understanding/sense'. *Sila* is an external force that interacts with the person and manifests itself in what we understand as intelligence and awareness. It is inextricably linked with *isuma*; 'mind/rationality'. *Sila* is present in every child in latent form and develops as the child grows and explores the surrounding world.

It is during play, either with other children or with adults, that the early socialization of children mainly takes place. I first observed the intensity of play and its significance for the development of a child's *sila* in Josepi's fishing camp. I was struck by the extent to which young children were given free rein to play near water, to scramble around rocky terrain risking injury, and to play rough and tumble games. Usually, as long as an older child was with younger children, and provided they did not stray too far from the sight of camp, parents tended to leave their children to their own devices.

During breaks from fishing and other tasks, adults spent a great deal of time involved in some form of play with children. The children regarded my presence as something of a novelty, gathering around my tent when I was getting dressed for a fishing trip, and running down to the shore when we returned. They considered teaching me Greenlandic words a game, continually testing my knowledge of an expanding vocabulary. Because of my rudimentary grasp of the language, my initial conversations were regarded as 'childish' by both adults and children. As I learned kinship terms and the names for features of the landscape, I became aware that questions about interpersonal relationships and knowledge of places were the most common that parents asked their children.

Throughout that first summer at Josepi's camp, the incessant questions about my own genealogical network and about places back home were not asked simply out of a healthy curiosity. Josepi's family certainly did acquire a good knowledge of my own kinship relationships and, with the help of photographs of my home town, I was able to develop a basic conversational style in response to queries about where I lived. More importantly, however, such constant quizzing ensured that I learned the diversity of kinship terms necessary for understanding the relationships of all those in the camp, especially as such terms are used in preference to personal names. It was when people began to quiz me on their own kin networks that I realized how my own 'upbringing' by Josepi's family mirrored Inuit styles of childrearing.

After some two weeks in the camp, I was expected to demonstrate a good knowledge of both the kinship relationships of those staying there, and of local geography. When I was asked who certain people were, I was not to identify them by their names, but by their positions in the kinship network, as 'David's sister's son', as 'Josepi's mother's cousin's son' and so on. When we sat outside the tents drinking tea, or worked on our equipment, I would be asked to name mountains and other features of the landscape. Early on, David had entrusted me with the responsibility of handling the outboard motor when we went fishing, and soon he expected me to be able to pick my way through the intricate pattern of bays and fjords without any directional advice. I was taught to identify the safe routes through stretches of shallow water, the places to fish for both halibut and capelin, and the sheltered harbours to head for in case of bad weather or difficulty. I soon came to expect a familiar pattern of being tested on my knowledge of both people and places. I was asked about the weather, about tides, wind direction and about animals. But I was not being given this knowledge so that I could write it down and later preserve it in an academic monograph. If I was to survive as a person, if I was to survive both physically and pyschologically in Greenland, then my prospects depended on an intimate knowledge of the social and natural environment.

Josepi's family knew this. From the first few days I was with them their strategy was to wear down my confidence and then 'raise' me in their own way. As it was, shorn of the props that went to make up my personality in my own society, together with the doubts and uncertainty that are part of anthropological fieldwork, it was not long before I hit the depths of despair. At the end of the first week, David told me he no longer needed my help. I was told to pack my tent and he would take me to Upernavik, from where, if I felt like returning home, I could catch a helicopter. On arriving in Upernavik, David told me to wait in the boat while he went to the store. When he came out with provisions to last several weeks, he informed me he still needed me and that I was welcome back in the camp. He added, 'Now you're homesick and depressed, you can start to learn how to be a Greenlander'. We returned to the camp via Kangersuatsiaq and I unpacked my tent.

My own experiences helped me to understand the value of the kinds of questions children are asked. Like my early interrogations, children are constantly questioned about their genealogical relationships. They are also asked about the people they are named after and they learn about their relationships with their *aqqa's* family. Children learn to identify their own places in the kinship networks of their parents, and where they fit into other patterns as *atsiat*. Through knowing the answers to such constant questions as 'Who is your father?', 'What are the names of your two mothers?' (i.e. the names of genealogical mother and the mother of the child's *aqqa*), 'Whose name does your sister have?', 'Why do you call your older brother "grandfather"'?, children learn to navigate their way across the social landscape.

Many of these questions are also concerned with testing a child's geographical knowledge. So a mother who asks her child 'Where is your father?', will expect the child to answer that he has gone hunting, or fishing or travelling to a particular place. In this way, the significant figures in a child's life are located in the physical landscape. Children become aware of the most prominent features in their locality through association with hunting and fishing activities, or by listening to adults tell stories about real or imagined events that happened at certain points in the landscape.

Knowledge of people and places, then, is central to the development of a child's awareness. In the changing environment of the Kangersuatsiarmiit, the ability to find one's way through the intricacies of both the social and physical worlds is vital for survival. Childrearing is a process whereby the child becomes aware of the instability and dangers inherent in the world. During play, the child is free to initiate explorations, with other people to some extent sitting on the sidelines, as the following example illustrates.

Three year old Aqqaluk was the centre of attention in his father's household. The love given to him by his parents and older brothers and sisters can only be described as intense. He was well known throughout Kangersuatsiaq as being 'cute' and 'sweet' (*meeraq inerqunartunnguaq*), and 'lovable' (*asanarpoq*). One day, I visited his parents but upon finding them out, I sat and waited in the living room. Aqqaluk had been entertaining himself with his father's *kamiks* (seal skin boots), but having grown tired of them he started to rummage through the chest of drawers that stood near the window. After a while, he produced a clear, empty plastic bag. He began to examine it, throwing it up into the air several times before deciding to open it. Aron, his nineteen year old brother, was also present. We were watching the interest Aqqaluk showed in the bag, with concern at least on my part. I was also watching Aron and his reactions. He sat expressionless, as Aqqaluk placed the bag over his head. I sat, gripping the edge of the chair, ready to leap to the other side of the room if Aqqaluk inhaled. Aron still sat and did nothing as Aqqaluk removed the bag and began to experiment with folding it into different shapes. After exhausting the possibilities of external form, he decided to take another look inside the bag, again by placing it over his head. This time, Aron snatched the bag away, just as his little brother opened his mouth as if to take a deep breath. Aron said nothing, placing the bag back inside the drawer while Aqqaluk gave a weak laugh and turned his attention back to his father's *kamiks*. Later, I mentioned this to Aqqaluk's teenage sister who, laughing, said 'How cute!'

Any ethnocentric feelings I had about the irresponsibility of Aqqaluk's brother and sister were dispelled a few days later when Martha, his five year old sister, discovered the same plastic bag. This time, Aron did not wait for the child to risk suffocation. Snatching the bag away, he shouted angrily: 'Martha! Are you out of your mind?' However, the same rebuke was not forthcoming during subsequent re-enactions from Aqqaluk. Martha was expected to know about playing with plastic bags and the inherent dangers, while Aqqaluk was just beginning to discover and appreciate such dangers. By the age of four this type of behaviour would be seen as a display of 'no sense' (*silaqanngilaq*). When Aron asked Martha if she was out of her mind (*silaqaraluarpit?*), he was demanding to know why she was not using her mind and her sense. At five years of age she was too old to experiment and play with polythene bags.

People regard such experimentation as efforts made by the child to train his/her mind. Such mind training is referred to as *silattorsarpaa*, a gradual achievement of consciousness, of being aware. Once this has been achieved, a child 'has sense' (*silaqarpoq*). As the above example is designed to show, playing with dangerous things can only be allowed to go so far. Aqqaluk will develop a sense of causality, an awareness that polythene bags should not be placed over his head. Until then he will not be severely rebuked, unless he demonstrates a extreme lack of *sila* which leads to injury.

A child who develops *sila* is said to be *ilisimmarpoq*, that is, 'has come around to consciousness'. A person who achieves a state of consciousness 'is aware', 'can think', and has the capacity to 'reason' by the correct use of mind (*isuma*). *Ilisimmarpoq* also means the ability to connect, to have knowledge (thus the term *ilisimatooq*; wise man, scientist), and to think about right action.

I was once present in a house when a four year old was threatening to pass his fingers through a candle flame. Hesitating a glance at his parents, who although watching him made no comment, he slowly lowered his hand over the top of the flame. Suddenly, he gave a shriek and holding his burned hand started to sob. His mother continued with her sewing, calmly asking: '*Ilisimmanngiliuk*?' i.e. 'Have you no awareness?' It is common to hear parents asking their children '*Ilisimmanngiliuk*?' It is the second person negative of *ilisimmarpoq*, (*ilisimmannqilaq*). People describe *ilisimmanngilaq* as the state someone gets into when they drink themselves into unconsciousness. A person coming out of that drunken state regains consciousness, that is returns to a state of *ilisimmaneq*. When a person is described as *ilisimmanngilaq*, reason and a state of awareness are temporarily absent.

Depending on the situation, a child will not be denied affection if they trip and fall and graze a knee, but if a two year old inserts a hair grip into an electric socket then, more often than not, this is ignored by an otherwise caring parent.

Once consciousness has been achieved, a boy becomes a *nukappiaraq* and a girl a *niviarsiaraq*. They then begin to learn their respective sex roles. Boys as young as four years old often accompany their fathers on short hunting and fishing trips. Active participation in subsistence activities will come when the boy is around ten years of age, when he helps with setting seal nets, fishing and spring hunting on the sea ice. Until then, he will familiarize himself with men's work by watching and learning. As mentioned above, children also learn about prime hunting areas through hearing stories.

Girls remain with their mothers and sisters, either in the village or in the spring and summer camps. From about the age of twelve, girls are expected to look after younger children in the family and are soon involved in household tasks, such as fetching ice. In the recent past, by the time girls reached their early teens they were usually expert in the butchering of seals and in the preparation of the skins. During the period of fieldwork, however, there were only two or three girls under the age of twenty who were competent in these tasks. Josepi's youngest daughter told me that her mother had first taught her how to scrape sealskins when she was nine years old. Most people tended to explain the lack of interest as a result of a school education and increasing external influence on village life.

During the first two or three years of a child's life, the personality and temperament of the child, until now dormant, will begin to reveal itself.

By joking and playing, adults and other significant others help to nurture personality and character. Such behaviour is also an effective way of reinforcing values and generating an awareness of dangerous situations (Briggs 1986). Jokes and games are not confined to childhood, but that is when children learn to be on the receiving end of jokes and also to retaliate by being jokers themselves. The same jokes and games are often re-expressed, sometimes with subtle variations. Following Briggs, one function seems to be the generation and maintenance of a sense of uncertainty, as the following illustrates:

> Susaat (five years old): What are you doing?
> Mother: Sewing Karl's (Susaat's brother) kamiks.
> Susaat: Let me do it.
> Mother: Susaat, go away! I'll send you to Denmark to live with your father.
> Susaat: Eh? My father? (looking across to her father). My father's here.
> Mother: Naa! Erik Andersen, your father.
> Susaat (confused): Who's Erik Andersen?
> Mother: Your father! A *qallunaaq* (Dane). You're Erik Andersen's daughter.

Although the style sometimes varied, the joke always entailed a rejection of Susaat and a denial of her father as her genitor. Even though she may have participated in this dialogue several times before, Susaat would always enquire about Erik Andersen. Occasionally, when her father was away, she would ask her mother if she was Erik Andersen's daughter, where Erik Andersen lived and when he was coming back. In reply to these questions, Susaat's mother would often say: 'Go away Erik Andersen's daughter!', seemingly denying affection when Susaat asked for it. I once heard Susaat ask 'Mother, am I really Erik Andersen's daughter?' completely out of the blue. Although the joke was expressed and re-expressed in playful mood, it seemed to me that Susaat was sometimes unable to judge whether her mother was or was not telling the truth. A feeling of uncertainty was generated on Susaat's part. She was constantly reminded of how little similarity there was between herself and her real father, that only a *qallunaaq*'s daughter would demand attention or behave the way she behaved. Often, when their father was out hunting, Susaat and her younger brother would be told that he had gone and would not be coming back. Their mother would add 'But Susaat is Erik Andersen's daughter, so that's all right', implying that only her brother's father would not be returning. This kind of play is carried out regularly. In this example it discusses the question of a little girl's paternity, but other characteristics are vulnerable as the following illustrates.

> Mother (to four year old daughter): You really are ugly!
> Daughter: I'm ugly?
> Mother: Very. Let me take away your face (reaching out for the child's face). Give it to me! (covering her face and gently squeezing).

or alternatively

Mother (to three year old son): What's that, a berry?
Son: No, it's my penis.
Mother: Let me look . . . it's a berry! Let me have it!
Son (laughing): It's my penis!
Mother (trying to grab it): I'm going to pick that berry!

A child can be picked up by an adult and dangled by the ankles over the edge of a pier, or told to fall into the water. Once, I was present when a five year old girl, standing on a slippery boulder down at the beach, was told by her father's brother: 'Go on, fall! Fall properly!' Children, though, are encouraged to participate and even to retaliate:

Uncle to girl: Aren't you ugly!
Uncle to girl's father: David, have you got an ugly daughter?
Girl's father: No, I've got a beautiful daughter.
Uncle: No, you've got an ugly daughter!
Girl (to uncle): It's just you who's ugly!
Uncle: You are really ugly, though you are lovable.
Girl: You aren't lovable. You're ugly.

Briggs argues that such styles of childrearing are 'consciousness-raising' experiences (1979). For Greenlandic Inuit, the nurturance of *sila* is the re-awakening of elements of consciousness that are contained in the name souls a child is given. This is not to say that a child will inherit bad aspects of another person's character, but that consciousness and reason are simply present and continue, just as the name soul itself remains on earth. In becoming a person, a child is integrated both psychologically with the environment, and socioculturally with a wide network of other persons, both living and dead. It is this relationship between the living and the dead that provides a sense of continuity, not only of the person but of social life.

Modernization in Greenland has had severe implications for kinship patterns and for the integration of the person in a wide and supportive network of interpersonal relationships. Urbanization, an imported education system, the influence of television and radio and the acceptance of Western values, have all contributed to alienation and the isolation of the person in the growing west coast towns. Changes in social structure have resulted in changing personal identities. Removed from a secure social environment, the individual no longer experiences a sense of continuity of both person and place. In the hunting districts, isolated from the process of economic development that took place in other parts of West Greenland during the 1950s and 1960s, people live within a cultural framework that carries the past through to the present. In Kangersuatsiaq, different levels of experience remain contiguous. Becoming a person means to become a participant in a dialogue of continuity with both the physical environment and with an enduring social world. How this gives rise to a complexity of social relationships will be considered in the next chapter.

6

Becoming kin

Kinship in Kangersuatsiaq

In this chapter, I discuss categories of kin and the application of kinship terminology. In collecting genealogies and learning terms, I found that the problem of kinship in Kangersuatsiaq and the rest of Upernavik district arises when one looks at the application of kin terms in situations of both reference and address. Terminology is not necessarily fixed and closed and cannot be understood by simply seeing it in concrete genealogical terms. Designation results from the possibilities available due to kinship being both a cultural and cosmological construct. Kinship has for long been a dominant and controversial topic in ethnography and anthropological theory yet, despite post-modernist trends, anthropologists should be wary of underestimating the significance of kinship, especially when it remains central to the way people conceptualize and define their social worlds.

In Kangersuatsiaq, kinship is characterized by the interplay between a pattern of equivalences and a network of inverted relationships that act as referents for the social construction of community. Concepts of kindred and descent based groups, as Inuit define them, articulate within a system that may appear to have distinct biological roots but depends ultimately on the integration of non-biological social relationships, influenced by naming and by personal choice. Although one can talk of a kinship system, in the sense that kin terms form a connected and complex whole, I am more interested in how such a system forms a non-prescribed unity by allowing extensive improvisation. Moreover, I want to try to avoid thinking in terms of a system and treat kinship in Kangersuatsiaq as a network or pattern of relationships. Kinship is a cultural reservoir from which individuals draw items that they can manipulate in strategic interaction and a continuing process of defining 'real' relationships.

The aim of this analysis of kinship in Kangersuatsiaq is to understand the meanings individual actors hold, rather than accepting as definition the terminologies used on the ground as concrete realities. This approach seems to fit in with a general sociological discussion of the fluidity of culture and kinship. But my material, although contributing to the view that Inuit culture is flexible (Guemple 1972), also shows that there is form rather than any random allocation, and that once defined, kinship is ultimately bounded. This may sound contradictory, but Guemple's notion of the 'disconcerting formlessness' of Eskimo social structure, (1972: 3), while apt in the Kangersuatsiaq case, also refers to a patterning which although fluid and negotiable, has a conceptual rather than concrete form.

My approach, then, is to concentrate on the meanings held by individuals instead of treating kinship in purely genealogical terms. Kinship is as real in a fictive sense as it is in a biological and genealogical one. Following Schneider (1968), I argue that there is nothing necessarily inherent in a kinship term that serves to inform individuals how to behave. This even applies to a core like mother and child. Guemple points out that children can adopt parents who they 'can relate to more effectively' when existing relations are incompatible (1979b: 101). The pattern is continually being adapted as fictive kin, name souls, name-sharers and adoption augment fundamental categories. Kinship in Kangersuatsiaq and throughout Upernavik district is a tangled skein of biological, social and cosmological intricacy. The problem is to discover the pattern within.

The 'Eskimo type' of kinship

One of the fiercest debates within the development of theoretical social anthropology has been concerned with attempts to devise a way of looking comparatively at descent groups and kinship generally. In the past, anthropologists have sought to construct a descent model that would equip them with the tools to translate in comparable terms the ethnographic information about kinship and descent groups from different parts of the world. Stemming from a tradition which saw social anthropology as shedding light on the idea of a common humanity, such an emphasis on comparison ignores the very diversity of human social behaviour. In particular, the perspective which held that poly-segmentary systems (such as those found in New Guinea) could be deciphered easily and quickly by making use of the understanding gained through the analysis of African political and kinship systems, illustrates how the distinctiveness of such societies can be obscured through attempts at comparison. In recent years, ethnography has shown that this influence of structural thinking, which ignored the distinctive non-African character of the New Guinea highlands, could not stand up to the data gathered from a wide range of societies studied there.

Traditional Eskimology and Inuit studies in general have not escaped from the ethnographer's tendency to play around with models. The interpretation of what goes on on the ground has always been seen in the light of a particular framework and theoretical perspective. This has helped to contain the study of Inuit culture as a rather narrow field, concerned with making comparisons across the whole Inuit area. The literature has imposed its own limitations on 'Eskimo culture', rather than culture in general. In a survey of anthropological research in the Canadian Arctic, Balikci explains how 'the possible links between Inuit ethnography and general theoretical developments are not clearly established.' Citing Mauss's *Seasonal Variation of the Eskimo* as the only exception, he goes on to say that '. . . northern ethnographies have not been included in the critical development and definition of theories and concepts' (Balikci 1986: 2).

Early accounts of Inuit kinship are characterized by shallow ethnography and a lack of thoroughness in the gathering of data. Deeply inspired by Lewis Henry Morgan, the literature stressed the importance of terminologies and, based on this, the 'Eskimo-type' kinship system was proposed by Spier (1925) as one of eight systems he identified for North America.

Spier's 'Eskimo-type' system groups cross and parallel cousins together by virtue of having one term to identify each, two terms for grandparents, four terms for parents' siblings, one term for grandchildren and simple nepotic terms. Furthermore, siblings are distinguished by age. This system was seen by Spier as characteristic of the whole Inuit area. In particular, the importance of the nuclear family is emphasized, i.e. the emphasis being on the terminology of the nuclear family. For Spier, cognatic descent groups are not of any significance, while matrilateral and patrilateral kin of ego are of symmetrical importance. Furthermore, Spier claimed that the 'Eskimo-type' system was static and immutable.

Murdoch went beyond Spier in his formulation of an 'Eskimo-type social organization' (1949: 226–228), with an emphasis on descent and the terminological separation of cousins and siblings. As previously mentioned, the 'Eskimo-type' kinship system was based on very little accurate ethnographic data and was formulated at a time when the Inuit area was believed to be reducible to a common unity. Although they do have compelling similarities, the very diversity of Inuit groups was ignored and misunderstood. The development of kinship studies in Alaska and Canada did illustrate this diversity, although the terminologies were often central to any research on kinship systems. Although they were often seen in reference to the 'Eskimo-type', many were seen as deviations (e.g. Damas 1975).

The anthropological study of kinship networks has tended to look for underlying structures and logic. One result has been the gradual development of an academic language rich in terminologies, descriptive models and concepts. Far too often anthropological descriptions of kinship networks reveal more about anthropologists and Western categories of thought than they do about the people anthropologists write about. Although this chapter considers the terminology in Upernavik, I am concerned with the contextual content of statuses and the conceptual layers of meaning that embellish terminologies, rather than with devising models. I shall seek to elucidate what it means, for example, when a person, in response to a question 'What are children?', replies 'My ancestors' ('*Siulakka*'), or when someone informs the ethnographer 'It's my mother's birthday, she's dead but she's still living. You're invited to visit her'.

The kinship network involves a continual redistribution of names (*atiit*), the establishment and re-establishment of relationships, the finding of similarity and equivalence between people (and the denial of difference and evasion of conflict) and performs an affective function. Central to this chapter is the idea that in the absence of much material wealth, the property an individual has is his/her relationship with another person. Upon an individual's death, this relationship (property) is passed down and inherited by a new-born child. The relationship is then able to continue. It is reaffirmed, re-expressed and cemented. It is modified in that the survivor of the original relationship continues that same relationship with the child who inherits the name soul. I shall show in a later chapter how this works.

It is precisely the unobservable in a kin term that gives it such potency. The implicit – the hidden meanings – are not objective or visible. A kin term may hold no particular significance for one person, but for another it may be suffused with memories. Kinship, by focusing on images, is about the realities of cherished relationships. It is only by seeing the terminology in social context that access may be gained to what is hidden and how a person 'thinks' with terminology and ultimately, to borrow from Lévi-Strauss again, how a person uses other people to think with. So kinship terminology is a memoryscape of persons in much the same way as the landscape is a repository of memories. Both kinship and landscape ensure continuity, thus negating finality.

Upernavik kinship terminology

Firstly, as a way of beginning to understand the social organization and cultural construction of Kangersuatsiaq, the terminology is sketched out below. The terms used in Kangersuatsiaq are also employed throughout Upernavik district.

Consanguineal kin:

Third ascending generation:

aataqqiut	– FaFaFa, MoFaFa, FaMoFa, MoMoFa
aanaqqiut	– FaFaMo, MoFaMo, MoMoMo, FaMoMo

Second ascending generation:

aatak	– FaFa, MoFa
aanaq	– FaMo, MoMo

First ascending generation:

ataata/aata	– Fa

anaana/aana	–	Mo
akkaq	–	FaBr
atsak	–	FaSi
angak	–	MoBr
aja	–	MoSi

Ego's generation:

angaju	–	older Br (male ego)
ani	–	older Br (female ego)
aleqa	–	older Si (male ego)
angaju	–	older Si (female ego)
nukaq	–	younger Br (male ego)
aqqaluk	–	younger Br (female ego)
najak	–	younger Si (male ego)
nukaq	–	younger Si (female ego)
illoq	–	cousin

First descending generation:

erneq	–	So
panik	–	Da
qangiak	–	BrCh
ujoroq/nuaraluaq	–	SiCh
illuusaq	–	second cousin

Second descending generation:

ernutaq/erngutaq	–	SoCh, DaCh

Third descending generation:

ernutaqqiut	–	SoChCh, DaChCh

Affinal kin:

aapaq	–	Spouse
ui	–	Hu
nuliaq	–	Wi
ukuaq	–	SoWi
ningaaq	–	DaHu
saki	–	WiFa, HuFa, WiMo, HuMo
		Informants told me that the term *saki* was also used for collaterals of ego's wife's first ascending generation.
sakiatsiaq	–	WiBr, HuBr, WiSi, HuSi

In addition there are two more terms for siblings:

aaju	–	older brother
aaqa	–	older sister

The term *nukarleq*, meaning youngest sibling, is also used quite extensively as a kin term.

Terms for relatives of the fourth ascending and fourth descending generations were difficult to determine. Three informants said that the fourth ascending generation lineal ancestors would be known as *aataqqiuqqiut* and *aanaqqiuqqiut*, while a fourteen year old girl replied 'Who's got one of those?' Nobody in Kangersuatsiaq could say for certain that there was any agreed term. There were several people in the village who had great-grandchildren, but again there were uncertainties as to what term would be applied to a fourth descending generation. It was assumed by most informants that *ernutaqqiut* (the term for the third descending generation) would be used. No terms could be agreed on for collaterals of those generations, possibly because such relatives had no place in people's immediate experience. As I will discuss below, name relationships and sociological preferences tend to cancel out the use of actual consanguineal and affinal terms in many cases.

As I mentioned in the previous chapter, personal names are avoided and kin terms are used as a form of address instead, usually in the possessive, e.g. *ataataga* (my father), *paniga* (my daughter). In addition, terms may be abbreviated (such as *nuka*, instead of *nukaq*, *aqqalu* instead of *aqqaluk*) or extended with a suffix, e.g. *nukannguaq* (*-nnguaq*, 'sweet/dear little', thus sweet/dear little brother), or *-kasik* ('sweet'; it is interesting to note that *-kasik* is also used as a negative suffix to mean 'bad'). The use of suffixes is a matter of individual choice and not all siblings, for example, call their grandfather *aatannguaq*, or both parents may use different postbases when addressing their children.

The avoidance of using a personal name as a term of address, and in some cases as a term of reference, may be a vestige of earlier name taboos that, until recently were still in evidence in East Greenland. When a person died, it was vital that their name would not be mentioned until the birth of a new child. In East Greenland, before the introduction of European names, people were commonly named after natural phenomena, such as stars and rocks, or after physical characteristics. So, for example, the death of a person who was called by the word for star resulted in a new word or metaphor to describe or refer to stars. The name taboo ensured that the language was in constant flux, with words changing each time a person died.

Family and relatives: choosing kin

Throughout Upernavik district, descent is bilateral and surnames are inherited patrilineally. Descent can be either real, in the sense of genealogical connection, or fictive, in the case of adoption and step-children. Genealogical descent is stressed by the use of the suffix *-piaq*, ('one's own', 'personal', 'real'), while those connected through fictive descent are identified by the suffix *-siaq* (meaning 'borrowed', 'bought', or 'found'). Quite often, such distinctions are only used as terms of reference rather than address. The use of a kin term is not usually suffixed in order to discriminate between categories of genealogical or fictive kin, so an adopted son, for example, will be addressed as *erneq* rather than *ernersiaq*. The use of such terminology suggests that the relationship is regarded as genealogical and that people respond accordingly.

Usually, children are adopted by people to whom they are already genealogically related, such as grandparents. While adoption is legal, within the definition of Danish law, it is still informed by Inuit ideals. I do not have any evidence that the identity of the biological parents will be concealed from the child. The adopted child will retain ties and obligations to the family into which it was born. One example is a boy adopted by his grandparents because his biological parents were not married when he was born and did not have a house of their own. The boy was brought up to address his adopted parents as *ataatannguaq* and *anaanannguaq* ('little father' and 'little mother'), yet he referred to them as his grandparents. When he was twelve his grandmother died. His grandfather was in his late sixties and was no longer able to hunt, although he continued to fish throughout the year and set seal nets under the ice in winter. The old man's daughter and her two sons were also living in his one-room house. By this time, the boy's biological parents had been married for some years and had four other children. The boy moved in with them because of the lack of space in his grandfather's house, although he continued to spend most of his time with his grandfather, including mealtimes.

The term which, anthropologically, we can use for a personal kindred is *ilaqutariit*. The root *ila-* means literally 'a part', or 'a companion'. The verb *ilaavoq* means 'to accompany', 'to be a part' (e.g. *'Hans ilaavutit'* – 'You accompanied Hans'). If someone is out travelling alone they are described as *ilaqanngilaq*, 'has nobody with him', but not in any negative sense of being lonely. A member of the immediate family is an *ilaqutaq*, 'someone who belongs'. Those who share this relationship with others form an *ilaqutariit*, a family. In its simplest form, the *ilaqutariit* comprises ego-centred patrilateral and matrilateral consanguineal kin.

Although the *ilaqutariit* includes a large number of persons related by descent, there are several categories of relationship that act to define the boundaries of the personal kindred. It is important to recognize the distinction between an *ilaqutaq* and an *eqqarleq*, a relative. For the latter there is a semantic link with *eqqaq*, 'the immediate vicinity/area', or 'close to'. *Eqqarleq* is not necessarily applied to distant kin, but its use depends on how an individual defines his relationship with another person. Burch's idea of 'cognitive limitation' (1975: 54) shows how people can choose to forget who their relatives are. In Kangersuatsiaq, cognitive limitation operates in several cases. It is common to hear someone consigning a member of their family (i.e. an *ilaqutaq*) to the status of relative (*eqqarleq*), or to dismiss a relative as a mere friend, denying any kin connection whatsoever. It is possible for people to consciously deactivate kinship relationships by simply ignoring them.

A thirty year old informant would constantly deny (both to other villagers as well as to the anthropologist) that his second cousin was a relative, because he had been involved in a sexual relationship with her some years before. Her brothers, however, were relatives to him and he would address them by the term for first cousin (*illoq*), while steadfastly refusing to acknowledge that their sister had the same consanguineal relationship to him. Occasionally, while discussing his choice of prospective marriage partners with me, he would often single her out as the most likely possibility for a wife: 'She's not my relative, she was my woman. Sometimes, when I think about her, I think about having her as a wife.'

Relationships can exist in consanguineal and affinal terms, but by wishing to deny it, or ignore it, the relationship does not exist on the ground. Rosaldo makes a similar point in her ethnography of Ilongot social life. She says that kin ties can be 'discovered' and then recognized with labour exchange. Similarly, 'the reverse is also true, and when people choose to "forget" or "cease to know" kinship, labor exchanges come to an end' (Rosaldo 1980: 183).

A seventeen year old girl once told me:

When I was a child, Aleqa would visit our house every day. I thought Aleqa and my mother were sisters and that Abel [Aleqa's father] was my grandfather. I called him aatannguaq [sweet little grandfather] and he called me ernutaq. When Mikhail [the girl's maternal grandfather, living in Upernavik town] heard about this, he got angry with me and said Abel was not my grandfather. But he is still my aatannguaq and he calls me ernutaq.

The girl's mother's father has had several children by different women and has not lived in Kangersuatsiaq during her lifetime. She calls him by his name, avoiding using the term for grandfather. She feels closer to her *aatannguaq*, with whom she has no consanguineal or affinal relationship, and carries a photograph of him together with those of her younger brother and sister. Again, this substantiates Guemple's point that incompatible relations can be remedied by substituting them for more effective ones (Guemple ibid).

An individual's *ilaqutariit* can differ from that of their siblings. As illustrated above, a person regarded as an *eqqarleq* by one person may be something else for another. Furthermore, one sibling may deactivate a relationship with a second cousin who may be regarded as a 'brother' by another because of a name relationship. By including or excluding relatives (either biological or social), personal choice allows for the continual development of a mosaic of possible relatives.

Each individual family household unit is suffixed with *-kkut* (for example Josepikkut; Josepi's household) and, with neolocal residence, there are usually several *-kkut* in an *ilaqutariit*. For example, three of Josepi's children have their own households. In turn, *-kkut* can be suffixed with *-miut*, so that Josepikkormiut would mean 'all those living in Josepi's household'. *Ilaqutariit* form quite distinct groups within Kangersuatsiaq, reflected in visiting patterns, mutual assistance, distribution and the sharing of meat and fish. Each household can usually rely on co-operation in economic activities from others in the same *ilaqutariit*. In summer, fishing camps are the exclusive preserve of individual *ilaqutariit* with each household occupying its own tent site. Sons inherit these tent sites, although they can be taken over by members of a separate *ilaqutariit* if they are not used regularly (see Chapter 4). The *ilaqutariit* also allows other kin, such as distant affines, access to tent sites.

In Kangersuatsiaq, people say 'we are all related', and 'all Kangersuat-siarmiit are like brothers and sisters'. While an individual can probably trace a genealogical connection with many people in the village, often such ties are not accorded much significance. Quite often genealogical knowledge is blurred the greater the distance across the generations. Few people know of the cousins of their great-grandparents, for example. But with bilateral descent, no rule of exogamy and name relationships, individual *ilaqutariit* tend to converge. Mutual co-operation and exchange often takes place, for example, between households of two different *ilaqutariit* related through marriage.

However, the existence of *ilaqutariit* as distinct groups also provides the basis for the possibility of factionalism. In Kangersuatsiaq there are no conflicting religious movements competing for people's allegiance and membership, nor are there differing ethnic groups that continually display their own sense of identity *vis-à-vis* one another, as in other parts of the Arctic and sub-Arctic (e.g. Kennedy 1982, Plaice 1990). Hostility, rivalry and conflict tend to be between individuals but in the past, if personal rivalry was ever bitter and deep, then whole families would stand opposed with each supporting their own. Informants told me that dispute between families was often due to conflict over hunting, such as rights over netting sites, or because of sexual jealousy and rivalry. Sometimes, in situations of uncertainty regarding hunting rights, there is discussion between family members as to whether specific actions could precipitate dispute with a household of a different *ilaqutariit*.

An example of this took place following one autumn expedition when I accompanied a hunter to the sealing grounds east of Kangersuatsiaq. It was October and we were hunting for harp seals as they migrated south in groups known as *amisut*. There are often several boats out at a time following one *amisut*, which means that several seals are shot at the same time. Once a seal has been shot, the hunter ties a small buoy to its tail flipper and leaves it in the water. The hunt is then resumed for more seals, and all the dead floating seals are collected at the end of the days hunt. After several hours, we had success in hunting three seals and were returning to Kangersuatsiaq when my companion spotted a dead seal floating in the water. There was no buoy tied to the seal, although there were several boats not too far from us. It was obvious from a piece of cord still tied to the tail flipper that it had been attached to a buoy, but had worked loose. The hunter told me to give him a hand to haul it out of the water, explaining that a seal found floating like this can be claimed by the first person to see it. A little further on we came across the buoy and we were able to identify the hunter who had killed the seal from his initials painted on it.

When we arrived back in Kangersuatsiaq, my companion related the events to his father and brother. His brother was unsure as to whether we had a right to take the seal, especially as the hunter who had killed it was not too far away at the time and had possibly seen us hauling it into the boat. The father told us that such events had caused hostility between people in the past, but that we did have a right to take an unattached floating seal. He suggested, however, that his son should share the meat with the hunter who had killed it. As it turned out, the man who had shot the seal accepted what had happened and the meat was shared. Such events may still have potential to cause conflict, but hunters accept a common code of unwritten hunting regulations and recognize that animals are not owned by any one individual (see Chapter 9). In modern times, factions within Kangersuatsiaq are seldom likely to arise because of conflict over hunting and, as the above example shows, dispute can be easily resolved.

Tensions that separate *ilaqutariit* from each other are more likely to stem from such divisions as those between drinkers and non-drinkers and those of differing political party allegiance. It is common that most members of the same family will support the same political party and interaction between *ilaqutariit* tends to be minimal if there is a difference of political opinion (see Chapter 10 for a fuller consideration of divisions within the community). Visiting tends to be restricted to a close circle of kin, but this is not to suggest that visiting patterns are determined by any conscious exclusion of other people. Quite often, socializing is done for the purpose of discussing hunting and visits between households of the same *ilaqutariit* are commonly made in order to plan hunting expeditions or for the distribution of meat.

Hunting partnerships and the social organization of fishing crews tend to remain within the *ilaqutariit*. Fathers share dogs and equipment with their sons, brothers will hunt with one another, or with cousins, and form partnerships for the purchase of fishing boats. For example, two brothers, Aron and Nuka G., regularly borrow each other's rifles and when their father was in need of a boat, both men shared Nuka's while he used Aron's. During the summer halibut fishery, David worked with his first cousin, while Eirik and Josepi fished together. It is rare for a man to hunt or fish with another to whom he does not apply a kin term or has no name-sharing relationship with.

Because of name relationships, and owing to the high degree of individual choice in selecting kin, the potential for conflict between *ilaqutariit* is reduced. Although certain families may not interact on a regular basis, they may still be linked in some way by genealogical, affinal, or fictive kinship, or by an *atsiaq*. Different types of alliance are important aspects of social organization in many Inuit communities and various groups form meat-sharing partnerships and exchange relationships.

In Kangersuatsiaq, the most common sort of affiliation with other *ilaqutariit*, apart from naming relationships, is through marriage. Over the last few decades, because of geographical mobility, marriages have taken place between people from other settlements, and men and women have not been restricted to finding a partner within Kangersuatsiaq. Usually this is because men travel throughout Upernavik district on hunting and fishing expeditions. Furthermore, the shortage of women of marriageable age in Kangersuatsiaq has often made journeys to other settlements necessary for men who wish to find themselves a wife. Marriage links have even been made across Melville Bay, with Avanersuaq district. Most notably people from Upernavik district (mainly, Kullorsuaq, Nuussuaq and Nutaarmiut) have intermarried with people from Savissivik and Moriussaq. In addition, other marriages have taken place between people from Kangersuatsiaq and parts of south Greenland, either as a result of people moving in from other areas, or because people from the village now live elsewhere. This results in a wider network of affinal kin in other parts of the country for some people, plus there is the possibility that *atsiat* may be named after people from villages and towns outside the district.

Returning kin

When a child is born, the mother will sing it a verse of affectionate words, or simply hum a tune, called an *aqaat*. This first happens soon after the birth, the mother cuddling the child and rocking it gently in her arms. Every mother sings an *aqaat* to her children, repeating the verse for several months and even years after the birth. The child's grandmother will also sing an *aqaat*. Informants can remember their fathers and other male relatives singing or humming an *aqaat*, although this is not common today.

Every *aqaat* is a mother's own personal possession and something she shares with the child. If a woman has several children, each will have its own *aqaat*. It is something that re-establishes and expresses the bond between a mother and her child which is temporarily severed with the cutting of the umbilical cord. They are connected through an endearment just as they are connected by the sharing of 'blood'.

As well as the mother and grandmother, there are other women who will sing an *aqaat* to the child. They may have no biological, genealogical or affinal relationship, but the new-born would be named after a deceased relative. In this situation, the endearment expresses the bond between the relative of the deceased and the *atsiaq*. Because a dead person has returned to the land of the living by virtue of a child receiving his/her name, the *aqaat* may be a word repeated over and over e.g. *angerlara* ('my one who has returned home'). Just as an *aqaat* replaces the umbilical cord, it also re-attaches a dead person to living relatives and is an expression of intense sentiment between adults and children.

I have previously mentioned that the personal name of the *atsiaq* is avoided by his/her *aqqa*'s family, with the appropriate kin term being used instead. This makes the actual use of terminology different from that sketched out above. A child is usually born into two families; that of his/her genitor and genitrix, and that of the deceased. It may be that an *atsiaq* belongs genealogically to the family of his/her *aqqa*, in which case terminology becomes more complex. For example, a child named after his grandfather is addressed as 'grandfather' by his genealogical cousins, as 'father' by his mother and her siblings, and himself calls his genitor 'son-in-law'. The biological dyadic relationship mother:son remains the same, but the terms of address correspond to the position occupied by the child as an *atsiaq*.

The genealogies I collected that correspond to the theoretical kinship terminology do not give us the true picture of what actually goes on, that is, conceptually. The person plays a wider and far richer range of social roles than can be seen if one restricts observations to kinship roles based on genealogy. If we sketch out the Upernavik kinship terminology and start from the point of ego, we would see that ego uses corresponding terms for each ascending and descending generation, siblings and collaterals, and affines. For the anthropologist attempting to understand terms of address, a considerable problem arises when ego is pointed out as his own father's brother, or his mother's father. Furthermore, ego's father may be named after his grandmother's brother, in which case terminology becomes even more tangled.

It is an important point to note that the terminology itself is not elaborate or confusing, but rather the actual use of terminology. Because of the multivocality of kinship terminology, a question arises as to whether this results in confusion. When a child calls its elder brother 'grandfather' or a younger sister is called 'father's elder sister', how does the child know what the true genealogical relationship is? Does the child come to think that his elder brother really is his grandfather? Such questions only really arise because Inuit kinship confuses non-Inuit ideas of order and social categories. Inuit themselves do not have any such problem. The key to understanding the application of Inuit kinship terminology is to recognize the difference between terms of reference and terms of address. So, a child addressing his elder brother as 'grandfather' will, in certain circumstances, refer to him as 'elder brother'. He will be aware that his elder brother is the *atsiaq* of his grandfather, just as he himself is the *atsiaq* of another person.

The recycling of names illustrates how the web of kinship allows extensive improvisation. A child is brought up to learn the terms s/he applies to consanguineal and affinal relatives, but throughout its life that child will never apply the correct genealogical terms to all of its close circle of kin. The kinship network is, in reality, a constant movement of people within a cosmological framework held together by names. Lévi-Strauss, discussing name avoidance, says that 'procreation is conceived not as the addition of a new being to those who exist already but as the substitute of the one for the others' (1972: 195). This is a useful starting point for a consideration of the relationship between the living and the dead in northwest Greenland.

Multiple name souls

I mentioned in the previous chapter that a dead person can have several *atsiat*, and that several dead people can share the same *atsiaq*. There is no limit as to how many names a person can be given or to put it another way, how many people can be reincarnated in a new-born child. One three year old boy has the names of five dead people; Jonas (his mother's brother), Pele (another of his mother's brothers), Tobias (the brother of a man named Knud), Robert (his mother's uncle), and Abel (his mother's grandfather). To his mother, the first name is the most important. The boy was born shortly after his mother's younger brother committed suicide. At the same time, Knud's younger brother died in the hospital in Upernavik after a long illness. Jonas's mother calls him *aqqaluk* (the term for female ego's younger brother), while Knud calls him Nuka (the term for male ego's younger brother). Jonas reciprocates with *aleqa* (older sister) as a term of address to his mother, while Knud is known as *angaju* (older brother). The names Robert and Abel are more distant. Both men each have their own *ateqqaataa* and the boy's mother told me she wanted to 'remember' her uncle and grandfather, and that her son was 'like them', but not as much as her brother. A child's first name is usually that of a recently deceased person while, as in this case, the other names are those of long dead relatives or others.

Similarly, a dead person can have many *atsiat*, not necessarily in the same community. Juditha, the wife of Abel L., had six children named after her throughout the district; two in Kangersuatsiaq (including her *ateqqaataa*), one in Upernavik, one in Upernavik Kujalleq, one in Aappilattoq, and one in Innaarsuit. As I have mentioned, the *ateqqaataa* is the most important. In addition, several children have Juditha as their third or even fourth name. Position of the name does not matter, and all these children have some kind of relationship with Juditha's husband. To Abel L., the *atsiat* living in Kangersuatsiaq are the most important. They visit him every day, whereas he is less likely to see the children who live in the other villages. Instead, photographs of the *atsiat* in Upernavik, Upernavik Kujalleq, Aappilattoq and Innaarsuit decorate the walls of his one room house.

If the *ateqqaataa* has been born in another village, the family of the deceased will make all possible efforts to visit the child on the day of the baptism. Often, inclement weather may hinder such plans, in which case gifts will be sent by post and the family will talk to the child's parents by telephone. A visit will then be made as soon as possible. Despite the birth of the *ateqqaataa*, the first same-sex child to be born in Kangersuatsiaq after a death will receive the name of that person. The *ateqqaataa* remains important to the family, but having an *atsiaq* in the village acquires deep significance.

As an example, shortly after Josepi died in October 1988, the news came through from Upernavik town that the wife of his sister's son had given birth to a baby boy. The family was overjoyed for, although it had not been formally announced what name the child was to receive, it was known that he would be called Josepi. Josepi's sons and daughters travelled through to Upernavik for the baptism in November and there was much celebrating afterwards. During this time, Josepi's youngest daughter Naja was pregnant, expecting her child in March. In February 1989, when I was back in England, I received a letter from Juuna telling me Naja had given birth to a son. He went on to say that the child was to receive his father's name (*'ataatama ateriniarpaa'*) and that 'we are all happy' (*'tamatta nuannaarpugut'*). From subsequent letters and from my experiences in the field, I can only surmise that this meant a great deal to Josepi's family. After her father's funeral, Naja had told her cousin (her mother's sister's daughter) she wished for a son so he could be Josepi's *atsiaq*. If she was to have a daughter, Naja said she would have her mother's name.

Such closeness ensures that a recently deceased person's presence can be experienced in the present. The idea of one person being re-born in several *atsiat* illustrates how the re-cycling of names is more a form of social reincarnation. While some aspect of the dead person passes to the child with the name (consciousness), what we seem to be dealing with here is the image and memory of a loved and valued member of both family and community. The succession of names ensures the replacement of one person with another, even to the point where someone is replaced several times. Greenlanders say 'the name doesn't die' (*'ateq toqussanngilaq'*). As the name is a person's life-stream, it links the new-born child in an existential network containing both the living and the dead. An *atsiaq* mediates between the living and the dead through physical and spiritual kinship.

Having been named, children learn the identities of the people they are named after and begin to acquire a knowledge of the various relationships that link them to an intricate pattern of genealogical and fictive kin. A child who has the names of four dead people can quite possibly be linked to four separate families as well as the one into which that child was born. As was illustrated above, however, this may not always be the case as the child may be named after immediate genealogical kin.

Whatever the situation, it remains that the child is named after people who had previously occupied positions in the kinship network. To some extent, because of the name, roles and interaction between *atsiat* and the family of the *aqqa* are prescribed. A child who is the *atsiaq* of someone's mother or wife will know how to behave when interacting with that person. *Atsiat* are expected to visit the surviving kin frequently, attend birthday celebrations, run errands, do housework, repair and loan hunting and fishing equipment and give regular gifts of meat.

This does not tell us anything, however, of the person's own sense of identity and feelings of being named. Other people do the naming, ensuring that they continue to experience the memory of a deceased loved one in the form of an *atsiaq*. There are a few cases in Kangersuatsiaq, though, where the *atsiaq* forms stronger attachments to particular people depending on their own preference to one of their names. One example is a five year old boy named David Peter. While being the *atteqqataa* of a man called David, the boy prefers Peter as a name for himself. As a result, he spends more time in the house of a woman whose husband Peter is the boy's other *aqqa*, than he does in the home of David's family. This theme will be returned to in Chapter 8.

Name-sharers and the seeking of similarity

Names are recycled and redistributed, allowing for the regeneration and continuation of families and the idea of community. But names are also something to be shared and an *atsiaq* not only enters into a relationship with his genealogical family and that of his/her *aqqa*, but with others who are name-sharers (*atiik*). Again, names are avoided and the reciprocal form of address is '*atiitsara*': 'my name-sharer'. While the dead continue their relationships with their close kin, they also continue their close social association with name-sharers. A child who is called Abel, for example, will be the name-sharer of all those who have the same name. The relationships will have already been established between his *aqqa* and other men called Abel. The child enters an existing order which is then able to continue.

Name-sharing is complex but it allows for the extension of kinship beyond the *ilaqutariit*. Indeed it is possible, at least theoretically, for an individual to include virtually everyone of the same sex as kin. If we take the example of the three year old mentioned earlier in this chapter, he addresses as '*atiitsara*' all those in the community who have Jonas, Pele, Tobias, Robert or Abel as a name in any order. Thus, in addition to all those he is related to as an *atsiaq*, he has a further sixteen people in Kangersuatsiaq as name-sharer relations. Furthermore, anyone in another part of Upernavik district (and theoretically in the whole of Greenland) who has the same name is also a name-sharer.

The same three year old addresses Abel L. (who is 68 years old) as '*atiitsara*' but Abel L.'s eleven year old grandson is also called Abel. All three are name-sharers, with the grandfather:grandson relationship subordinate to that based on shared names. This is an important point, as name-sharers regard one another as equals then terminology is also equated. A person will also address the relatives of his name-sharer by the terminology they themselves use. Thus, a man will address the younger sister of his name-sharer as '*najak*', and his father as '*ataata*'. If the younger sister happens to be the *atsiaq* of his name-sharer's mother's sister, then he will call her '*aja*' (mother's sister). She will then reciprocate with '*ujoroq*' (sister's child), just as she does with her brother. In this way, a person will address as many other people with kin terms as s/he has name-sharers. Parents refer to the name-sharers of their offspring as 'our son' or 'our daughter' and may give them gifts on birthdays and at Christmas, although this is not obligatory. It is incumbent on name-sharers to exchange gifts on these occasions, however.

Through a name-sharing relationship there is an enormous range of other possible relationships to enter into. Again, it can be simply a matter of choice how far, for example, a person wishes to develop something based on kin terms applied to a name-sharer's father or sister. It may be nothing more than a way of addressing one another, or possibly it may be something a little more significant. As a child, one informant used to spend more time in the house of her name-sharer (six years her senior) than in her own home. Quite often, she would eat, play and sleep there. As a result, she has grown up with two 'mothers' and two 'fathers'. The two families have no genealogical connection and nothing passes between them. Indeed, the girl's own parents are members of the temperance movement and support the Atassut political party, while her name-sharer's parents are known as notorious drinkers and are loyal to the Siumut party. It is not that there is any friction between them, but as a result of differing views they have very little contact with one another. However, this has not prevented the girl from developing a meaningful relationship with them.

The various combinations and possibilities available are too numerous to set down here. The intricacies of name-sharing are not always available for immediate study, and during my fieldwork I did not gather all the material on this. Just as a picture began to take shape, new twists and turns would blur it a little. For example, someone defined as distant consanguineal kin (*eqqarleq*) by several siblings would often turn out to be a name-sharer of one of them who, privately, would regard the relationship as rather more meaningful. Despite the use of appropriate reciprocal terminology, there would sometimes be no more in this as far as the other siblings were concerned. Such idiosyncrasies apart, more distant kin can be brought 'closer' through sharing names.

Earlier in this chapter, I mentioned that kin terms are often applied to people who have no consanguineal or affinal connection. If a person looks upon another as a brother, sister, grandfather or daughter, then there is nothing to prevent them from sealing this preference with the use of a kin term. Similarly, kinship can also be deactivated, or forgotten about. Informants told me that it was possible for name-sharers to 'forget one another', but it is rare for people to ignore the sharing of a name and I have no example of this. There is a fundamental difference between kin terms and names, the latter belonging to both a social and spiritual network.

In some cases, sharing a name is not a prerequisite for establishing a name-sharing relationship. People who have a close association as friends, hunting and fishing partners, or who are even genealogically related may address each other as '*atiitsara*'. Such people are 'fictive' name-sharers usually on the basis of some shared experience. Rosaldo also makes the point that, for the Ilongot of the Philippines, reciprocal names are used 'in commemoration of experiences they have shared' (1980: 11). An example of this in Kangersuatsiaq is the lifelong relationship between Josepi and Jens. Both men were born in Kangersuatsiaq, where Jens married Josepi's mother's cousin before moving to Upernavik town. Their sons and daughters are defined as Josepi's cousins.

Both Josepi and Jens grew up in the village and often travelled and hunted together as young men. They shared a profound knowledge of hunting and of the local environment and were regarded as *piniartorsuit* (big hunters) by the rest of the community. They were often asked advice by other younger hunters, especially about weather, equipment and hunting areas. In addition, both had a strong reputation as story-tellers. Because both men were such firm friends, they addressed each other as name-sharers despite the fact they did not share a name. However they did share a relationship and many experiences which they recognized and cemented by regarding each other as an *atiik*. The creation of other kinship ties followed as a result. For example, Jens' oldest daughter has always called Josepi 'father'. One of his sons has never avoided Josepi's name, but he told me he had often thought of him 'like my father' ('*soorlu ataataga*').

As might be suspected, the importance of names raises many questions about the meaning of kinship not only in Greenland, but for kinship theory in general. In a sense, I have tried to outline, albeit somewhat briefly, what are seen as 'real' kin relationships. These are the relationships that individuals give meaning to, either idiosyncratically or collectively in the case of an *atsiaq*. This does not mean that actual kinship, that is kinship based on putative biology, is entirely forgotten about. Non-biological ties defined as meaningful are ultimately recognized as fictive when sexual relationships and inheritance are taken into consideration. The equivalence of terminology through name-sharing does not mean the equivalence of blood, so there are no incest taboos which apply between an individual and the actual kin of his/her name-sharer (unlike the Azande incest taboo which is extended to include blood-brothers; see Evans-Pritchard 1963). As I have mentioned, theoretically a kin tie can be created with virtually every other person in the community. The absence of an incest taboo illustrates how this broader set of relatives is perceived as a cultural construction where kin terms and genealogy do not necessarily coincide. The existence of an incest prohibition for immediate genealogical kin extending as far as second cousins, however, draws a neat line between categories resting on biological or sociological criteria.

Inheritance also recognizes the importance of genealogical connection. A son (including adopted sons) inherits seal, beluga and salmon netting sites from his father. Campsites also go the same way. Equipment and material wealth become the property of offspring but *atsiat* and name-sharers have no claim and expect no hereditary succession to property. The continual expanding of the universe of kin contracts and emphasis is strictly genealogical.

Name-sharing is only part of a perpetual seeking of similarity between people which, in its way, is bound up with the evasion of difference. Name-sharers are essentially blood brothers/sisters and the same is true for people born the same year (*peqatigiit*; age-sets) and those who share the same birthday (*nallioqatigiit*). Both categories involve the exchange of gifts; on New Year's Day in the case of *peqatigiit*, and on birthdays in the case of *nalliuqatigiit*. The oft heard phrase '*Kangersuatsiarmiit soorlu ataaseq*' ('The Kangersuatsiarmiit are like one') is no mere rhetorical statement of egalitarianism. It is a denial of difference and, ultimately, of individualism. In a society where privacy is simply not available and where solitude is equated with loneliness, the notion of community dominates and finds its expression through kinship.

Name-sharing, the recycling of names and the possibility of choosing kin make kinship a network of intimacy and equality. It is not only name-sharers who enjoy a symmetrical relationship. In practice, kinship is not founded on the asymmetrical relationships of senior–junior, especially when a man's son is his 'grandfather', or a woman's younger sister is her mother's sister. As Chapter 5 showed, a child's consciousness (*sila*) is allowed to develop because it is already present in latent form and that some aspect of the *aqqa* has passed with the name to the *atsiaq*. In this way, people are involved with one another in a pattern of inverted and continuing relationships.

Kinship and the construction of community

So where does this leave kinship in northwest Greenland? The theme running through this book is that community is not defined in terms of social structure, but that it belongs to the realm of ideas. The physical entity of the village is immediately observable to any who arrive there, but the meanings held by its inhabitants that make community a cultural construct are elusive and implicit in how people think, feel and behave.

This chapter has sketched out briefly the kinship network found in Kangersuatsiaq. It is multi-faceted, embracing genealogy, friendship, name-sharing, age-sets, birthday partners, chosen kin and name souls. It is the means for the expression of the whole person and central for the way people orientate themselves in relation to their social and spiritual worlds. In this sense, kinship is a collection of symbols highly charged with emotional energy. The recording and listing of terms does not mean that designation will follow accordingly (Schneider 1968). Rather, kin terms are symbols that allow for the imputation of idiosyncratic meaning. They form part of a much larger set of symbols and implicit meanings that actively construct the idea of community, here perceived as containing both the living and the dead. Names and, implicitly, people do not die. Children enter an already existing place in the cosmos which allows for the continuity of the person, the continuity of the family and the continuity of community.

Kin categories vary in meaning, but their significance lies in the way they permit individuals freedom to employ them in any way they choose. It is in this sense that kinship is symbolic. Through it, people find expression in their social world and it becomes a map of real and meaningful interpersonal relationships. Cultural items, such as kin terms, are not accepted by people in Kangersuatsiaq at face value. The reluctance to regard kin terms and genealogy as coterminous results in an elaborate construct: a universe of relatives transcending 'biology'. Learning every kin tie is impossible and this has been noted in other parts of the Arctic (e.g. Briggs 1979). Even the Kangersuatsiarmiit have not worked out their entire kin reckoning as it differs from person to person. Furthermore, it may be problematic to talk of 'extension' of the kinship network and better to see it in terms of improvisation and existing possibilities. Talking of Inuit kinship, Guemple holds that social relatedness begins in the local group, not in kinship ties, because people are recognized as kin and relatives if they live in the same community. Kinship is therefore, inherently socio-cultural rather than biological (Guemple 1979b). Consanguinity and affinity are only two ways of expressing these relationships. The recycling of names, name-sharing and improvisation in the use of terms is, in one sense, 'a symbolic conferral that emerges out of the need to convert a person who is in the local group . . . into a relative' (ibid: 94). People become kin and strengthen the feeling of community.

Kangersuatsiaq

Upernavik

Summer fishing camp in the fjords east of Kangersuatsiaq

Preparing seal meat for winter storage

Mitaartut

Elderly hunter with his daughter and his wife's atsiaq, a four year old girl named after his deceased wife

The individual or collective catch of large sea mammals, such as walrus, is a community event, with the meat shared out between all households

Melville Bay

Making salmon nets in preparation for the autumn fishery

Each hunter requires an understanding of the behaviour and movement of sea-ice

Jigging for Arctic char in early autumn

In spring, hunters use a small white screen for approaching basking ringed seals

7

Strangers

Strangers and community

Essentially, kinship is juxtaposed to non-kinship and the previous chapter showed how people can choose others as kin by employing a kinship term to cement a particular relationship. People can be converted into relatives in this way. However, in Kangersuatsiaq, there is a category of person that remains distinct from kin. This is the stranger. The importance of kin terms for community and group solidarity is illustrated by the stranger as a figure who is unable to demonstrate any kin ties in the community. There is a significant distinction, which will emerge later, between lonely people who have no kin (as shall be shown in the next chapter this can be remedied) and strangers who can never establish kin ties.

In the past, a stranger who crossed over another community's boundary ran the risk of being killed by members of that community. In north Alaska, the stranger who arrived in an Eskimo community was 'immediately catechized as to his relationships . . . The stranger, subject to such rough treatment as being pummelled and having his clothes torn by the residents of the settlement he entered, in any case, would attempt to get the names of house or tent owners in the community. In this way, he might be able to claim relationship and protection being thus able to establish some connection in the community' (Spencer 1959: 72). This situation was not unique to Inuit society. Among the Tallensi of Ghana, for example, strangers from other tribes were enslaved if they ventured into Tallensi settlements. Strangers were only safe from captivity if they had kinsmen, affines or friends in the community who were able to put in a good word for them (Fortes 1975).

As this chapter shows, strangers are feared and pose a threat to everyday social life in the community. The outside world impinges increasingly on the lives of the Kangersuatsiarmiit, a theme that will be returned to in Chapter 10. Strangers are regarded as representatives of the outside world and I illustrate this by showing how death can be potentially disruptive, not only owing to the loss of a valued member of the community, but because of the involvement with outsiders during illness and mortuary ritual. I also show how funerary procedure has a symbolic importance for community construction by excluding the outside.

The Greenlandic word for stranger is *takornartaq*; 'one who has not been seen before'. Later in this chapter I explore the significance of this literal meaning by discussing the appearance of symbolic strangers in the form of disguised figures during the period leading up to Epiphany. Although a neat distinction can be made between the community and strangers, the latter category is ambiguous because strangers cannot be identified as just being Danes, or people from other villages. There is also a supernatural element and the stranger becomes a metaphor for everything that is threatening to community.

Qallunaat – the Danes

By 1782 the Inuit population along the west coast, from Cape Farewell in the south to Upernavik in the north, had come into permanent contact with Danes and other Europeans. As well as the missionary activities of Lutherans and Moravians, explorers and whalers had far-reaching influence on Inuit culture both economically, through bartering activities, and genetically as a result of liaisons with Greenlandic women. But, above all, the year-round presence of Danes (*qallunaat*; sing. *qallunaaq*) was felt in the hierarchy of authority that, as well as the missionary, included inspectors, traders, assistants and the colony crew. The inspector and trader were each known by the Inuit as a *naalagaq*; 'someone to be obeyed'.

In each settlement the trader occupied a position of power over the lives of the Inuit. This power was based on a responsibility for the distribution of trade goods and provisions, and for the payment of wages in kind. The trader, and other Danes who came to work in the colonies, seldom stayed longer than six years or so before returning to Denmark and being replaced by new civil servants and employees of the KGH.

The Order of 1782 (see Chapter 2) laid down rules for KGH employees as a guide to moral conduct in their interaction with Greenlanders. Indeed, free and easy interaction between the two groups was prohibited. It was generally believed that contact between Danes and Greenlanders had resulted in laziness and a decline of hunting. As such interaction was regarded as having an adverse effect on the trade economy, Danes were prohibited from having sexual intercourse with Greenlandic women and banned from supplying Greenlanders with any form of alcohol. It was possible for KGH employees to be given permission to marry Greenlandic women however, provided they were of mixed descent. Of central importance to the Danes was the protection of Inuit culture and the continuity of the trade economy. By the end of the eighteenth century the fortunes of the missionaries, the traders and the Inuit were inextricably bound up with the survival of the hunting way of life.

As a result, the KGH attempted to prevent the Inuit becoming too dependent on the Danes by ensuring that all basic necessities could be satisfied by hunting. The polarization of the two groups was maintained, although it was difficult to avoid mixed marriages. Those who did marry Greenlanders tended to stay on in Greenland, but the turnover of Danish employees stationed in Greenland for short periods continued.

Until the 1950s the majority of Danes in Greenland were involved with either the KGH or the Lutheran Church, or were teachers, administrators, doctors and nurses. Following the abolition of colonial status in 1953 there was a greater influx of Danes, including large numbers of construction workers. As a result of migration from the villages to the towns in the 1960s more Greenlanders came into contact with Danes, resulting in ethnic and ideological conflicts. Since Home Rule the numbers of Danes in Greenland has increased and there are now some 10,000 living and working there. By far the largest number of Danes, almost 4,000 out of a total population of 12,000, live in Nuuk.

Most Danes go to Greenland on two-year contracts as teachers, doctors and administrators. Some renew their contracts, but many return to Denmark and quite often have no further association with Greenland. Others choose to stay in Greenland, settling in the towns and marrying Greenlandic women. Very few Greenlandic men marry Danish women. In addition to those on contracts of a couple of years or more, the number of Danes increases mainly in the summer months when skilled and unskilled workers arrive to work on construction projects directed by Nuna-Tek, the former Greenland Technical Organization (GTO).

Few Danes live in the villages, which remain predominantly Greenlandic and monolingual. Danes who do work in the villages tend to be teachers and most Greenlanders will only interact with a large number of Danes in the towns. In Upernavik town there are just over one hundred Danes resident throughout the year. Most are employed by the municipal council, the KNI and Nuna-Tek. Others are teachers or work in the hospital.

The majority of Danes in Upernavik do not interact with Greenlanders on a casual basis. To the native population they remain strangers (*takornartat*) and are regarded as belonging elsewhere. Danes on contract work know they will return to Denmark and Greenlanders are usually critical of the fact that they come to Greenland to earn big money and make no attempt to learn the Greenlandic language. The Danes tend to be self-contained, distant from their close social associates back home in Denmark yet retaining a set of values that maintains the social distance between themselves and the Greenlandic community.

Greenlanders tend to regard Danes as sojourners who have little incentive to assimilate into the host community. Their stay is brief and they usually explain their reasons for being in Greenland as a wish to combine work experience with travel and adventure. Like expatriates throughout the world, they regard their jobs as means to an end rather than an act of benevolence for the future well-being of the native population. While working publicly with Greenlanders in schools, hospitals and administration, Danes live intensely private lives shared only with other Danes.

As sojourners who interact with fellow sojourners, Danes enjoy constant reminders of home in the form of Danish food, TV, music, annual holidays back to Denmark, the Danish language, comfortable furniture and good housing. By not aspiring to membership of the host community Danes remain strangers to the majority of Greenlanders. They do not share a language of membership, and social relations between the two groups are not based on familiarity. They are strangers who are both inside and outside the host community (Fortes ibid.) – inside as short or long term residents, yet outside due to ethnic and cultural differences. When Danes occasionally came to Kangersuatsiaq to work on brief construction projects, I was used by the villagers as a way of approaching them, usually for cadging wood, nails, pieces of scrap metal and other materials. Similarly, I was asked by Danes to arrange for them to be taken out on hunting trips by local people. Not all hunters welcomed such passengers and many only agreed to a expedition providing that I also accompanied them in the boat. Once, when two Danish biologists spent two weeks collecting blood, meat, kidney and stomach samples from seals the hunters had caught, I was used as both translator and mediator for both business and social transactions.

The absence of a well-defined social proximity between the two groups can result in tension and distrust. For Greenlanders this is most obviously felt during intensely traumatic experiences such as bereavement. What follows is a consideration of bereavement and subsequent funeral procedure as a way of illustrating the place occupied by Danes as a category of community thought.

Death and the involvement of outsiders

In Kangersuatsiaq, as in other Greenlandic villages, news of a death is something that cannot be concealed. The first murmurs that a death has occurred spread rapidly through the village. Even those who do not hear immediately are alerted by the flag that flies at half-mast outside the house of the deceased's immediate family. As the death becomes widely reported, a group of men begins to gather outside the old meeting house. They begin to express shock and surprise (*tupinaq*). Incidences of violent death and suicide are high in Greenland and news of a death by drowning or accident is always met with disbelief. An unexpected death leads to a discussion that centres on how and where that person died.

Similarly, a person who has died because of an illness (an expected death) will become the focus of a verbal post-mortem. Every aspect of the deceased's illness comes under scrutiny; the length of the illness, the number of times the person either recovered or was judged to be near death, the movement of the patient between the village and the hospital in Upernavik town (or possibly also to Nuuk or Denmark), the role played by the doctor.

Because most people who die through illness do so in hospital, there is a feeling of remoteness between village and town. As one elderly informant commented on his wife's illness and isolation from her family 'Poor Sofia, the hospital is really so very far away' ('*Sofia nallinnaq. Napparsimavik ungasipallaaqaaq*'). The verbal post-mortem pieces together whatever scraps of information there are which filter through from the town. The feeling of distance is intensified by the role of midwife (*juumooq*, which comes from the Danish *jordmoder*) who acts as intermediary between the hospital and the immediate family of the deceased. It is the midwife who informs relatives of the death of a family member. As a Greenlander (and native of Kangersuatsiaq), she is a member of the community by birth and kinship. However, her experiences of other parts of Greenland (such as Nuuk), and of Denmark, her education and training as a midwife, her status and lifestyle put her at one remove from the other villagers. Once a death has occurred she assumes a role that puts her at a further distance precisely because death and subsequent mortuary procedure have become institutionalized features of modern Greenlandic life.

There is usually a long period of waiting for the deceased's family while the midwife is trying to find out what news there is from the hospital. Often, in winter, the geographical distance from the town is most marked by frequent difficulties with the telephone. The absence of news and details of the death complements the social distance of the midwife.

People are usually unable to travel easily and cheaply to visit loved ones in hospital. They also feel constrained by their inability to deal directly with the doctor and to discuss the return of the body after death. The doctor in the town is a Dane and most people will only see him as patients when he visits the village, normally twice a year during his rounds of the district. On these visits the midwife again acts as intermediary, this time as interpreter. Most informants, while acknowledging the importance of the doctor, admitted they felt *ajukkuppoq*, which translates as a feeling of shyness because of a sense of inferiority and unworthiness while in his presence.

Most people's experiences of the doctor are brief and infrequent. The majority of villagers have no knowledge of Danish and the doctor cannot speak Greenlandic. Furthermore, because he is a Dane (and a figure of authority) the doctor is an outsider and stranger in community cognition. He is also a transient worker, remaining in Greenland only a couple of years. Here, Simmel's (1950) idea that the stranger is a person 'who comes today and stays tomorrow' does not apply. Because of the regular turnover of Danish doctors, the villagers are denied the chance to develop feelings of trust and such transience does little to ameliorate a sense of inferiority (*naalagasiorpoq*: see Chapter 10 for a fuller consideration of this).

As a Danish speaking outsider, the doctor has no established role in village life, except as a rather remote figure from the town who can only be approached through the midwife. Berger and Luckmann's succinct observation that 'to underline its authority the medical profession shrouds itself in the age-old symbols of power and mystery, from outlandish costume to incomprehensible language' (1984: 105) shows how the doctor, as outsider, can intimidate people into feeling *ajukkuppoq*. By maintaining distance the boundary between villager/patient and doctor, or Greenlander and Dane, insider and outsider in a wider context, is given particular salience. The ethnic boundary may be invoked to strengthen the feeling of distance. Shyness can be exploited as a characteristic of Greenlanders when confronted by Danes, and it is the manipulation (either consciously or unconsciously) of this characteristic that helps to keep the insiders (Greenlanders) and the outsiders (Danes) apart. Shyness and feelings of inferiority legitimate the doctor–patient relationship.

To the Kangersuatsiarmiit, the doctor plays a leading role in the scenario of the hospital, particularly when a death has occurred. Kin and other villagers seek to discover where he was at the time of death, if the patient was being attended to or neglected. The doctor is not bereaved (*aliasunngilaq*) and is therefore distanced even further from the community. He is relegated to a status of geographical and social isolation. Such segregation is possible because the deceased's kin need not have any contact with the doctor, except through the midwife.

Institutionalization of mortuary procedure and ritual involves strangers (doctors, nurses, others) as necessary participants. Even when a death has occurred in Kangersuatsiaq, the preparation of the corpse involves the participation of the midwife. In cases where the midwife can trace no genealogical relationship to the deceased she, like the doctor, is not said to be bereaved. In the past, the immediate female relatives would wash and dress the corpse, and although they may still be involved, nowadays the midwife assumes responsibility. Participation of immediate kin in preparing the corpse for burial is reduced. This aspect of mortuary ritual has been removed from the sphere of kinship, as has initial contact with the dead in many cases.

While the group of men gathers to discuss all they know and have heard, a steady stream of people call on the deceased's family to express their sympathies. Usually, women are the first to call, followed by all those who had a close social association with the deceased. Expressing sympathies simply involves entering the house and sitting down. Coffee is served and general conversation or silence follow. Bereaved women are kept company by other women soon after the death and this may continue for up to a week after the funeral.

Immediate male relatives such as sons and brothers begin to discuss the making of the coffin. Almost as soon as the death is announced, arrangements are made to bring the body back to Kangersuatsiaq for burial. Again the midwife acts as go-between for family and hospital. Arrangements must be made for the supply boat (or in exceptional circumstances the police boat) to make a special journey from town to village to transport the body at least a day before the funeral.

The catechist is responsible for fixing the date of the funeral, which must be approved by the priest in Upernavik town. The burial usually takes place on the third or fourth day after death. Of the four villagers who died during the period of my fieldwork, none died in Kangersuatsiaq. Three deaths were in the hospital, while the fourth was the result of an accident in Upernavik harbour. When a death does occur in the village itself, the doctor may be required to visit and examine the body before burial takes place.

Symbolizing the boundary: returning the body

On the second day, the closest male relatives purchase wood from the store and begin to make the coffin in the village workshop. Any activity in the workshop is always an attraction for men, teenage boys and children, and interest is intense when a coffin is being made. There is a steady stream of visitors to inspect the work and to comment on how well the coffin is coming along. Advice is offered on construction and tools are often taken up by others. Teenagers and children are to be seen helping by smoothing pieces of wood with sandpaper. Coffin making has an air of haste and intensity about it. The men work well into the night and usually continue into the small hours of the morning. In this way coffins are finished normally within two days. The making of the coffin contrasts with the institutionalized aspects of mortuary procedure because it remains in the sphere of kinship. Although a coffin can be purchased, if need be, it is one feature that can avoid the participation of outsiders, or more specifically strangers. Close female relatives may involve themselves in the washing and dressing of the corpse, but the participation of the midwife excludes the possibility of it remaining the private business of kin and close associates.

Coffin making, on the other hand, remains the property of kin and, by extension, the property of the community. A woman commenting on the coffin her sons made for their father said 'They made it very beautiful'. This remark contains a poignancy in a society characterized by subsistence hunting and fishing where families are both units of production and consumption. Families provide for their members when living and dead. While other areas of life and death are gradually being appropriated by the wider society of modern Greenland, coffin making assumes a significance that is informed by it being the concern of close kin who can exclude and deny the outside world.

As I have mentioned, in most cases even the act of dying has been consigned to an institution. The coffin making signals the beginning of a local funeral procedure that, looking forward to the return of the body, expresses the idea of community. The death of a member of the community sets in motion a series of events that culminate in that person's return to the village, both for the funeral and through the transfer of the name to an *atsiaq*.

While the coffin is being made, one or two men are employed by the municipal council to dig the grave. Because of the permafrost and stony ground this is done with a shovel and pneumatic drill. The grave is usually only about two or three feet deep. Where the ground is exceedingly hard, a space is cleared and no grave is dug.

On the day the body is due to be brought back to the village, people keep a constant lookout for the KNI boat. Once in sight, all work is suspended, the shop and school are closed and people line the pier to await the boat's arrival. The boat is crewed by people from Upernavik town and owned by the KNI which, to the ethnographer at least, intensifies the feeling that until now the deceased has been anything but the concern of kin. The body is carried from the boat by close male relatives and a long line of people forms. The body is then carried up to the church and the procession winds its way through the village, collecting more people (those who could find no place on the pier). The body is placed in the small chapel next to the church and the group begins to dissipate as villagers return to their work and other tasks. The close kin are left behind with the catechist and arrangements are made for the washing and preparation of the body for viewing.

Later on, there is a pre-funeral invitation for coffee and cake and people visit throughout the day to sit and spend some time with the bereaved. Again, it is important to point out that the expressing of condolences and sympathy is inherent in the actual visit itself. Visiting contains within it a set of statements which express community norms and values. Once the body has been washed and dressed, people go up to view it in the chapel, starting with immediate kin and close associates. After viewing, a few people re-visit the deceased's family.

Funerals

On the day of the funeral, groups of men gather below the church and at the side of the meeting house. The Greenlandic national flag is flown at half-mast outside the church half an hour before the service is due to begin. While the men are gathering, there is general talk about the weather and about recent hunting and fishing. Some fifteen minutes before the service, the immediate kin go up to the church, followed shortly after by the other villagers. While the catechist, his assistant and the main body of villagers take their places in the church, the close circle of kin and associates gather in the chapel for one last look at the deceased. The coffin lid is then fastened down and wreathes of plastic flowers are placed on top. The coffin is then carried from the chapel into the church by the deceased's sons, brothers or nephews, followed by other kin and close associates. The whole community attends the funeral and burial. The exceptions are people who are away from the village and cannot return, and those too ill to leave their homes.

Following the service in the church, the funeral procession moves to the graveyard on the far side of the village. Again, the coffin is carried by the closest male relatives of the deceased. The procession is led by a kinsman or other close associate who walks in front carrying the simple white wooden cross that will be placed at the head of the grave.

For the ethnographer, one of the most striking features of the funeral procession is the clothing worn by the mourners. The close kin dress in the Greenlandic national costume. The men wear a white cotton anorak, black trousers and black shoes. The women wear a red silk anorak fitted with bead collar, short sealskin trousers and knee-length white sealskin *kamiks* trimmed with white lace. The other villagers dress in their every-day clothes and some in their workclothes. This gives the Greenlandic village funeral something of an air of normality. This feeling of normality cuts through the solemnity as people light cigarettes and gentle chatter can be heard as the procession makes its way towards the graveyard.

The villagers gather around the grave to hear the burial service given by the catechist. The coffin is placed in the grave and sprinkled with holy earth. At this point, the bereaved kin can be seen apart from the rest of the community. They cluster around the graveside while other people begin to break off from the main group and gather in several places. Children can be seen wandering around and playing among the graves. There is an increase in the level of quiet talk, contrasting with the proceedings at the graveside. After the burial service is complete, the catechist and the villagers return to the village, leaving the mourning kin who start to shovel earth over the coffin and to cover the grave with large stones. Once this is done, the family gathers around the grave and takes a series of photographs. An enlargement of a graveside photograph is hung later in the homes of close kin.

The close kin remain in a bereaved state (*aliasunneq*) after the funeral has taken place, with other close associates and name-sharers of the deceased only marginally so. As I have mentioned, the rest of the community return to their everyday tasks with rapidity. Even as the bereaved kinsmen are filling in the grave, men are making their way to the harbour to complete necessary work on their boats and equipment. If the weather is bad, boats need to be secured. In good weather, opportunities for a successful day's hunting are taken. Women return to household duties and children are soon to be seen playing out of doors.

Death and subsequent mortuary procedure show how the distance between village and town is intensified by the role of hospital and doctor, symbols of the wider society that has appropriated aspects of mortuary procedure. The funeral gives the boundary particular saliency and illustrates this distance by the sense of locality with which it is charged. All members of the community are involved in the funeral proceedings and the sense of locality is, I believe, the key to understanding the significance of normal everyday behaviour. The funeral becomes a community occasion as well as a family occasion, that centres around the return and burial of a loved and valued member. Outsiders from Uper-navik town do not participate in the funeral. Their involvement stops at the hospital (in the case of the doctor) and the pier (in the case of the KNI or police boat that brings the body back). However, there is an occasion when strangers and threats from the outside go so far as to intrude into the warmth and familiarity of people's homes. It is consideration of this to which I now turn.

Scaring the host, insulting the stranger: *mitaarneq*

Once a year, disguised figures known as *mitaartut* roam the village over a three day period leading up to Epiphany. This is an elaborate event known as *mitaarneq*, meaning the 'act/state of being disguised'. Deriving from the intransitive *mitaarpoq* ('is disguised'), *mitaartut* is the plural of *mitaartoq*, meaning 'one who is disguised'.

In the early literature (e.g. Birket-Smith 1924: 402) *mitaarneq* is mentioned in the context of ritual mask dances, wife-exchange ceremonies and as an imitation of the sexual act, or as a pre-Christian remnant of the Sea-Woman cult (Kleivan 1960). The latter was a widespread Inuit ceremony to appease the wrath of the Sea-Woman who guarded over animal souls 'that have been offended by transgression of taboos' (Boas 1901: 139). In the ceremony, the Sea-Woman would send her servant to visit the Inuit. She was represented by a man dressed as a woman who was dumb and wore a mask of sealskin. Other Inuit groups, such as the Nugumiut of Frobisher Bay, had similar ceremonies with three masked persons representing supernatural beings (Boas ibid.). However, relatively little has been written about *mitaarneq*, especially from an anthropological perspective. Nelleman (1960) has described his observations in West Greenland, while Nooter (1975) and Gessain (1984) reported on the very similar mask performances, known as *uajarteq* in East Greenland.

As it appears today, *mitaarneq* is a blend of Greenlandic custom and the practice of mumming once found in Scandinavia (Kleivan ibid: 25–28), which explains why it takes place at Epiphany. Greenlanders also call the event *kongepingasut* ('the Three Kings'), thus relating it to the journey of the Magi. Although Kleivan attempts to link *mitaarneq* with other customs such as the Alaskan Eskimo asking festival and the Baffin Island Sedna feasts (ibid: 11–14), the only other Inuit figures bearing any similarity to *mitaartut* are the Labrador *nalyuks* (Ben-Dor 1966: 121). They appear on Twelfth Night and probably have their origins in Newfoundland Christmas mumming customs (e.g. as described by Robertson 1984).

In Kangersuatsiaq, Christmas time is a celebration that involves the entire community. On December 24, 25 and 26, and again at New Year, groups of people go from house to house for coffee and cake. Ideally, every house must be visited at least once during this period. People enter the homes of those with whom they have very little interaction during the rest of the year. Christmas visiting thus contrasts with regular mutual visits for coffee, which are usually confined to kin and other close associates. In addition, disorderly and drunken behaviour is condoned and children stay up late. Some men and women drink alcohol and participate in drinking binges, even if they usually do not (except members of the temperance movement), and at New Year children are given cigarettes. Christmas time provides a licence for deviance and this establishes a liminal framework within which *mitaartut* appear.

Several days before the first *mitaartut* are expected to be seen, people begin to make preparations for the disguises. The aim is for the *mitaartoq* to be disguised sufficiently so as to be genuinely unrecognizable by others. Emphasis is on the grotesque with the distortion and exaggeration of physical features. Men, women and children take part, although informants told me that old people no longer appear as *mitaartut*, as they did in the past.

Costumes consist of masks made from seal or dog skin, pieces of cloth, pillow cases and sacks. Cheap plastic masks can also be bought from the store, as the manager orders a large quantity especially for the occasion. When masks are not used, faces are blackened with soot from kerosene heaters, mouths are stuffed with cotton wool and string is often used to flatten the nose. Clothes are usually old or made from curtains, sheets, skins and plastic bin liners. Children wear their parents's anoraks, boots and other large items of clothing. Through the wearing of these costumes a person's sex becomes either ambiguous or reversed, with men dressing as women and vice versa. Sexual characteristics are emphasized, wigs are made, or the hair is concealed by a hat or balaclava. A lot of thought and preparation goes into the disguises and family members will usually help the *mitaartoq* to dress up. This provides much entertainment while people amuse themselves at the thought of others trying to guess their identity.

At this time of year the days are dark with extremely low temperatures. The sun does not reappear above the horizon until the end of January. However, men are still to be found outside working on their sleds, or returning from setting seal nets under the ice. Children are also out playing and, when the first *mitaartut* are to be seen moving through the village, they give shrieks of hysterical laughter and scatter to hiding places. The drama of *mitaarneq*, however, takes place indoors and most houses are visited at one time or another by several different figures during the three days.

Mitaartut usually visit people's homes in pairs, or in groups of three. Sometimes there is just one disguised figure, often accompanied by two or three people who are not disguised. Before entering a house, the *mitaartoq* will knock loudly on the door. Sticks and brooms are carried for this purpose. Immediately, this creates a sense of surprise and tension inside the house as only strangers knock, while the people of Kangersuatsiaq usually just walk in and out of each others' homes with no formalities.

On entering the house, the *mitaartut* remain silent while those inside ask 'Who is it? Who has come in?' ('*Kinaana? Kina iserpa?*'). The *mitaartut* do not reply. Although initially they do not make threatening gestures, their very appearance and disguises are enough to make any children in the house scream and try to hide behind adults. *Mitaartut* are strangers (*takornartat*) and children are said to be *takornarput*; 'become afraid because of seeing a stranger'. While adults do not say they are afraid, there is little laughter on their part. As the immediate object of the host is to discover the identity (*kinaassuseq*) of the *mitaartut* and to establish their kin ties, the questions continue: 'Who are you?', 'Who is your father?', 'Where do you come from?', 'Are you from the north?' If the visitors are still giving away no clues, the questions become a little more direct, with a hint of insult: 'Your father must have been a Dane, is that right?', or 'How did you travel from Kullorsuaq in darkness, *mitaartoq*?'

If the *mitaartut* still refuse to talk or laugh, then more personal insults are hurled: 'You smell, *mitaartoq*!', 'Your father is a *tuneq* (i.e. a tall figure from legend), but what is your mother?', 'Didn't I see you flirting with so and so's daughter down on the pier last night?' At this point, the *mitaartut* respond by scaring the children, or by sitting next to an adult and trying to kiss them. It is now the turn of the visitors to frighten and amuse their hosts, by waving their sticks and brooms and making aggressive gestures. This brings screams and laughter from all those assembled and continues until the visitors' identities are guessed, or until the host finally offers the *mitaartut* coffee and cake, or tea, cigarettes and other gifts such as tinned fruit and sweets. These have been bought several days before to give to the *mitaartut*. However, the host tells the visitors that they must dance if they wish to receive anything. The *mitaartut* then dance and reveal who they are, before being given the gifts and leaving for the next house.

As strangers, *mitaartut* express the idea of the 'other'. While most costumes are ambiguous, some dress as Danes (notably, as a doctor), or as a *qivittoq* (pl. *qivittut*). A *qivittoq* is a mysterious, supernatural wanderer, a person who has left the warmth and security of their home community to live alone in the mountains. In the past this was said to be a response to personal pressures and problems with others. The most common explanation is that *qivittut* are mainly men who have been unlucky in love. The Kangersuatsiarmiit say that there are also female *qivittut* and even whole families of *qivittut*, although stories tend to focus only on the solitary nature and habits of the *qivittoq*.

The root *qivit-* means 'disappointed' and the *qivittoq* has become something of a metaphor for the rejection of community. In popular impressions, particularly those of children, a *qivittoq* tries to cover up his disappearance, making it seem the result of a fatal accident. He does this by smashing his kayak on rocks or by abandoning his boat. After some time living alone in the mountains, the senses of the *qivittoq* have sharpened; his eyes, ears and nostrils have grown larger to enable him to see, hear and smell animals, and his teeth and fingernails are long and sharp. His body becomes covered in a thick coating of fur and his head hair is long and matted. *Qivittut* are believed to live in caves in the mountains and in summer they move down to the coastline. During winter, *qivittut* are said to return to the village in order to steal food and dogs, and to peer through the windows of people's houses. For most of the year, however, they tend to keep themselves hidden and shy away from human contact. Despite their solitary and retiring natures, there have been several sightings of *qivittut* in the Kangersuatsiaq area in recent years. People talk of seeing tall, strange figures clambering over rocks when out fishing, or of seeing someone walking on the ice in the darkness of winter.

Qivittut are always seen from a distance, but there are several occasions when people from Kangersuatsiaq have had near close encounters with them. In Chapter 4, I noted the story of the hunters who found two of Eirik's dogs dead on the floor of a hunting hut, together with footprints in the snow leading away up into the mountain. This was explained as the action of a *qivittoq*. In February 1988, an elderly man awoke one morning to discover that one of his three sled dogs had been killed. There was a deep wound to the dog's skull, as if caused by a swift blow of an axe. There was widespread disbelief throughout Kangersuatsiaq as to who would commit such an act and it was rumoured to be the work of a *qivittoq* who had wandered about the village looking for food. Having resorted to taking a dog, people supposed that he had been disturbed and had fled before he was discovered, and without having had the chance to steal away with his kill.

Each hunter seems to have a story of strange happenings, such as char and halibut disappearing from drying racks at fishing camps, or of hearing human noises, such as coughing, outside the tent when a hunter is alone and many miles from home. In autumn, women and children would often return from berry picking expeditions with a tale of someone having seen a distant figure wearing animal skins, or of rocks stained with the evidence of a meal of berries – a sign that a *qivittoq* had been in the area. Specific places are associated with stories or sightings of *qivittut* and, because there are large areas of the landscape where nobody ventures, such places are imagined to be their most likely haunts.

Qivittut are feared and the possibility of them coming down from their mountain homes, especially in winter when they can walk on the ice, is used as an effective socializer of children. Adults also scare one another with stories about *qivittut* and I noticed that this kind of storytelling intensified with the onset of winter or when people moved out to the summer camps. During my stay in the village, I welcomed the opportunity to walk alone in the mountains as a respite from the strains of fieldwork. I would leave details of my route with Josepi's family, always to be told that I should be wary of the possibility of encountering a *qivittoq*. I was told that, although a hunter travelling alone may never see a *qivittoq*, this does not exclude the possibility that a *qivittoq* is not watching the hunter, keeping a careful distance and waiting for an opportunity to pilfer some seal meat or freshly caught fish.

When *qivittut* die they are said to remain on earth as ghosts. Many children equate *qivittut* with *mitaartut* and, for Labrador, Ben-Dor says that the *nalyuk* is the 'most prominent of the Eskimo bogey figures' (1966: 122). So as well as symbolizing strangers, there is also a strong feeling of the supernatural surrounding *mitaarneq*.

Qivittut, however, are threatening because they stand in complete opposition to the secure human world, which they found disappointing enough to have rejected. In a superficial sense, this rejection results in the reversion of humanity to nature, where a person takes on raw animal characteristics and depends on himself for survival, with none of the trappings of hunting technology. But the figure of the *qivittoq* illustrates the close proximity between the human and natural worlds, rather than stressing any well-defined gap between them. *Qivittut* and other spirits that 'people' the landscape are metaphors that make the natural world intelligible, expressing and giving further meaning to the physical environment as a central feature of the cultural world of the Kangersuatsiarmiit, and as a window on human nature. In turn, this cultural world is an integral feature of the physical environment.

The *qivittoq* does not symbolize a rigid dichotomy between nature and culture but, in its essential loneliness, it does suggest the possibility that human alienation from the secure world of one's home community is ever present. As will be shown in the next chapter, loneliness is negative to both individual and community. The *qivittoq* is loneliness personified, the expression of all that is feared about rejection and isolation, destined to wander as both a living being and as a ghost. It is a figure in the landscape that has aspects of both humanity and animality and one that belongs to both the phenomenal and spirit worlds. In the human world it rejected, the *qivittoq* was once a person who was part of a wide network of kin. Having severed those cultural bonds, the *qivittoq* has no place in the community, which no longer has any genealogical knowledge to identify it as a social person. Whether it has remained as a human, or has become an animal, ghost or wandering spirit, the *qivittoq* is now a stranger. The symbolic appearance in the form of *mitaartut* reinforces the potency of this powerful imagery and serves to remind people that, as strangers, *qivittut* are also similar to themselves and are never far away.

Mitaartut are not only feared figures, however, they are insulted and made a mockery of (*mitarpaa* means 'mocks him/her') by the people they visit. As strangers, they are not treated as guests who are welcomed and given food freely, because they may be a god, for example (Hocart 1970). Rather, they embody elements of fear and amusement, tension and entertainment and provide 'an institutionalized way of releasing hostility' (Ben-Dor ibid: 125). There is a sense of the familiar and unknown, the sacred and mundane. The ambiguity of the disguises and of the response in the houses (from fear to amusement) suggests a feeling of liminality. *Mitaartut* have no social reality and are released from daily constraints. Turner's emphasis on structureless liminality (1969: 94–98) reinforces the idea of ambiguous rather than reversed roles, as Leach sees masquerading (1961: 135). While an opposition can be set up between community and strangers, it is not clear who the strangers are. *Mitaartut* are ambiguous because the strangers they represent are Danes, people from other villages, characters from legend and the supernatural in the form of *qivittut*. In order to understand this ambiguity, a little needs to be said about visiting and hospitality.

In Kangersuatsiaq, as throughout Greenland, the tradition of *pulaataqattaarneq* is a central form of hospitality and expression of fellowship. It refers to regular visits to households. Theoretically, households are open for all to visit, although on the ground informal visits are confined to those who have a close social association, i.e., the type mentioned in Chapter 6; sons, daughters, grandchildren, hunting and fishing partners, name-sharers, age-mates and *atsiat*. Central to *pulaataqattaarneq* is coffee as a symbol of hospitality. In every household there is always a flask of fresh, hot coffee ready for visitors, who call at any time during the day.

The more formal *kappimik* (a gathering for coffee) is held on special events such as birthdays, Christmas, New Year, first catch celebrations and at baptisms and funerals. These involve the entire community. The most regular are birthdays, and with 200 people in Kangersuatsiaq, there are some two to three birthdays every week. All *kappimik* require an invitation, contrasting with the more relaxed mutual *pulaartaqattaarneq*. Invitations come from children, who call around, or by telephone.

An important contrast is made between two categories of visitor; *pulaartoq* and *tikeraaq*. The *pulaartoq* is known and, as mentioned above, can trace a kin connection or has some other social association with the host. Even if the *pulaartoq* has no kin connection, he or she is still known as a member of the community. However, a *tikeraaq* is a 'visitor from another place'. The word is related to the verb *tikippoq*; 'has come', in the sense of arriving or returning. Both the verbs *tikeraarpoq* and *pulaarpoq* mean 'is/goes visiting', although the former is what a *tikeraaq* does, while the latter describes the visit of the *pulaartoq*.

A *tikeraaq* from another village in the district usually has at least one relative in Kangersuatsiaq. There may also be *atsiat* named after dead relatives. Summertime sees the arrival of people from other places and most visit in order to see relatives. But the term *tikeraaq* conveys a sense of both social and geographical distance. Most are unable to trace kin ties with more than a few villagers. There is also a feeling of transience and impermanence because while the *tikeraaq* has come, he/she will also 'go out' (*aallarniarpoq*). So the difference is between visitors who are from other places and those who live in the community.

Within this fine distinction between categories of visitor, a *mitaartoq* is a *tikeraaq*. Metaphorically, the disguised figures have come from other places. In one house where I was present a woman, dressed as a hunter complete with blackened face, visited her brother who exclaimed: 'It's a visitor (*tikeraaq*) from the far north!' Mockery and insults mainly take the form of making reference to coming from other villages in the district, or to some biological connection to Danes, or figures from legend. But despite symbolizing the outside, the visit of *mitaartut* also emphasizes core moral, cultural and religious values of hospitality. All visitors must be given coffee and possibly fed. Faris sees hospitality as 'more akin to fear: by feeding a stranger one learns more about him and his purpose, and one also puts oneself in good stead with him' (1973: 163). By knocking on the door and generating an initial atmosphere of fear, the behaviour of *mitaartut* is the inverse of societal norms. In treating the stranger as a guest, such fear is dealt with because the ritual and moral nature of hospitality acts to establish temporary bonds commensurate with kinship, friendship and obligation.

Attempts by the host to establish kin ties are ways of creating a sense of familiarity with what is strange and potentially threatening. The atmosphere of clowning and carnival that develops, however, only seems to emphasize the feeling of unfamiliarity. Clowning with strangers is possible because 'real rules only apply to real people' (Goffman 1972:

155). *Mitaarneq* brings a threat that creates a disturbance owing to the confrontation of an unrecognizable figure. The Greenlandic word for mask is *kiinarpak*, meaning 'over-face'. A disguise is meant to be deceptive,

> regardless of its kind or genre, be it the threatening mask of an ogre, or the clownish appearance of a circus performer. There are indeed false faces that aim to perplex the spectator. The masker's objective is always calculated for effect, be it playful or awesome, ritual or malevolent. Whatever the wearer's intention, the critical factors are always to avoid recognition and to create uncertainty in the viewer. The masker enacts a role that differs from his everyday one; the mask shields him from identifiability by redefining his physiognomy, even his entire body [Muensterberger 1989: 262]

Muensterberger also says that, when confronted with a masked figure, 'one recognizes a presentiment of discomfort because one cannot "read" the face'. Greenlanders say they 'read' faces. During my first few months in Kangersuatsiaq, people would ask how I was and I would return the question. One day, a man in his early thirties asked: 'Why do you keep asking how I am? You can *see* how I am.'

The significance of *mitaartut* lies in the transformation of a known person to someone who cannot be identified, someone who has no kin connection in the community and therefore has no social reality in terms of everyday life. The threat comes from a modification of a relationship that is known and mundane and everyday. The outside intrudes on the inside.

Strangers stand apart from the kinship network, are socially distant and excluded from what is stable, known and shared. But the word for stranger, *takornartaq*, in meaning 'one who has not been seen before', suggests the possibility that strangers could be related in some way to the host community. It is just that they are not known, or have not been seen before, hence the importance of being able to establish a kin connection in the past when a person wandered into another community. Similarly, the questions that the host asks the *mitaartoq* are in order to discover its identity, not so much as a person, but as a member of the kinship network.

Danes, as it has been noted, are strangers on the inside of the wider Greenlandic community because of residence, yet they are on the outside owing to their marginality and transience, and the absence of kinship ties. In the context of Home Rule, which does not discriminate on ethnic lines, Danes are politically part of the Greenlandic system, yet culturally apart from other Greenlanders who are, none the less, fellow citizens.

On the other hand, people from Kangersuatsiaq who are no longer resident in the village still remain part of the community. Although physically absent, they retain ties of kinship and remain on the social horizon because of name-relationships. This is also true of the dead, who continue to occupy their place in community memory through *atsiat*. While the stranger presents the host community with the problem of possibly incorporating, either temporarily or long term, 'one who has not been seen before' into a well established network of relationships, death and the physical absence of community members causes people to ensure that they continue to play a part in an elaborate social context. How the dead and the absent remain in this social context provides the basis for the next chapter.

8

Loss, loneliness and return

Names and emotional expression

As the previous chapter showed, strangers are people who are unable to demonstrate kin ties. This chapter considers the temporary loss of kin ties through death, the return of dead relatives as *atsiat*, and the association of living, yet absent, people as *atsiat*. This develops themes concerning naming which were introduced in Chapters 5 and 6. While Chapter 7 also discussed the relationship between Kangersuatsiaq and the outside world by using the institutionalization of death as an example, its treatment of the funeral focused on an observable ritual. Although I was concerned with demonstrating its local nature, the action and symbolism of the funeral, as of most other rituals which are the concern of symbolic anthropology, takes place 'in visibly bounded arenas' (Rosaldo 1984: 185). Writing about the anthropological treatment of death, Rosaldo says that '. . . placing the accent on the routine aspects of ritual conveniently conceals the agony of such unexpected early deaths as parents losing a grown child or a mother dying in childbirth' (ibid: 186). Those who are bereaved experience a wide range of emotions and the emphasis on ritual can actually go so far as to obscure the emotional force of bereavement.

In their concern with objectivity and interpretation, Rosaldo accuses anthropologists of remaining detached when having to report back about funeral and mortuary procedure. Ethnographic accounts, in translating 'exotic' cultures, usually eliminate emotions (ibid: 189). But grief and mourning are not confined to periods of ritual activity and 'human beings mourn both in ritual settings and in the settings of everyday life' (Wilson 1939: 22–23). People grieve when alone, or with close kin or other close social associates and while this may be widely recognized, Rosaldo urges anthropologists to be aware of this as well if they are to grasp the cultural force of extremely emotional states. Both the formal and the informal practices of daily life should be looked at, he argues, rather than focusing on colourful rituals which have definite locations in space.

In this chapter I attempt to show something of the emotional significance of *atsiat* for people who have experienced bereavement and are affected by loss and loneliness. I say 'attempt' because my initial feeling, if I was to write about this at all, was to retreat behind the relative safety of objectivity that Rosaldo urges against. The deaths of Greenlandic friends, while I was in the field, forced me to question my position as an anthropologist in the community. Although I did not actually sit in the homes of bereaved people and take notes following a funeral, I remained aware that it was 'material' to write up later. I was sickened and depressed by this thought. I was associated with a family that had lost, firstly, a mother and later a father during the time I lived with them. Also the death of a young man with whom I had established a close friendship left me at a loss as to how to interact with his family. In such situations I felt a tension between analytical detachment and personal involvement.

The case studies that appear in this chapter are presented as 'data' because I want to convey an idea, however superficially done, of how *atsiat* are thought about in different ways by different people. An understanding of the emotional significance of *atsiat* also allows a greater appreciation of themes to be discussed in Chapters 8 and 9. This chapter also moves on another level because the significance of *atsiat* makes a statement about community. I hope to create an atmosphere of what the return of loved ones and the sharing of names means to those who are bereaved and are, or are perceived by others to be, lonely. Such an approach is inspired by a desire to 'understand culture by trying to capture its experiential sense' (Cohen 1982: 4). Names can, and do, mean different things for different people. One woman told me

> You ask me about my grandmother's atsiaq? She's Peter's daughter . . . do you know her? But she's not my grandmother, she only has her name, not her soul [i.e. in this sense tarneq]. Only her anersaaq is still here.

In contrast, a forty year old woman has her mother's *atsiaq* as a visitor to her house for long periods each day. A sixty-nine year old man has the walls of his house decorated with photographs of the six young children named after his dead wife. Two of them live in Kangersuatsiaq and are to be found in his house on any given day. There are numerous similar examples.

While the form may be held in common, naming is imprecise because it does not tell people how to act, just as kinship allows for improvisation and the creation of idiosyncratic networks. There is no cultural determinism implied here, but rather a recognition of experience and fluidity. When Josepi died in October 1988, I abandoned anthropological detachment because I felt bereaved for the first time in my life. I was having breakfast with Juuna when Eirik came to tell us the news. I left Juuna, because I thought he might want to be alone, and went for a walk through the village. I felt a great deal of sadness at the passing of a man who had decided to trust an outsider, an initial stranger, and consider me a 'son'. As I walked down to the pier, I tried to think who was pregnant because I hoped a baby boy would be born, so that I could continue my relationship with Josepi through his *atsiaq*. I walked around outside for about an hour and then went to Josepi's house.

One old man was sitting with the family and later several older men and women walked in. Some questions were asked about the time and cause of death (a heart attack). During this time the family were sitting in the living room, receiving fellow villagers against the incessant noise of successive videos shown to occupy the children. One of Josepi's nieces was busy helping to make coffee, wash cups and saucers and put out cake on the table. My impression was one of normality, at least initially, but the atmosphere in the house was punctuated with prolonged bouts of silence and emotion as the women showed their grief with periodic bursts of crying. Three days later, at Josepi's funeral, I was full of feelings of loneliness and isolation as we moved up to the cemetery. It was snowing, the mountains were white against the grey sky and a cold wind coming from the east injected a sense of emptiness.

The day after the funeral, news came through to Josepi's family that a baby boy had been born in Upernavik Kujalleq. The news created intense excitement and a fervour of activity followed as presents were bought for the child. The supply boat was due to call at Kangersuatsiaq later that afternoon and it was arranged that the presents would be taken by someone travelling with it to Upernavik Kujalleq. Our talk revolved around plans to visit Upernavik Kujalleq for the baby's baptism at the end of October.

While I am aware that such personal feeling may influence the presentation of my material, I believe it allows an understanding of what follows in the rest of this chapter. Josepi died towards the end of my residence in Kangersuatsiaq and, because of the nature of anthropological experience, I would inevitably find it difficult to write like many other anthropologists who are 'positioned as uninvolved spectators' (Rosaldo ibid: 193). Firstly, I shall discuss a context of bereavement and how *atsiaq* beliefs were put into practice by one family, Josepi's, within that context.

Marie's death and the birth of her *ateqqaataa*

In the summer of 1987 Marie, Josepi's wife, left her village and her home for the hospital in Upernavik. She was sixty-one years old and had been suffering from cancer for some time. My first few weeks with Josepi's family were dominated by talk of her illness. Recently, her condition had deteriorated and it had become harder for her daughters to look after her. During the third week of August, the midwife consulted with the family and a decision was reached that Marie should travel to town with the next boat. Although her sons and daughters were reluctant to release Marie from their care, they were aware that, apart from love and warmth, they could not provide the kind of care she now needed.

During the first few days following Marie's departure, the family was in regular contact with the hospital through the midwife. After some two weeks, the doctor decided to move Marie to hospital in Denmark, where she could receive specialist treatment that was unavailable in Greenland. Immediately, the family began to fear the worst. When the decision was taken, I was travelling with David and Aninnguaq and visiting Aninnguaq's family in Nutaarmiut. David heard the news from his sister, Naja, over the telephone. Immediately, he showed visible signs of depression and helplessness. For the next two days he went for several walks away from the village, sometimes alone and sometimes with Aninnguaq.

One morning, he told me he had decided to return to his father's house in Kangersuatsiaq and that we would leave Nutaarmiut the following day. He asked me if I understood the situation and explained that his father would be kiserliorpoq (i.e. 'living in loneliness') because '*Ataataga kipilerpoq, immaqa*' ('Maybe my father is longing after his wife'). In this sense, *kipilerpoq* is used as an expression of longing/aching to see or hear someone, especially a loved one. Shortly after Marie had left for the hospital, Eirik had also left the village to find seasonal work in the Disko Bay area. His departure had increased David's feeling of the fragmentation of his family. Now it was clear to David that his father would be 'living in loneliness' even though he still had two daughters, one son and nine grandchildren with him in Kangersuatsiaq.

Because I had been fishing and travelling with David, I had not yet taken up residence in Juuna's house. We had all moved away from the summer camp in the first week of August when most of the family had returned to Kangersuatsiaq. On arrival from Nutaarmiut, I found Naja in Juuna's house, cleaning, and washing his clothes. Over the next two weeks she became a regular visitor. She would come to Juuna's house every day, around midday, and sit quietly for five minutes or so. Without saying anything, she would simply come in, sit and then leave. One day she broke her silence by saying: 'Father's house is depressing. Mother's going to die.' Juuna did not reply. At this time the midwife was unable to provide very much news about Marie's condition. Possibly because she was in Denmark, communication was not as frequent, adding to the distance between Marie and her family.

In the first week of September, Marie was moved back to Greenland and eventually back to the hospital in Upernavik. During this period of movement, the family lost track of Marie's precise whereabouts as she was flown from Denmark to Kangerlussuaq (Søndre Strømfjord), Ilulissat and Upernavik. When she did eventually return to Upernavik, Josepi travelled there to be with her.

When the news came through in the first week of October that she had died, I was present in Juuna's house when David came to tell him. Juuna nodded, his face showing no visible change. David looked at me and repeated the news, simply adding: 'You understand, don't you?' ('*Paasivat ilaa?*'). Immediately, the two brothers began to discuss plans for the coffin making. David said he would go and buy the wood from the store, while Juuna went to get the key for the village workshop.

The news spread rapidly through the village and people began to visit the house. The family kept in constant touch with Josepi and arrangements were made through the midwife concerning the return of

Marie's body for burial. For the next two days the workshop was alive with activity, as the two brothers struggled to finish the coffin before the police boat was due to arrive with Josepi and their mother's body.

On the day of the funeral, the men began to gather outside the meeting house half-an-hour or so before the service. Other villagers ambled along the road, some alone, others in groups. One man, Piitaaq K., (who will appear later in this chapter) joined the main group of men. He was drunk, unshaven, unwashed and clutched a very tatty wreath of plastic flowers in his right hand. To the group of men, which included both young and old, Piitaaq cut a comic figure. The men had been commenting on the weather, the availability of seals and discussing the end of the season's salmon fishing. Piitaaq's arrival transformed the scene and the tone of conversation. Stumbling around, his breath smelling of *immiaq* (Greenlandic homebrew beer), Piitaaq laughed hysterically as he waved the plastic wreath with his right hand. One or two of the men said 'Hello Piitaaq!', the sarcasm in their voices producing a response of loud laughter from the others. Piitaaq mumbled something incomprehensible to the group and twice welcomed me to Greenland, despite having first invited me to his house some three months previously. Grabbing my hand and shaking it vigorously, he continued to repeat 'What's your name?' in English, turning to the group and announcing his linguistic prowess.

The situation generated considerable laughter. As a drinker, Piitaaq occupied a marginal position in the community (this theme will be explored in Chapter 9) and his tatty appearance, complemented by the tatty wreath seemed to exemplify this. It was clearly enjoyed by the others. When drunk, his usual way of walking (arms thrust back, with the upper half of his body leaning backwards) was often exaggerated. Outside the meeting house, this caused even more laughter as he staggered about, arms in the air.

It was the first time I had experienced a Greenlandic funeral and I still had to shed a little ethnocentrism. There were no comments from the men about how shocking or unacceptable it was that Piitaaq was drunk on the day of Marie's funeral. In fact it was I who was expecting and looking for such remarks. Because Piitaaq was going to attend the service and burial in a drunken stupor, his condition offended only what I thought were accepted ways of behaving. Before Piitaaq had joined the group, I was struck by the normality of the men's conversation and by playing his accepted community role, Piitaaq seemed to strengthen this sense of everyday normality.

While the catechist conducted the service, I sat at the back of the church and watched as children fidgeted and made paper aeroplanes from the hymn sheets. Apart from the coffin and the solemnity of the catechist it did not seem like a funeral. The funeral procession and the burial service at the graveside had something of an air of hilarity about it. Young people and children shuffled about and laughed among themselves.

At the graveside, children were running around and one mother turned her three year old away from the proceedings while he urinated on the snow. A fine sleet started and people shivered with the cold. The burial service over, the catechist and most of the villagers hurried away back down to the warmth of their houses. Josepi and his family were left alone to fill in the grave. Once this was done, Juuna started to take photographs as the rest of the family posed in an icy wind at the head of the grave. Shortly after, they returned to Josepi's house to prepare for the post-funeral gathering for coffee.

During the evening Juuna got drunk. He had left his father's house sometime in the late afternoon and I had stayed away, thinking he wanted to be on his own. I could not escape the intense feeling of intrusiveness which had clung to me throughout Marie's illness and had certainly not been ameliorated since her death. My involvement with her family had only been for some four months. During this time we had lived cheek by jowl, firstly in the fishing camp and latterly in the village. My personal belief that I was progressing with the language was rudely overturned when I found myself struggling to find words of comfort, particularly for Josepi and Juuna. My immediate reaction was to shy away from Josepi and his family. At a time of bereavement, I felt they did not need an intrusive outsider.

I returned to Juuna's house rather late in the evening to find he had made good progress with a bottle of whisky and several cans of beer. Inviting me to have a drink, he told me he was happy, in reply to the only thing I could think of saying ('How are you?'). He poured himself a generous measure of whisky and handed me a can of beer. He looked at me and said:

> When my mother died I thought I would cry. David told us the news, you were here, he told the two of us. Even when I was making the coffin with David, I thought I would cry. Today we put the coffin in the ground and covered it with stones, but I still didn't cry.

He continued to tell me he felt happy, despite his mother's death. He was happy that a baby girl would soon be born and would be given his mother's name. At this time I felt it must have comforted Juuna to say this, but I could not be sure if he was denying his mother's death. What did he think would return with his mother's name? I did not and could not have access to Juuna's thoughts.

One week later, Juuna had managed to acquire more alcohol. He seemed to get drunk more easily and broke down in tears. He started to tell me how much he was missing his mother (*maqaasineq*), continuing to drink until he finally got up and walked over to his bed. Lying down, he fell into a deep sleep. The following morning, Naja came to Juuna's house to tell him that Margrethe, a woman from Kangersuatsiaq, had just given birth to a baby girl in the hospital in Upernavik. To the family it was clear what this meant. The baby would be Marie's *ateqqaataa*, the first child who would receive Marie's name. Almost immediately, there was a noticeable change in the moods of various family members, parti-cularly the women. Talk was of the forthcoming baptism, which was to take place on the 29th November, and the weeks before were devoted to embroidery and the making of clothes for the baby. About one week after the birth, Margrethe returned to the village and took her new daughter to Josepi's house. A great deal of fuss was made of the child as she was passed from family member to family member. Margrethe was given gifts for the child, photographs were taken and the women talked of the baptism.

On the day of the baptism, the family of the child gathered together with the godmother for photographs, coffee and cake following the church service. During the afternoon and throughout the evening the whole community visited for coffee and cake. All people in Kangersuatsiaq normally visit on such occasions, to congratulate the parents and to see the child. The community celebrates the birth of a child, a new person. But at the same time there is an awareness that the child is also a recently deceased person's *atsiaq*. The community is thus celebrating the return of that deceased person. In doing so, the community is celebrating itself, however unconsciously. The celebration is, in a sense, a celebration of the continuity of both person and community. But what must not be forgotten is that the deceased's family is also celebrating its own continuity. The inclusion of an *atsiaq* in private celebrations has an important function, as the next section shows.

A first catch celebration and the inclusion of deceased loved ones

In January 1988, David set a seal net under the ice for Jonas, his seven year old son. Jonas was not yet old enough to learn how to make and set seal nets himself, so he would often accompany his father on hunting expeditions to watch and help. They would walk out on the ice each day in the winter's darkness to check David's nets. On the way home Jonas's netting site was always the last one to be checked. For several days, Jonas showed his disappointment when no seal was found in his net. David explained to his son that the seals preferred to give themselves up to older hunters. Jonas would have to wait. A seal would come to his net in time and then he could start to learn about seals and hunting.

Some ten days after setting the net, father and son walked out on to the ice during early evening. This time Jonas had a seal in his net and shrieked with excitement as he helped his father haul it out of the water through the hole in the ice. David went to check one of his own nets, where he also found a seal. Both then set off for home, dragging their seals over the ice with Jonas struggling, but determined, to take his first catch back to the village himself.

When Jonas arrived home, Aninnguaq arranged a first catch celebration. Overjoyed, she telephoned her parents in Nutaarmiut to tell them their grandson had become a hunter. Aninnguaq then flensed the seal and began to cook the meat amid scenes of excitement, as Jonas recounted his hunting adventures to his little sister and cousins. With the meat almost cooked, Aninnguaq told Jonas to run and invite Josepi and the rest of the family. Although it was an important event, Jonas would not be recognized as a hunter by the rest of the village until he had gone out and actually caught a seal without assistance from his father. This particular first catch party was to be a closed, private family celebration, a celebration that other members of the community were not permitted to attend.

Naja was the first to arrive and sat down without removing her coat. A few minutes later, she rose and made her way to the door. Turning to Aninnguaq, she said 'I'll go and invite mother.' She left the house as Eirik, Lydia and Juuna walked in. Shortly after, Josepi arrived with Jonas. He sat down and Aninnguaq poured him some coffee. Josepi then asked 'Is my wife sleeping?' Aninnguaq replied that Naja had gone to fetch her. Seal meat was then offered to Josepi and the others, while David made another flask of coffee and opened several packets of biscuits. The good quality and taste of the meat was commented upon and Josepi congratulated Jonas for catching such a tasty seal. Not long after, Naja returned carrying Marie, her mother's three month old *ateqqaataa*. Naja said 'Here's mother' and Aninnguaq, addressing the baby, said 'Come in, sit down and have some coffee. It's cold outside and we have some fresh meat from Jonas.'

The baby's warm clothes were taken off and she was sat upon Aninnguaq's lap. Aninnguaq said 'Have some coffee, mother.' Dipping a sugar lump in cold coffee, she raised it to the baby's mouth for a brief moment, allowing the sugar to touch the baby's lips. She did the same with the cup of coffee, but making sure the baby did not drink. Finally, Aninnguaq asked 'Mother, would you like some meat? It's your grandson's catch, his first seal.' She cut up the seal meat into small pieces, placing it on a plate together with one small potato and some boiled onion. She 'gave' the baby some meat, again making sure it only touched her lips. Once this was done, Aninnguaq looked at the child for a short while, then she said 'It tastes good. What do you think? Your grandson's catch is a tasty one, isn't it?'

The child was then passed around the room, with each member of the family taking it in turns to hold her. David, Juuna, Lydia and Naja all addressed her as 'mother', commenting on her 'grandson's' success. Naja took the baby in her arms and asked if she wanted to go home, that she should say when she was ready to leave. At one point, the baby looked across at me and I responded with cooing sounds. Naja immediately retorted: 'Don't make leching sounds at my mother! If you're going to flirt with someone, flirt with me!' Almost hurriedly, Naja started to dress the child saying: 'Come on mother, I'll take you home.' Marie's *ateqqaataa* had been in the house for about forty minutes before she was taken back to her parents. During this time she had been spoken to and treated as an adult. As a family celebration of Jonas having his first catch, the family gathering had been complete due to the inclusion of the *atsiaq*. She was included as a participant by symbolically drinking coffee and eating the meat.

It had been three months since Marie's death and family and community celebrations at Christmas and New Year had been tainted by her absence. David openly displayed his sense of loss on many occasions by telling people he was depressed by his mother's death. At the end of December, Aninnguaq told me:

> Christmas was a little depressing this year. We all remembered Marie. David still dreams she is sitting in her chair, smoking but not speaking. He says the dream always seems real.

On Christmas Day, Josepi and the rest of the family went up to Marie's grave immediately after the Christmas service in the church had ended. They said a few prayers and placed a new plastic wreath on the grave before returning to the house. During the early afternoon, both Marie's *ateqqaataa* and her second *atsiaq* were taken to Josepi's house by their parents. Both babies were given several presents and stayed for about an hour, before they were taken back to their respective homes.

Such scenes are common in the village, illustrating the constant inclusion of *atsiat* in private as well as public events and situations. The return of a deceased relative as an *atsiaq* allows the continuation of warm and loving relationships between kin and other close associates. In Chapter 4, I mentioned how it was important that the name soul does not remain lonely and homeless for too long. Similarly, the birth of an *atsiaq* ensures that the bereaved do not live in loneliness (*kiserliorneq*). As well as the transmigration of names, emphasis is on those who are left behind. Hertz has said that 'we cannot bring ourselves to consider the deceased as dead straight away' (1960: 81) and there is a sense whereby reincarnating names negates the finality of death. Names are used as references to a past state prior to the disruption death brings. Leach (1961: 124–136) argues that conceptions of time are ambiguous in that death follows birth just as night follows day. But the opposite is also true, for birth follows death and day follows night. The movement of names from the dead to the living, together with the promise of resurrection in Christianity (in the sense of resurrection on earth rather than immortality in heaven) ensures immortality in the form of social continuity.

I have argued that the name is a distinct and vital part of the person. Here, I extend this argument to include it as a distinct and vital part of the community. The sharing and returning of names gives a feeling of community and the person, as an *atsiaq*, belongs to an elaborate social context which embraces the living and those who have gone before. The birth of a child and its baptism is an important event for all the people of Kangersuatsiaq, not only those who are bereaved. In celebrating the return of a loved and valued member, the community celebrates itself by symbolically constructing its membership. By concentrating on continuity and the returning of name souls, grief and loss are managed and find their expression in *atsiaq* beliefs. These beliefs can be explored in a variety of situations, where bereavement, loss and loneliness can be examined within a context of private and public notions of person and community.

The spiritual components of the person (*ateq, tarneq, anersaaq*) are conceptualized in various ways which are related, in turn, to a wide variety of life situations. These find expression in different levels of meaning and metaphor. Different people think different things about *atsiat*. The changes in a person's understanding, due to particular experiences, mean that a person may think different things at various points in their life. In addition, a person may think different things about *atsiat* in different contexts, particularly when faced with birth and death.

When people say a dead person has 'come home', the initial disruption caused by the death results in an eventual period of renewal once the name soul has reached home as the final resolution of its journey. In this way, provision is made for both the dead and the living. Crantz said that the migration of souls played an important function for the Greenlanders in 'weaning them by degrees from their excessive grief' (1820: 342). In 1988, an informant in Upernavik town expressed a similar, but less severe thought about his eight month old son, who had been given the name of an old woman's recently deceased son. As an *atsiaq*, his son was important to the woman because 'he is something she can give her heart to.'

Loneliness

A person who lives in loneliness (*kiserliortoq*) makes others feel 'pity' and 'sorry for him/her' (*nalligaa*). Death brings loneliness because a loved person is missed (*maqaasineq*) and longed for. Edvard M. told me 'a person does not say "I'm missing someone", but we can see it in their face. We know.' It is far too simplistic to suggest that grief is forgotten about with the birth of an *atsiaq*. It is commonly held that, because *tarneq* goes to God, the complete person does not return. But people are always watching out for characteristics of dead relatives in their *atsiat* as they grow and develop. In encounters with the relatives of deceased people, *atsiat* are asked such questions as 'Who's this? Do you remember your daughter?', or told 'Look! Your big brother is fishing. Is he clever? You're his little brother aren't you?'

Almost from birth, children become regular visitors in the homes of the people whose relatives they are named after. The three year old 'wife' of Abel L., for example, visits her 'husband' every day and, when she is older, she will carry out household tasks for him. Old people, in particular those who live alone, are said to be 'happy' if they have 'sons', 'daughters', 'husbands' or 'wives' who can bring them gifts of meat or fish, or who come simply to visit. Loneliness exemplifies the antithesis to the 'warmth' of community. To be alone is 'unpleasant' (*nuanninngilaq*) just like hunger or extreme cold. Two weeks after Josepi's death, Juuna told me:

> I envy you. You've got a mother and a father. I feel alone in the world now. Where can I go to? Like when my mother was alive, she'd cook every day at midday and I'd go to eat. I had my own house, but I'd go and eat anyway. The last week father was alive, I visited and he was ill in bed. He asked me if I was hungry and told me to help myself. He never used to ask that. I was surprised because he was like mother, asking me like that.

A lonely person will receive visitors, or will visit other households for comfort. Women whose husbands are away on overnight trips will be kept company, usually by female relatives, and a man who spends a night alone on the ice is imagined by others to be 'depressed' (*tujormivoq*) because of his situation. Separation from loved ones, even for a very short time, makes people 'ache with longing' (*kipilerpoq*) to see them. The episode that follows describes a lonely person with no genealogical kin.

On his fiftieth birthday, Piitaaq K. invited me to his house for coffee and cake. It was a Sunday in July and the annual confirmation of young people had also taken place. Piitaaq's birthday celebration was thus overshadowed by several other parties in the village. When I entered his one room house, Piitaaq poured me a cup of weak, cold coffee and told me to help myself to cake. As usual, his house was dirty, untidy and stalesmelling. The two burning candles barely penetrated the dark, and the only sound was the lit jet of Piitaaq's gas cooker. He was boiling some lamb given as a birthday present by Rasmine, his mother's eighteen year old *atsiaq*. He gave me a can of soda pop, poured more coffee and asked if I would like to eat with him that evening. Conversation limped along and we remained alone, although Piitaaq said he had invited many more people. He had been drinking steadily since the morning and was showing signs of depression. On many occasions, I had been present when Piitaaq had broken down emotionally, often as a result of having spoken about his past life and present position in Kangersuatsiaq. Such occasions had always started with a drink.

To the others in the community, Piitaaq was a *kiserliortoq* (someone who lives in loneliness). An only child, he was born in Kangersuatsiaq but left for an education in Nuuk while in his early teens. Having worked in Nuuk for several years, he then spent long periods in some of the other big towns along the west coast. Piitaaq earned his living mainly by taking casual work in the fishing industry, but his real love became art. Many of the paintings and drawings he did during this period away from the north depict scenes from the hunting life he remembered as a child. By the time he chose to return to Kangersuatsiaq at the age of forty, both his parents were dead. He took up residence in the same house in which he was born and soon acquired a reputation as a storyteller.

His house also became the venue for regular drinking binges and Piitaaq began to spend his waking hours either very drunk, or getting there. Sometimes he would lock his door and remain inside for several days. These periods of isolation would end abruptly with another session of heavy drinking with a few others. Most of the money Piitaaq earned was spent on alcohol and he usually had very little left for food. While it was agreed that he was stupid (*sianiik*) in this respect, he received regular gifts of meat from people who said he induced feelings of 'pity' in them (*nallinaq*). However, it was Piitaaq's own sense of being alone that had intensified the longer he remained in the village. He often told me he was going to return to Nuuk, because Kangersuatsiaq was 'unpleasant to live in' ('*tujorminarpoq*'). Juuna said that he had once bought

Piitaaq paper and drawing materials from the store in Upernavik in an effort to encourage his art. The paper had never been touched and Juuna felt that Piitaaq 'probably desires to be alone' ('*kiserliorniaq*').

Whatever the reasons for his loneliness and sense of alienation from the community, I did not see any evidence to suggest antipathy towards him coming from anyone. However, his drunken behaviour in public often produced scenes of hilarity (as during the funeral above), particularly when he was seen to be angry. On the occasion of his fiftieth birthday, a feeling of helplessness led to a spontaneous expression of anger that I interpret as illustrating how Piitaaq perceived his own position.

When the lamb was only half-cooked, the gas ran out. Piitaaq's immediate reaction was to kick the cooker and curse the empty gas bottle in Danish. I told him I would help him collect a new one from the store. Being Sunday, the store was closed but Piitaaq thought the manager would let him pay for it on Monday. The gas bottles were kept down on the pier, so it would just be a matter of picking one up. It turned out that the manager was out hunting, so Piitaaq and I went to ask Nuka K., the assistant KNI manager. Nuka told Piitaaq that it was impossible for him to allow a bottle of gas to be taken on a Sunday without the manager's permission. Piitaaq protested that it was his birthday and the gas was needed so that he could finish his cooking. Nuka would not be swayed and so we left with Piitaaq muttering the Greenlandic curse '*saatan, tiaavalu, toornaarsuk*' (meaning 'Satan, Devil, Demon').

On the way along the path to his house, he kicked over an empty oil drum and sent it tumbling down to the store with a crash. In trying to calm him I suggested we go and find someone who would cook the meat, but Piitaaq replied: '"Mother" will know, "mother" can help me.' We then tried to find Rasmine, unsuccessfully as she was out visiting. Piitaaq then called on Rasmine I., an older woman who had been his own mother's name-sharer. He explained the situation and she offered to cook the lamb. Piitaaq addressed this older woman as 'mother', something he did not usually do, temporarily equating her as his mother's *atsiaq*. I suspect he did so because, unable to buy gas, he turned to somebody whom he could regard as being close to him for help. We returned to his house and fetched the meat, during which time Piitaaq's anger and curses had subsided. Rasmine I. then invited him to her daughter's house, where her granddaughter's confirmation was being celebrated.

Name-sharers as *atsiat*

Such an association of a dead person's name-sharer, that is one who was alive before the death, as an *atsiaq* is quite common. I witnessed similar episodes not only in Kangersuatsiaq, but in other parts of Upernavik district. For example, in May 1988 I was visiting Kullorsuaq, having arrived there from Savissivik in Avanersuaq district. A family from Savissivik had also recently arrived by dogsledge and planned to spend the summer in Upernavik. At Whitsuntide there was a party in the house of a young hunter who was related to the Savissivik people. There was much drinking and eating of Greenlandic food, particularly rancid seal meat known as *mikiaq*. The homebrew beer flowed and the dancing started to the accompaniment of an accordion player. Almost immediately Mikhael, a fifty-eight year old hunter from Savissivik, got up from his chair and went over to a young woman who had just walked in. He gave her a hug and a kiss and then they started to dance. The dance over, Mikhael came across to the other side of the room and sat down by me. He explained that Susaat, the woman he danced with, was the *atsiaq* of his older sister's daughter. He said he loved her very much and had not seen her since the death of his niece five years previously. As Susaat was 32 years old, I wondered what Mikhael had meant when he said she was named after his dead niece. He spent a large part of the evening talking and dancing with her, until his wife said: 'You dance with your *ujoroq* (sister's child), why not with me?'

The next day, I was visiting Susaat's house when Mikhael walked in suffering from a hangover. I noticed he called Susaat by her name, rather than using the term for sister's child as he had done the previous evening. Mikhael elaborated on what he had told me at the party, explaining that Susaat was his niece's name-sharer (his niece had been one year older), but that she 'was like her *atsiaq*' ('*soorlu Susaap atiia*'). Mikhael now thought of Susaat in this way, transforming the name-sharer of a deceased loved one into an *atsiaq*.

Chapter 6 showed that a child enters into name-sharing relationships with all those who shared the name of his/her *aqqa*. As the above examples illustrate, people can also continue relationships with a dead close associate through someone who is already living. They do not have to wait for the birth of an *atsiaq*. It does not necessarily suggest the replacement of the dead with a living person, but rather a more implicit way of coping or dealing with loneliness and loss. In a sense, through the name, people share something of each other, as the following example shows.

Aqqaluk was a forty two year old hunter whose sister, Elisabeth, died of cancer in the spring of 1988. She lived in Upernavik town and died in the hospital there. It had been some months since Aqqaluk had last seen her. Soon after receiving the news, Aqqaluk set out alone on a hunting expedition. The following day, he returned to the village and made no mention of his sister, and his wife told me he showed no visible signs of grief. Four days after the death, it was Aqqaluk's birthday. I was visiting for coffee with several other people when Aqqaluk told us he had now missed both his father's and his sister's funeral. He was getting a little drunk and had started to slur his words, when his one year old daughter came into the room. She was also named Elisabeth, her paternal aunt's name-sharer. Aqqaluk called to her: 'Sweet little older sister, come here.' ('*Aleqannguaq qaagit*'). He usually called her by the term for daughter (*panik*), but spent the rest of the day addressing her as his older sister (*aleqa*).

The following week, a woman returned to the village having given birth to a daughter in the hospital. She took the baby to Aqqaluk's house, where a celebration was taking place to mark the naming of the child as Elisabeth's *atsiaq*. The mother drank coffee while the child was made a fuss of. It was interesting to note that Aqqaluk avoided addressing the baby in any way. Instead, his daughter was given a central role and encouraged to play with 'your little name-sharer', and asked 'Who is this? Do you remember your father's sister (*atsak*), your name-sharer?' Elisabeth and her name-sharer were sat side by side while Aqqaluk took photographs of them. Throughout, emphasis was placed on the relationship between the baby and Elisabeth and I did not hear Aqqaluk refer to the *atsiaq* as his 'older sister'. However, he did continue to use the term in addressing his own daughter, and I heard him do so during the rest of my stay.

Chapter 6 also showed how kinship terms allow for idiosyncratic variation. Similarly, names acquire symbolic significance in that they have the capacity to make meaning. People not only become *atsiat* because others regard them as such (as the above examples show), but they also allow themselves to be equated with dead people, whether temporarily or long term. Just as people are fictive kin, there are also fictive *atsiat*. It is recognition that loneliness is negative to a person's wellbeing, for example, that allows a woman to become a 'mother' to the son of her name-sharer, as well as the fact that a person addresses relatives of name-sharers by the terms they themselves use. The sharing of names means Piitaaq could theoretically call Rasmine I. 'mother' because of the customary use of an equivalence of kinship terminology. But Piitaaq's mother had an *atsiaq* who was important to him in daily life. Unable to find her, he chose to regard his mother's name-sharer as her *atsiaq*. In the case of Aqqaluk, he chose to regard his daughter as the *atsiaq* of his recently deceased sister rather than the *ateqqaataa*. However, I have no evidence to suggest that Elisabeth would stop using the term for father and reciprocate with 'younger brother' (which would be *aqqaluk*).

A person who becomes a fictive *atsiaq*, for either a long or short period, allows a glimpse of how they regard their name and their own identity. So far, my discussion of naming and kinship has concentrated on the location of the person within a social matrix that defines and circumscribes them. To some extent this would seem to suggest the imposition of an identity that denies the person, as an *atsiaq*, any sense of self-definition. In grappling with the complexities of naming I was concerned with trying to get an idea of an individual's conceptualization of self as much as I struggled to understand the ideas other people had of the individual as an *atsiaq*. This was no easy task, partly because of language difficulties and partly because people were probably forced to consider unnecessary distinctions between individual and social notions of the self when questioned.

While some people did regard themselves as just having the name of a dead person, others felt that being an *atsiaq* meant that some part of their self also encompassed part of the person they were named after. A seventeen year old girl named after her mother's mother told me that she felt sure she had lived before, and that she had inherited the mental strength of her grandmother. One woman told me that she had named her five year old son Peter Abel, but when 'Abel' (the name of his mother's brother) was the first word the boy ever uttered she considered that he knew whose *atsiaq* he was. Gert, the brother of Peter, the boy's *ateqqaataa*, regarded him as just that. Although the boy did not enjoy being called Peter, he none the less visited Gert and allowed himself to be equated with his brother, while calling himself Abel. While individuals can contest and define their own identities, attributing their own meanings to their names does not necessarily result in conflict. Thus, a man can consider a woman to be his mother's *atsiaq* when in fact she is not, or someone can regard a child as his brother when that child regards itself as the *atsiaq* of another person.

These examples are by no means isolated episodes, but I have chosen to use them in trying to show something of the cultural imagination, as opposed to the social structure, of Kangersuatsiaq. The flow of events (and as we shall see, the giving of meat) allows a glimpse of how relations between people are articulated. The data I present is contextual, an interpretation of statement and sentiment. At first glance, together with answers to the ethnographer's persistent questions, it is easy to report that an *atsiaq* is someone named after a dead person. But the form should not be taken to suggest meaning (e.g. Turner 1969, Cohen 1987); meaning something which is expressed privately (Firth 1951) and implicitly (Douglas 1975). Naming does not tell people how to act towards or perceive another person, but it gives them the capacity to do so in whichever way they choose, depending on the situation.

Angerlartoqut

As I have shown, an *atsiaq* can be either someone who has no genealogical connection to the family of the deceased, or can be someone who is named after his/her dead relative. I have discussed how, for example, a grandfather–grandson relationship can be that of elder brother–younger brother if the grandson is his grandfather's brother's *atsiaq*. On a very general level, the relationship between two people within the naming network is defined with reference to the relationship which existed prior to a person's death. The deceased returns as an *atsiaq* and can re-enter anywhere in the community, depending on who happens to be pregnant. The parents of a child who becomes an *atsiaq* need not necessarily have had any previous relationship with either the deceased or the deceased's family.

In Kangersuatsiaq, the naming of children after dead people is not done in order to seek personal advantage or favour from others, or practised 'by helpless widows in order to obtain treatment' (Crantz 1820: 185). Crantz regarded the transmigration of names as superstition and wrote that

> If a widow can persuade any parent that the soul of her deceased child has migrated to his son, or that the spirit of his deceased offspring animates the body of one of her children, the man will always do his best to befriend the supposed soul of his child, or in the other case consider himself nearly related to the widow [ibid]

Similarly, Søby quotes the tale of Kasiagsak the Great Liar from Rink's (1875) collection of Greenlandic tales. Upon meeting a couple who had recently lost a daughter named Nepisanguak, Kasiagsak claimed that his own daughter had the same name. The couple gave him gifts, only to discover the following day that Kasiagsak had no daughter and had exploited them for personal gain (Søby 1986: 288–289). Such episodes do not seem to have been widespread, however. While naming may extend a person's kin relationships, there is no conscious political strategy or manipulative broadening of social horizons as is the case with much fictive kinship (such as *compadrazgo*).

Within families, a dead child can 'return home' as an especially emotionally powerful category of *atsiaq*, called an *angerlartoqut*. An *angerlartoqut* is a child named after its dead sibling. *Angerlartoq* means 'one who has returned home', deriving from the verb *angerlarpoq*; 'is/has come home'. The suffix *-qut* means 'belongs'.

If a child dies, the first same-sex child born to its mother will become its dead sibling's *atsiaq*. The child is said to 'have come home' to its mother and father. There is a certain power of emotional expression contained in the word *angerlartoqut*. An *angerlartoqut* has particular significance for its parents and there seems to be a stronger emotional attachment. The child's name is avoided and any other siblings will address him/her with the appropriate kin term used for the dead child. In this way an older brother or sister becomes a 'younger' sibling but the senior term is applied. However, the parents avoid using a kin term such as 'son' or 'daughter' and will address their child as '*angerlartoqut*'. Quite often the address is in the possessive form, such as *angerlara/angerlaga* (my *angerlartoqut*), or *angerlartoput* (our *angerlartoqut*).

While there is a deep significance for the bereaved parents in having a returned child, in some cases an *angerlartoqut* may not fill the void left by the death of a loved son or daughter. As an *angerlartoqut* develops its personality and character parents and others pay special attention to any similarities to the dead child.

In 1975, Ane K.'s three year old daughter died following a short illness. One year later, Ane gave birth to a baby girl, an *angerlartoqut*. Ane would wrap her *angerlartoqut* in love, overjoyed that her dead daughter had returned home. However, the *angerlartoqut* began to show a different character to that of her dead sibling. Ane would comment on this to her family and friends. It became known throughout Kangersuatsiaq that Ane had not got over the death of her daughter. She would tell others that her *angerlartoqut* was not Susaat (her dead child), but that she simply had Susaat's name.

Seven years after the birth of Ane's *angerlartoqut*, Juditha L. had a baby girl whom she named Susaat, after Ane's first daughter. Ane was overjoyed that Juditha's daughter was Susaat's *atsiaq*. Juditha explained to me that she had named her child after Ane's dead daughter because Ane was 'still looking' ('*suli ujarlerpoq*') for her daughter.

There are also *angerlartoqut* who may have returned several times. There are two couples in the village for whom the emotional bond with their *angerlartoqut* can only be described as powerful and intense. Andreas and Lydia P. have an eleven year old son who was born only after their first two sons had died shortly after birth. They both told me their son had 'come home twice'. Another couple, Knud and Mette, have a daughter in her mid-twenties who had 'followed' (*sinnerpaa*) after the deaths of three other daughters.

It is also possible, however, that a child can become an *angerlartoqut* without being named after a dead sibling. An example is Pavia, an eleven year old boy who had been critically ill for several weeks following his birth. Pavia's parents told me his heart had stopped sometime during his first few minutes of life. He had been 'brought back home' by the doctor, but it was some months before his mother was able to take him from the hospital to Kangersuatsiaq. Pavia was given only one name as a way of marking his position as a special child. To his parents he is an *angerlartoqut*.

A few days after his eleventh birthday, during spring 1988, Pavia went hunting with his father and shot his first seal. During the evening there was a first catch celebration in his parents' house. Pavia distributed gifts of meat to each household in the community and every member was invited for coffee and cake and to taste the meat. Gifts were given to Pavia in recognition of his first catch. The celebrations continued until late in the evening and much of the conversation was concerned with Pavia's early illness. There was talk among some elderly people that Pavia had not only returned home to his parents, but had come home to Kangersuatsiaq so that one day he could become a hunter who would feed the community.

Nalliuttuusaartoq; birthdays, the happiness of old people and the continuation of community

In Greenlandic villages all birthdays are celebrated by raising a flag outside the house and inviting everybody for coffee and cake. A person who celebrates a birthday (*nalliuppoq*) is called a *nalliuttoq*. A child will celebrate its first 'birthday' at six months of age (*qiteqquttoorput*), followed by a proper first birthday at twelve months. However, *atsiat* also celebrate the birthdays of the people they are named after and an *angerlartoqut* will celebrate the birthday of his/her dead sibling. An *atsiaq* who celebrates an *aqqa*'s birthday is known as a *nalliuttuusaartoq*. Because *atsiat* have the names of several dead people, there are several birthdays to be celebrated each year. So apart from a few fixed Christian festivals, the calendar is composed almost entirely of these events and affirmations.

The *nalliuttuusaartoq* receives gifts from the dead person's nearest consanguineal kin, such as sons, daughters, husband, wife, brothers and sisters. Usually, this takes the form of a small cash gift. For example, one woman, Juditha L., has two daughters who are the *atsiat* of her mother and mother's sister. I was present on the birthdays of the dead women and both times saw Juditha wish her daughters happy birthday. Each girl received a gift of 20 Dkr. In addition, Juditha gave 10 Dkr to the other *atsiat* of her mother and mother's sister.

Because a *nalliuttuusaartoq* celebrates the birthday of a dead person, the number of birthdays celebrated in Kangersuatsiaq increases beyond the number of living people celebrating their own birthdays. Where a person has six children named after him/her, those children will be *nalliuttuusaartut* on that person's birthday. However, such birthday celebrations are difficult to observe. There is no flag raised and no formal invitation for coffee and cake. However, there are some visitors to the house of the *nalliuttuusaartoq*. These include name-sharers, age-mates and people born on the same day as the dead person, as well as that person's close kin.

But just as there are fictive *atsiat*, a person, particularly a child, can be a fictive *nalliuttuusaartoq*. This is usually the case when an old person has left the village to go and live in Upernavik town, or has moved to another part of Greenland. When Maren J., a woman in her late sixties, left Kangersuatsiaq to live with her son in Upernavik in 1984, the next baby girl born in the village was given her name. This child was regarded as Maren's *atsiaq* by everybody in the village. On Maren's birthday the girl dresses in the Greenlandic national costume and invites several of Maren's relatives and close associates for coffee in her parents' home. I was told that old people who leave Kangersuatsiaq have *atsiat* 'because they are happy knowing a child has their name'. When Maren re-visits Kangersuatsiaq the *aqqa–atsiaq* relationship becomes that of name-sharers, with corresponding terms of address.

While children are named after people who are still living, yet become *atsiat* rather than name-sharers (*atiik*), I suspect it is done as much for the sake of the community as it is to ensure the happiness of old people. A loved and valued member of the community who leaves will be missed just as deceased people are. When someone takes up residence elsewhere, whether for a brief or prolonged period, they none the less remain part of the social context that defines and embraces them as a social person.

An absent person continues to be 'present' in the community in the same way that a dead person's presence can be experienced in everyday life, showing that absence is the essence of death. The link between person and name is inseparable and the same is true of person and community. It is not an arbitrary association which is severed at death, or departure for a different place, but a bond that integrates each and every person, both living and dead, present and absent, in a social and psychological network of interpersonal relationships. In the rest of this book I will develop this theme within a context of the ideology of subsistence and current changes taking place in Kangersuatsiaq.

9

Sharing and the ideology of subsistence

The previous chapters have discussed the idea of community as expressed in kinship relations, names, sociability and continuity, as well as in perceptions of landscape. A person sees his/her identity in terms of memories, as references to the past and to other people; memories that provide a link to the present. A recurrent theme of this book is that of sharing. Inuit share a sense of continuity as revealed in collective representations of the natural environment and expressed in stories and place names. They also share a sense of continuity with each other through the return of dead relatives and close associates as *atsiat*. Moreover, they share names, experiences and sentiments that find emotive power in altruism together with making provision for the living and the dead.

In this chapter I elaborate further on sharing as an expression of community, by exploring the meaning and ideology of subsistence in Kangersuatsiaq. Central to this is a consideration of the relationship between hunters and animals, 'respect' for animals and the environment, and the cultural value of meat and fish. The cultural viability of subsistence hunting depends on these interrelated elements. An understanding of them provides the basis for Chapter 10, which will discuss the compatibility of subsistence hunting with economic development in the context of the persistence of community in Upernavik district.

The hunter and the hunted: 'the living have souls'

Hunting is more than economic exploitation of resources, it is an interaction with the natural world. Survival depends on extensive knowledge of animals and their movement, together with deep understanding of the environment. As a result, the hunter is involved in a relationship of

136

intimacy with his surroundings that involves a moral code which recognizes the source of this intimacy as resting on a spiritual balance.

According to this, animals and some inanimate objects in nature are imbued with potent spiritual power, manifested in a spirit owner or guardian known as *inua* ('it's owner'). Hunting and human action within the natural world involves a dialogue and moral interplay with various *inua*. In this way hunting is a complex of social relations between humans, animals and spirit owners. I have already made brief references to the idea that seals give themselves up to hunters. The hunter requests that *inua* release the animals in their care, but in return the hunter must ensure the correct treatment of the animal during death and subsequent butchering, disposal and consumption.

In Greenlandic the word for animal, *uumasoq*, means 'living thing' and is derived from *uumavoq*; 'is alive' (the Greenlandic word for heart, *uummat*, is formed from the root of this verb). The Kangersuatsiamiit say animals also have souls (*tarnit*) just as people do. The literature on Inuit religion stresses the importance placed on the propitiation of animal souls (e.g. Rasmussen 1930, Søby 1969/70) as one of the central concerns of human life. Correct treatment of animals not only displays a reverence for them, it also appeases their spirit owners.

In pre-Christian Inuit cosmology, the Sea-Woman was said to guard over all sea mammals, giving them to humans to convert into food providing they observed the taboos necessary for maintaining harmony in the natural world. Failure to propitiate the souls of seals, for example, would result in the Sea-Woman punishing the Inuit with failure in hunting. Starvation and famine could then follow. In such cases, the Sea-Woman could be appeased by the Inuit in using the *angakkoq* as mediator, together with daily observances which showed respect for animals and ensured their souls did not return as 'crooked' spirits (Balikci 1970: 200).

The behaviour of every person in the community had an effect on the outcome of the hunt. All over West Greenland, for example, women had to remain indoors in darkness while the men went out whale hunting (Søby 1969/70). Propitiation of animals souls usually took the form of gratitude to the dead animal, expressed in giving it a drink of fresh water before flensing. Older informants in Upernavik remembered that seals would only be brought into the house if this had been done. Sometimes the seal was given a drink in the house, but only if it had been brought in through the window.

Once the soul had been properly cared for, it would return to the sea and to its *inua*, and find a new body. The same seal would then allow itself to be killed again by the same hunter. Some Inuit groups had elaborate rituals such as the Bladder Ceremony in Alaska (Fienup-Riordan 1983), although this was not the case in Greenland. However, in Upernavik district today, successful hunting still depends on right action and respect for animals. While there may not be colourful and observable rituals to ensure success in hunting, recognition that seals must come to the hunter is implicit in pragmatic behaviour and unspoken attitudes that imply respect and dependence. To ill-treat an animal is to offend both that animal's spirit owner and the balance between the human and natural worlds necessary for sustaining life itself.

Success in hunting is perceived as entailing a reciprocity based on the exchange of respect, a belief that finds expression in the idea of seals being 'frightened' and 'shy' of young, inexperienced hunters. A kill is only possible as the result of a change in status between hunter and seal. When a seal is first spotted, a good hunter assumes a position of deference in recognition of the animal's intelligence. The aim is not to scare the seal by assuming a position of superiority, but to wait until the seal has allowed itself a subordinate position to the hunter in giving itself freely.

The change in status from the initial self-perceived inferiority of the hunter to the inferiority of the animal is a feature of other hunting societies, such as the Mistassini Cree of Quebec (Tanner 1979: 136). Here, the relationship between the hunter and the hunted is interpreted in anthropomorphic terms. Animals are seen as having social relations not only with themselves, but with hunters. Similarly, in recognizing the seal's intelligence the Greenlandic hunter begins from the perspective of the seal in 'thinking' its movements through. The outcome of a hunt depends on knowledge of the seal's potential movement.

During the open water season, which lasts from late spring through to late autumn, successful hunters travel out to a stretch of water where currents are likely to create favourable conditions for seals. If the seal dives, the hunter switches off his outboard motor and waits. He then looks around, not in the hope of seeing the seal by chance, but instead 'imagining' where it will come up. Two or three spots are chosen as likely areas where the seal will surface for air, and the hunter then imagines it swimming. He relies on knowledge that the same seal will not return to the same place where it was scared or wounded. There is a consensus of opinion, especially among older hunters, that the decline in the use of the kayak and its replacement with speedboats has had an effect on the seals. They are less likely to come to the hunter freely because of the noise.

When I first went out seal hunting with David, in the summer of 1987, I was allocated the task of handling the outboard motor. Because I had to wait for visual, rather than verbal cues, I was given plenty of opportunity to watch how David 'thought' his way to the spot where he anticipated the seal would surface. Often, we would pursue the same seal for up to an hour with David seemingly trying to outwit it by waiting purposefully over a chosen spot. When he was successful in killing a seal, we would both pull it into the boat, with David saying 'Thank you' once the seal was securely out of the water. I would respond with a quiet 'You're welcome' and then we would continue on our way. I had been David's hunting partner for about three weeks when he turned to me and asked: 'Why do you keep saying "you're welcome"? I'm not thanking you.'

Despite the absence of the ritual observances of the past, David's quiet 'thank you' illustrates both a respect for animals and an acknowledgement of seals coming freely to a good hunter that, however implicit, is still profound. It is present in the way a woman throws away the seal's kidneys uttering 'let there be more', or in the way she spills a cup of warm blood on the ground near the seal's head. The influence of a Christian notion of God as the giver of daily 'bread' cannot be ignored, but such propitiations are not empty platitudes and have remained similar and consistent despite the introduction of modern technology.

Seals, men, women and meat

Dependence on seals for survival is reflected in the language that has evolved to accommodate animals as a configuration of human thought. The generic term for seal, *puisi*, is derived from the verb *puivoq*; 'to raise its head out of the water'. Words for different species of seal are numerous, such as *natseq* (pl. *natsiit*) for ringed seal and *aataaq* (pl. *aataat*) for harp seal. In addition they are distinguished further by age and position. For example, the word for bearded seal (*Erignathus barbatus*) is *taqammuaq* ('makes a splashing sound in the water'), but in spring it becomes *taqammuaq qassimasoq* ('one that has crept up on to the ice to bask'). A young bearded seal is called *teqilluk* ('small and narrow'). Any rutting male seal is known as *tiggak*, while an old male seal with a foul smell is a *tigganitsoq*. A seal in a breathing hole is a *puisartortoq* and the first seal that arrives in spring is *tikeqqammeq*. Hunting strategies differ to take account of particular types of seal. Young harp seals (*aataavaraq*) heading south to the whelping grounds off Newfoundland are said to be easier to kill than adults that may have experienced several migrations, surviving the intensive October hunt in Greenlandic waters. These seals are said to stay away from the hunter because they may have been scared or wounded in previous years.

Hunting is an exclusively male activity, linguistically endorsed by the verb *anguvoq*, which means 'kills a seal' and is derived from the masculine root *angu-* (*angut* meaning 'man'). Similarly, the harpoon used for seal hunting is a *anguvigaq*. During the hunt, as described above, a relationship is established between hunter and seal. But the ideological expression of hunting reaches its apogee in the post-hunt processing of the catch and in the preparation and consumption of the meat. The return of the hunter to the village ends the male-oriented activities, illustrated by the giving of the seal to a woman, usually the hunter's wife, mother or sister.

Traditionally it was the woman who flensed the seal, although now it is quite common for men to do this down on the beach or outside the house. The reason given for a change in an otherwise rigid sexual subdivision of labour was that it helped ease the heavy nature of women's work. As well as childrearing, cooking, housework and the fetching of ice for drinking water, the preparation of meat and skins is the responsibility of women. Most hunters said they started to flense seals when the effects of the collapse of the international fur market began to bite into the local economy in the early 1980s. Women now receive little or no remuneration for preparing skins for trading to the KNI. The participation of men in the processing of the catch is confined to butchering, while other tasks remain in the sphere of women's work.

But the cultural significance of this sharing of a previously female duty is best understood in light of the gender specific nature of subsistence. Hunting is differentiated from 'work' (*suliaq*) in that it is shaped by immediate needs. *Piniartoq*, the word for hunter, literally translates as 'one who wants', or 'one who makes an effort to get'. To hunt (*piniarpoq*) is to strive for something one wants and needs, and another meaning of *piniartoq* is 'provider'. In terms of organization and strategy, hunting differs from manual labour in the village and from the tasks carried out by women. Whereas the hunter makes an effort to provide what is needed, a woman's role in subsistence activities falls within the category of 'work' (*suliaq*). *Suliaq* refers to 'action', something that must be finished, in the sense of a task such as scraping sealskins. It also has the sense of meaning that somebody is occupied with a task, such as fetching ice to melt for water needed to wash clothes. Furthermore, there are usually several sealskins to be scraped and washed at a given time, thereby investing women's work with a repetitive nature.

Hunting generates intense interest in others because, unlike the preparation of meat, it always produces stories. It takes place in an environment that both gives meaning to and derives meaning from hunting (see Chapter 4). Furthermore, there is a sense of uncertainty about the outcome of each hunt. When a hunter returns he is expected to relate the events of the hunt to other hunters. This involves a complete description of the route taken, the number of seals spotted, the amount of time taken to secure the catch, and the number of bullets fired. No detail is spared and many past hunts have become celebrated events which are remembered and re-told. In complete opposition, women's work belongs to the known domestic sphere within the community. Besides being necessary, it complements the seeking and striving of the hunter in transforming his catch into meat.

Flensing seals can be a lengthy and demanding procedure. The seal is laid on its back and, starting with a slit at the throat, the whole skin is gradually removed. Women use a crescent-shaped knife called an *ulu*, which has advantages in ensuring both skin and fat are separated cleanly. Care is taken to ensure the stomach is not cut open until the skin has been removed. This done, the lungs, intestines and bladder are cut out first and placed in a bucket. They are not consumed by humans but are later fed to the dogs. The intestines are sometimes kept and dried for making into dog whips or, in exceptional circumstances, boiled and eaten as a delicacy, but it is only a few old people who profess a liking for the latter. The flesh is then cut into packages for preparation later, starting with the ribs and hind quarters. Depending on individual preference, flippers are kept, are given away or fed to the dogs. The same goes for the head, but the liver and heart are kept while, as I have mentioned, the kidneys are thrown away.

140

Each household has its own meat drying rack or a shed (*qui*) where meat is stored for later use. In winter, the exceedingly low temperatures allow meat to be stored outside without need for cover, providing it is out of the reach of dogs. Only meat for the household's immediate needs is kept indoors. Skins are not scraped until the following day, when several may be done at the same time. Again, an *ulu* is used to remove all the fat from the underside, which is kept and either boiled for human consumption or fed to the dogs. The skins are washed, dried and stretched before being taken to the KNI for trading.

When a man gives a seal to a woman, a neat line is drawn separating the male and solitary nature of the hunt from addressing what Fienup-Riordan calls 'the problem of social meaning' (ibid xxxv). Knowledge of seal hunting becomes public in that people go down to the pier or the beach to welcome returning hunters. The size of the kill, or the number of seals caught comes under the admiring or critical gaze of the onlookers. The news of either a successful or poor hunting trip soon spreads through the community, so as to build up a complete picture of the day's events to store in the collective memory. Thus, reputations are established and publicly endorsed without, interestingly enough, harming the essential statements of egalitarianism – although, privately, this may not be the case (as will be illustrated in the next chapter). Hunters do not brag about their success, which is not self-ascribed but expressed in an unspoken recognition by the community. This is not to deny that hunters vie with one another in a more implicit fashion, but to announce publicly that one is a 'big hunter' conflicts with the community norm. Recent and increasing use of the telephone also means that news of hunting spreads throughout the district, giving a modern twist to the term 'bush telegraph'.

Sharing and giving

The emphasis on kin is reflected in economic practices, in that the *ilaqutariit* and component households are more or less independent units based on subsistence, at least in terms of production for the household economy. Seal hunting no longer means complete self-sufficiency for subsistence needs, but I shall show later how more readily remunerated activities are pursued primarily to supplement subsistence. It remains that hunting, together with the preparation of meat and skins, is the exclusive preserve of each household, with daily tasks the concern of individuals carrying out their allotted roles within the division of labour.

But when meat is shared out between households beyond the *ilaqutariit* or simply given away to others, then it expresses mutual aid and distribution and stands as a metaphor of community. If a hunter returns with several seals, then it is quite common to see people making their way to his house carrying plastic buckets or polythene bags, thus expressing a request for meat. If the hunter has meat to give, then he will give it freely, although it is his wife who decides on what shares are given out. Those who want meat need not ask formally, as simply arriving during flensing or walking into the house with something to carry the meat back in is enough. Requests for meat can not be denied by the hunter or his wife, ensuring that there is always an obligation to give.

This is central to an understanding of the ideology of subsistence in northwest Greenland. There is a recognition that some people are unable to hunt for themselves, possibly because of old age or illness, or even owing to incompetence or laziness. These people generate feelings of 'pity' in others and collectively the community ensures nobody goes hungry. Gifts of meat or fish are often taken to people's homes even if they have not been requested but it is felt they are needed. But the obligation to give is not simply born of a strong sense of compassion and overt generosity. It parallels the giving of the seal to the hunter, in that what comes freely must be given away freely.

In Chapter 4, reference was made to the conflict between, on the one hand the right of the individual to hunt wherever he chooses and, on the other hand access to hunting territory being controlled by the community. As it works on the ground, individual hunters are free to hunt where they like within a recognized and bounded area, the physical expression of their own community. There is nothing to stop hunters from Kangersuatsiaq going sealing near Upernavik Kujalleq, or vice versa, but the fact that they do not reflects an awareness of local boundary. When boats or dogsledges from Upernavik Kujalleq come dangerously close to the Kangersuatsiaq boundary, suspicions are raised if they are seen to be hunting. There is never public dispute, but there is plenty of silent complaint as when three large boats came up from Uummannaq district to fish east of Kangersuatsiaq in the summers of 1987 and 1988.

This prompted general talk of enough fish in Uummannaq and a feeling of resentment that these boats should travel north to take Greenland halibut from Upernavik district. Such feelings were exacerbated each time the boats came to Kangersuatsiaq for supplies. People would go down to the pier to hear news of the fishing, or to admire the boats. After a little conversation, there would be a lot of joking and teasing, based on the reciprocal mimicking of the Upernavik and Uummannaq dialects. Once or twice I heard references to the effect that some hunters would be making a visit to Uummannaq to 'steal' a few seals.

With the increase in commercial fishing more vessels are moving into Upernavik waters from south Greenland. In particular, they spend several months of the year exploiting the rich shrimp and prawn grounds. Any ideas about 'stealing' are responses to outsiders coming into local waters. People in Kangersuatsiaq know that seals and fish cannot be stolen precisely because animals are not owned by anyone. This is a crucial difference between domesticated and non-domesticated animals and the part they play in the structure of social relations. While certain persons have ownership and control of access to domesticated animals in agricultural and pastoral societies, hunting peoples depend on non-domesticated animals. As a result, access to animals is collective.

Because they give themselves up to hunters, it is incumbent on the hunter to give them in turn to other people. This, probably above anything else, creates an obligation to give meat to those who ask for it or are known to need it. The obligation to give is also an obligation to the community because, despite individual procurement of seals, it is the community that has the ultimate claim on the animals its members catch. This is illustrated most vividly by *ningeq*, the distribution of catch shares from large sea mammals such as whales, walrus and bearded seals.

If a hunter has shot a bearded seal, for example, others are entitled to a share simply by arriving on the scene. Usually they make a claim by touching the seal with the toe of a boot, or by helping to haul the seal out of the water or bring it to shore. In Kangersuatsiaq it is common for the flensing to be directed by the first hunter to arrive on the scene, or by one of the older men in the village, with the man who actually made the kill assisting. In spring, the seal is flensed out on the ice, but during the open water season it will be taken back to the village for all to admire. The shares are divided according to the order of arrival or the first to touch the seal. The hunter who has claimed the kill receives the head and upper left hand side (including the left flipper), while the first to arrive at the scene receives the upper right hand side. The second to have made a claim gets a share from the lower left part of the body, while the third receives part of the lower right. The rest of the seal is divided according to the the number of claimants and the butchering is usually interrupted while long discussions take place about this. The skin of the bearded seal is also distributed amongst all those who share the meat. It is cut from the seal in diagonal strips and used for *kamik* (sealskin boots) soles.

On the rare occasions when walrus are caught, every household in the community receives a share because the butchering is carried out in the village where everybody can make a claim on some of the meat. In the autumn of 1988, Edvard K. caught a walrus in a beluga net. His brother returned to Kangersuatsiaq ahead of him, in his own boat, and spread the news. By the time Edvard reached home with his catch, the school and store had been closed and everyone was down on the pier with buckets and plastic tubs. Six days later, most households were still living off the shares of walrus meat they had received. Whatever form the distribution takes, the hunter who made the kill always ends up with more than enough meat for his own needs.

Through sharing and giving meat, what was an individual success in hunting becomes a distinctive statement of community. I also see it as reinforcing my arguments in Chapter 6 about the fluidity of kinship because the carcass is not a genealogical diagram. Because seals and other marine mammals are non-domesticated they do not act as the basis for social relations between persons, households or groups as domesticated animals do in ranching and pastoral societies (Ingold 1980). Free distribution is an acknowledgement of the debt owed to the animal in coming to the hunter and a denial that any one person has exclusive claims to ownership of the animals that are caught.

Today, though, sharing is also seen as something of an ideal or as symbolic of traditional distribution. No hunter is isolated from the need for bullets, rifles, benzine, boats and other equipment. He and his family are also dependent on a certain amount of store bought food, electricity and kerosene used for heating. Households have to generate enough income to provide a steady flow of cash to pay for all these necessities. Despite the low prices paid for sealskins, they still provide an important source of money which is now supplemented by income from summer fishing and from casual labour. Thus there remains only a minor commercial element in seal hunting, the main reason being to secure meat for the household.

By contrast, there is an increasing commoditization as regards whaling. It is now more likely that hunters will sell meat from narwhal and beluga whale hunting than distribute the meat freely to people other than their immediate family. Reasons for this are twofold. Firstly, beluga are hunted only in autumn in the northern part of Upernavik district. Only those hunters with larger fishing boats can participate and, because of the running costs, they need to sell a large part of what they catch. The surplus is then kept for their own household consumption. As the hunting crews on these expeditions are fathers and sons, brothers or cousins, then shares are divided between households of the *ilaqutariit*. Secondly, an increasing incentive to hunt beluga is the high reward paid for each whale by the KNI. In autumn 1988, several hunters received upward of 10,000 Dkr (about one thousand pounds) for a single whale. With *mattak* (raw whale skin) selling at 100 Dkr per kilo, hunters use this as a yardstick when selling it privately. Throughout the 1980s there has been an increase in the trade of *mattak* from both beluga and narwhals (Born 1987), with private sales of whale meat fetching around 30 Dkr per kilo. The signs are that this has arisen as a result of the fall in sealskin prices.

The gradual intrusion of a commercial element into a previously self-contained whale hunt has produced a mixed response in the villages. While many recognize that going north for beluga is economically lucrative, there is a feeling that money is now more important than sharing and distributing the meat on returning home from the hunt. In December 1987, one hunter brought in four belugas he had caught in nets set close to Kangersuatsiaq. He sold the *mattak* and meat to other villagers, but many people complained that the meat should have been given away as the whales had been caught locally in nets. The hunter in question responded that he had exclusive use of the netting sites and added that people were no longer hungry, as they were in the past. Privately, there were complaints that the hunter was 'thinking like a Dane' because he already enjoyed a regular income from his job with the Upernavik municipal authorities. The day after the whales had been landed, I was taking a class in the school when one fourteen year old girl asked me if I had bought any *mattak*. When I replied that I had, she added that her father would give me *mattak* next time he caught a beluga, because it should be 'given freely'.

So far, commercialization of hunting seems limited to whales, with demand for meat and *mattak* providing a domestic market. The commercial element has necessitated a change in attitude among hunters. It has also created a dilemma for those who seek to serve the best interests of the hunters, but are now involved in appropriate redefinitions of 'subsistence hunting' for the purposes of policy making. In the future, it can be expected that criticism will be made of this type of hunting from not only anti-whaling groups, but even from Greenlanders who spearhead the anti-hunter lobby in Nuuk.

At the local level, however, a conflict has arisen between the giving of meat, where the individual stands in a relationship to the whole community, and the selling of meat which is expressed in a transaction between two people, or one person and an agency (the KNI). Whereas sharing and distribution sustains the whole community, selling meat only benefits the buyer and the seller. This tension between generalized and balanced reciprocity will be discussed in more detail below, but firstly it is worth mentioning an episode that illustrates the negative response to the potential commercialization of seal hunting.

The tinned seal meat factory plan

In the early autumn of 1988, I received a letter from a Danish engineer working in Upernavik town on contract with the municipal council. She asked if I would, as a social anthropologist, provide an assessment of a plan to build a factory in the town that would produce a ready-made seal meat product. The idea was to have small chunks of seal meat mixed with potatoes, onion and rice in gravy, which is already a Greenlandic dish (known as *suaasat*) eaten as a staple in the hunting districts. The product would be sold to the rest of Greenland, with the factory in the town gradually expanding output as demand increased. It would not only provide much needed employment in Upernavik, but hunters throughout the district would benefit as suppliers of seal meat. The site for the factory had been decided upon, the number of employees worked out, and it had been estimated that two or three hundred thousand tins would need to be produced and sold annually to make it a viable proposition. All of this presupposed the participation of hunters in what the plan called 'increased productivity' in providing several thousand kilos of meat.

Despite personal reservations, I put the idea to the Kangersuatsiaq Hunters' Association. It was met with scepticism and criticized for the lack of understanding on the part of the municipality. The hunters felt that both Greenlanders and Danes involved with bureaucracy in Upernavik had failed to grasp both the realities and meaning of seal hunting. Not only could a hunter go for days without catching a seal for his own family, but the idea of selling seal meat goes against the ideology of subsistence. Because seal hunting continues throughout the year and, reducing all reasons to the most basic, is done to provide the hunter's household with meat, it does not expect any direct material return. The primarily commercial nature of the autumn beluga hunt, on the other hand can be equated with the summer halibut fishery in that it is seasonal, involving a different technology and supporting secondary industries with a complex division of labour. To develop this further, it is necessary to understand how the nature of reciprocity and the ideal of the giver, figure prominently within the ideology of subsistence.

Sharing, kin, names and sociability – the 'pure gift' and being a kalak

The sharing and giving of meat comes close to Malinowski's 'pure gift' in the Trobriand Islands (1922: 177–178), itself Sahlins' ideal type of generalized reciprocity (1974: 194). Because requests for meat are never turned down, or shares are distributed according to need, there is a strong sense of altruism, generosity and aid that underlies this. Meat is food, it gives and sustains life. It is the most powerful and culturally significant, but also the most commonplace, gift that can be given. As an element of generalized reciprocity, the obligation to give does involve a counter-obligation to return, although the reciprocal expectation is imprecise and makes no demand of a definite time and equivalence of the returned gift. Indeed, this 'weak reciprocity' (Price 1962) allows the obligation to return to be forgotten about.

A hunting household that provides regular meat to an alcoholic renowned for laziness, for example, will not expect any reciprocation precisely because the gifts are not given with any in mind. Rather than a desire to accumulate wealth, for some people sharing establishes 'a conceptual foundation for the ascription of renown by effecting an ideological separation between the categories of "givers" and "receivers" of harvested produce' (Ingold 1986: 210). But while giving more than can be returned does enhance a sense of prestige and affirms the reputation of 'big hunters', morality and feelings of compassion for others are also implicit in the nature of sharing and giving (Firth 1951: 144).

If a return can be made, the one who receives accepts what the giver can afford to give. Those who give normally do end up with something in return, although this could sometimes be months or even years later, as reciprocity in this case is 'a whole class of exchanges, a continuum of forms' (Sahlins ibid: 191). The return may be the equivalent in meat, or hospitality in the form of a cup of coffee, the loan of a rifle or boat, looking after children, or fetching water as a favour. Everything that is shared, given and returned is an expression of sociability. To quote Sahlins again, seen in this way the material side of transaction 'is repressed by the social' (ibid: 194).

A direct equivalent in return for seal meat, then, is neither necessary or expected. Shares of seal meat are not distributed as gifts in the sense of being part of Mauss's debt economy, where personal relations are desired instead of the gifts themselves. Mauss (1966) saw no clear cut distinction between persons and things; with gifts containing an element of the giver's personality. In this sense, in Kangersuatsiaq seal meat is inalienable, containing an element of the giver and is something that is

146

intrinsically socially desirable. Its value extends far beyond nutrition and maintaining life, because in cultural terms it sustains the community. As a gift, seal meat symbolizes cultural continuity and sustains close social networks.

However, as the examples above show, if meat becomes a commodity it can actually harm social relationships and the cultural fabric of community. In this sense it becomes an alienable commodity exchanged between independent parties. The selling of whale meat and *mattak* belongs to the realm of balanced reciprocity in that it is based on direct exchange. By selling meat, the hunter receives an immediate return in the form of money. The transaction is short, involving a different kind of partner, and favours those who can afford to pay the required price. Money transactions distance the transactors and are final between them rather than ongoing. Because of the alienation of the product there is no connection to the producer; likewise there is no strong connection between transactors.

In many Inuit societies there has been no tradition of using food as a trade item (e.g. Spencer 1959: 204), although in Greenland the recent development of a commercial fishery as the main industry has meant the growth of direct material return based on food. Whaling is now going the same way. However, in Upernavik district, the persistence of seal meat remaining outside a sphere of balanced reciprocity is reinforced further by kinship, names and ideas of being a 'genuine' Greenlander.

When seal meat is shared beyond the *ilaqutariit*, a large proportion of those who receive are likely to have some form of genealogical, fictive kin or name relationship to those who are doing the giving. There is a strong case for a correlation between generalized reciprocity and close kinship and social association (Sahlins ibid: 196). At the other extreme, the remoter the kin tie and the greater the social distance, the trend is possibly towards balanced reciprocity. The giver has a wide range of potential relatives to share meat with (see Chapter 6), people named after dead relatives may possibly receive regular gifts of the same part of the seal, while name-sharers may each receive a rib. This may continue to work in the villages, but in the large towns, where the few people who hunt sell their catch in markets known as *kalaaliminerniarfiit* or *kalaaliaraq*, a degree of social isolation restricts opportunities to establish a wider network of kin. In addition, most people in the towns do not have meat to share.

In the towns, where people enjoy salaried employment, a balanced reciprocity of buying and selling exemplifies the essentially fragmentary nature of urban Greenland. When meat is shared, the meat sharing relationships are more inclusive and balanced and stand outside a wide framework of potential and actual social alignments. Balanced reciprocity involves partnerships between individuals representing the needs of their respective families. In the past some Inuit groups, such as the Copper and Netsilik of the Central Canadian Arctic, established exchange relations based on seal-sharing partnerships (Damas 1972). Sharing did not involve the whole community, but tied a number of individual families together.

Damas sees meat sharing as an alliance supporting an already existing system of kinship alliances.

In Greenland the idea of sharing as an institutionalized means of establishing alliances seems weak. Social relations are expressed in terms of being either kin or non-kin. In Chapter 6 I discussed how kin relationships can be created if individuals perceive their existing relationship in the sense of feeling themselves to be like kin. On the other hand, a relationship based on genealogy can be forgotten about if a person regards that relationship as unsatisfactory. A person already stands in a relationship to many people other than genealogical kin because of the complex network of name souls, name-sharers, age-mates, birthday partners and affines. It may well be that sharing and gift giving goes some way to 'legitimize the linkage' between those who use kin terminology for non-genealogical relationships (Fienup-Riordan ibid: 361). But sharing is more a statement of relationships that already exist, or have the potential to exist. To share and give meat away is a reaffirmation of values guiding attitudes towards animals and an expression of community.

Petersen sees the introduction of money into the Greenlandic nature of distribution as a way of maintaining the 'traditional system' (Petersen 1989: 116). This presupposes that distribution has been based on a balanced exchange in the past, with money replacing whatever it was that people with different opportunities were previously expected to return. In Kangersuatsiaq, however, direct exchange is thought to negate community and indicates, to my eyes, a change in thinking influenced by the wider society. With knowledge of town life, most immediately Upernavik town, such previously pragmatic aspects of village life as sharing, generosity and hospitality take on a new, almost symbolic, significance in being regarded as 'genuine' and 'real' Greenlandic cultural traits. Within modern Greenlandic society, there is a general feeling that the villages are more traditional and therefore more Greenlandic than the larger urban centres. The search for a Greenlandic 'soul' expressed in an appraisal of village life finds a voice in literature, poetry and art (the novels of Otto Rosing and Ole Brandt, for example, are set in the past and take the hunting life as their themes). Similarly, the denunciation of modern urban life is a favourite musical subject for many young rock bands.

In Kangersuatsiaq, sharing is imputed with a meaning that sees it as a metaphor of village life. To give is to be a *kalak*, a 'real' or 'genuine' Greenlander. When people say somebody is 'like a Dane' ('*soorlu qallunaaq*'), it is used as a symbol of the values perceived to be pervasive in the dominant society, values that are beginning to take a hold in the community. The attitude is quite clear: Greenlanders give freely, Danes sell. However, today only real Greenlanders give freely, while Greenlanders who act like Danes sell.

In south Greenland the term *kalak* is applied in a derogatory manner when people talk about the old hunting life. It is synonymous with *eskimuut* (eskimos), a term that I have even heard used by people in Upernavik town to describe those who live in the outlying villages.

In Kangersuatsiaq, though, as some people use the term, to be a *kalak* conveys the quintessential features of *kalaaliussuseq*; 'identity as a Greenlander'. In this way they make a distinction with *kalaaleq* (Greenlander), and with *inuk* (person). It encapsulates the Greenlandic conception of tradition and stresses the ideals, skills, personality, values and symbols of the Greenlander as held during the colonial period of 1721–1953 (Kleivan 1969/70), Langgaard 1986). During this time, the Greenlanders were perceived to be free from a pervasive Danish lifestyle, value system and way of thinking, excepting an imported and influential Lutheranism. The turning point came with abolition of colonial status in 1953 (see Chapter 2).

High-rise living in the fast growing towns meant that it was possible to be a *kalak* only in the remoter villages, particularly in the hunting districts. Just as the *inummariit* of the Canadian Eastern Arctic stand for the time before settlement life (Brody 1975), the *kalak* is a powerful symbol against a 'modernity that is antagonistic to "real" things – for these real things are, in the conscience of most Eskimos, representations of human goodness, honesty and strength' (Brody 1975: 126). The Greenlandic concept of what it means to be a person (see Chapter 5) informs contemporary definitions of *kalaaliussuseq* within an emerging nationalistic Greenland.

Conversations about being a *kalak* tend to dwell on the past, emphasizing aspects of character and expertise that most claim are absent in today's young:

When I was a young man, all the men here hunted from kayaks. They would go out alone for many hours, catching maybe two or three seals. The old hunters didn't take any food with them when they went out by kayak. But they didn't feel the cold because they would eat seal meat before going out. Their skin clothes also kept them warm. Now a lot of things have changed. People hunt by speedboat and take soda water and Danish food with them. Some older men still know how to hunt without having to go to the store [i.e. without having to supplement their diet with store bought food], but we can't expect that our children will want to continue the old ways. They have the taste of another culture.

G.J. (47)

You ask me what it means to be a *kalak*. Sometimes I ask 'who am I?' Maybe an Englishman, maybe an American, maybe a German. The dogsled in winter, that's Greenlandic. In summer, sitting in a speedboat . . . that's European. We've been given a factory . . . that's European. If it's dark when I walk in the house, I switch on the lights . . . that's European. The old stone lamp . . . we used seal fat. How warm it was!

M.L. (78)

The *kalak*! I long for the past, for the old people who are dead. I would wake up, get up and drink a little coffee, but wouldn't eat. I would go out in my kayak for twelve hours. During this time I didn't feel hungry. I would go home with the seals I caught and then I would eat. They tasted good!

A.L. (68)

The thing I most remember about my grandmother is her strength. You think I work hard in the house, helping my mother? Grandmother always worked, just like all the other women who are dead now. But her strength was inside her, in her soul (*tarneq*) and in her blood.

A.J. (17)

The *kalak* is also recognized as having knowledge of a specialized language, one that has evolved as a result of a profound experience of the environment, animals, and of the subtle moods of the weather (*sila*). The publicly ascribed role of *ilisimatooq* ('one who has much knowledge/wisdom') to men such as Josepi is an acknowledgement of this. However, much of this language has now disappeared because certain hunting equipment and methods are no longer used, or because particular animals are not hunted anymore (e.g. caribou, see Chapter 4). Furthermore, the increase in the popularity of television and video has reduced the role of storytelling as an effective medium for the transmission of the language of the *kalak*.

But defining *kalaaliussuseq* is not necessarily determined by a romantic attachment to the past. It derives from values and symbols of a past colonial period that are, none the less, recognized as having persisted in the villages, particularly in the hunting districts. The villages are not fossilized in any sense, but as the last bastions of a pre-1953 Greenlandic culture they are held to be 'only slightly adapted versions of late colonial period equivalents' (Langgaard 1986: 299). While many do define themselves in terms of the past, others see the *kalak* in the light of what they regard to be a qualitative difference between life in the towns and villages, as the following case study shows.

In the late autumn of 1985, Eirik returned to Kangersuatsiaq after ten years in Nuuk, two years in Aasiaat, and a six month period spent in Copenhagen. He was eighteen years old when he left his home village, having been taught to live as a hunter by Josepi. After three years in Nuuk, he married a girl from south Greenland, with whom he was to have two children. For some time, Eirik drifted through a succession of jobs before finally settling with an audio-visual equipment retailer repairing radios and video cassette recorders. He enjoyed what he called a Danish lifestyle, living in a new apartment, driving a car and earning a large salary. Fluency in Danish enabled him to mix socially with Danes. However, Eirik began to spend most of his money on alcohol and marijuana, with the result that his marriage broke down. His wife moved to Aasiaat with their two children. Eirik remained in Nuuk but later went to Copenhagen with a Danish woman he had met in a bar. The relationship did not last, and Eirik experienced racial discrimination when attempting to find work in Denmark. He moved back to Greenland, this time to Aasiaat in order to be near his children. Eventually, unable to hold down a steady job, he returned to Kangersuatsiaq intending to live as a hunter. Living in his father's house, he spent seven unsuccessful hunting months while he attempted to re-learn the skills of his youth. During this time he was dependent on his father and two brothers. He also received regular gifts of meat and hospitality from several people whose dead relatives he was named after. Eirik explained his decision to leave town life as follows:

Sometimes I think it is a better life in Nuuk. It's a hard life being a hunter. In Nuuk I could earn a lot of money, but you get no money from selling sealskins. But I can trust people here. In Nuuk there is a lot of drinking and a lot of fighting. I drank and smoked a lot of hash, so I came back here. You don't get big money and I have to live in my father's house, which is hard for me. But in Kangersuatsiaq you can be a *kalak*. Here, I can eat Greenlandic food every day. In Nuuk I longed for seal meat, all the time because you only eat Danish food. You have Denmark in your mind and in your stomach.

Whatever Eirik's own personal ideas of being a 'genuine' Greenlander his return to the village was not without its difficulties. There were many who felt he acted and thought 'like a Dane'. His presence also created an uneasy situation in his father's house, particularly because he maintained a tense relationship with his youngest sister, Naja. David once told me that he attributed Eirik's way of thinking to his use of marijuana in Nuuk, adding that Eirik was sometimes a 'different' Greenlander compared to others in the village.

It was also the relationship between David and Eirik that highlighted the conflict of values perceived as characteristic of the difference between town and village. I was once present in Josepi's house when David asked Eirik for some acrylic tape so he could make dog harnesses. Eirik said he wanted paying for it as it was available in the store. Being evening, the store was closed and David then said he would not have asked if it had been possible to buy some himself. Reluctantly, Eirik gave David a roll of tape and suggested he either paid for it, or buy some the following day as a replacement. David quietly agreed and put the tape in his pocket. Naja then said to Eirik 'He's your brother, give it to him.' Eirik responded that it was expensive and that things do not come freely. At this point, Josepi disagreed and said that things should be shared. It was David's quiet acceptance of Eirik's attitude, however, that seemed significant. It also indicates an acceptance, that these values are also operative in the village. His reserve compared to the assertiveness of his brother is indicative of a reluctance to engage in overt conflict that is pervasive in Greenland. Confrontation is attributed a negative sanction as being non-Greenlandic. An example of this again involved Eirik.

In January 1988 I spent several days with five hunters (including David and Eirik) in a hut to the north of Kangersuatsiaq. We spent the first evening discussing the possibilities for good hunting during the next few days. Conditions in the hut were basic and cramped, each man occupying a tiny space. Every now and then somebody would go and fetch snow for melting into water. This was done quietly and unprompted by the others. The following morning, Eirik awoke in a bad mood and shook the young hunter sleeping next to him, telling him to go and fetch snow so that we could make some tea. The younger man said that he would do it, but Eirik persisted in telling him to hurry up while remaining in his sleeping bag. David told Eirik to leave the other man alone. Eirik replied that hunters should be fresh and ready for work in the morning. While this was going on, the younger man had put on his kamiks, but, in heading for the door, kicked over the primus stove. This gave Eirik further ammunition for attack, this time calling the man 'stupid' (*sianiik*). By this time we were all awake and, including Eirik, making no attempt to rise from the warmth of our sleeping bags. Eirik said to us all: 'Isn't he stupid!', and David told him once more to ease off. Eirik then turned to the object of his abuse and shouted: 'You're stupid! Get some snow!' Up until now the younger man had said nothing to Eirik, but picking up a pot, he slammed the door as he left the hut. While he was outside, David and Eirik engaged in a quiet argument. Eirik accused the other hunter of getting angry by slamming the door when he should have gone to get the snow without complaint. On re-entering the hut, the other hunter made a comment about the weather and seemed in a cheerful mood as he began to melt the snow over the primus. Eirik, however, continued to brood over the morning's events throughout the day.

Negative attitudes to anger and conflict among the Inuit have been written about in detail elsewhere (e.g. most notably by Briggs 1970). The potential for tension that close proximity generates needs to be managed effectively or it results in uncomfortable situations. The sense of negativity becomes acute when individual assertiveness is seen as exemplary of foreign values and norms. Eirik's inability to fit back into life in Kangersuatsiaq is at variance with accepted ways of thinking and behaving. To sell to a brother something he needs, for example, goes against the grain of community attitudes to sharing and giving. To vent one's anger in a crowded hunting hut is to ignore legitimate codes of equanimity endorsed by a cultural consensus committed to the idea of community, to which conflict is antithetical.

Ecology, community and identity

In the literature and in more popular accounts, Inuit have long been portrayed as living in a barren, inhospitable wilderness, regarded as 'one of the most desolate environments on earth, particularly inappropriate for human occupation' (Balikci 1970: xviii). Studies have concentrated on cultural responses and adaptations to the environment, although this is not to imply the acceptance of an environmental determinism. Rather, there has been an emphasis on pointing out the strategies employed in ensuring an ecological fit. Even in the realm of kinship and alliance theory, kinship in all its forms is seen as organized to accommodate the needs of ecology (Damas 1971). Mauss's theory of an increased social life correlating to a high density of population fits within his framework of seasonal constraint and adaptation (Mauss 1979). Due to the constant idealization of Inuit life as a supreme example of how human beings deal with an extreme environment, 'the students of Malthus and Darwin are continually drawn to the contemplation of the lifeways of the inhabitants of the arctic' (Fienup-Riordan, ibid: xi).

Haller's study of Nuussuaq, in the northern part of Upernavik district, extended the ideas of Boas in its concern with showing how hunters exhibit patterns of spatial organization with respect to their action space

(Haller 1986). Haller defines action space as an annual subsistence resource area, which is the 'total resource area utilized by hunters during the annual cycle of hunting activities' (ibid: 43). In this sense, Haller sees hunting as a 'biobehaviour' system with its use of space as a highly specialized elaboration of culture. Haller's thesis is that, despite technological change, a hunter's action space has remained consistent over time.

For Greenland generally, Petersen argues that there are a number of regulating factors to ensure an ecological fit between hunting and the environment. When talking of the distribution of meat shares, he sees *ningeq* as an 'expression of common attitude to the hunting area' (1965: 119) but, more importantly, he argues that it is a regulating factor to prevent too many seals from being killed on the same day. Recently, he has written that it is a 'wise utilization of renewable resources' (1989: 105).

However, these studies do not give the whole picture because they do not consider the type of data I have tried to present throughout this book. The meaning of survival and subsistence is expressed in the values and ideas inherent in the notion of community. Fienup-Riordan regards an orthodox emphasis on ecology as redundant in the study of subsistence. By focusing on social structure and ritual exchange her concern is 'cultural imagination' rather than leaning towards a narrow environmental determinism (ibid: xi). I have tried to show how the giving and sharing of meat is informed by a mixture of belief, altruism, generosity and allegiance to community. Chapter 8 also showed the power of sentiment and concern for the emotional and physical welfare of others. In this sense, ecology becomes subordinate to the recognition of need. Furthermore, the giving of catch shares to *atsiat* and name-sharers is a powerful statement of recognizing the significance of names.

To argue against Petersen, *ningeq* illustrates the fundamental conflict between individual freedom to hunt and access to hunting areas based on affiliation to community. Furthermore, it is an implicit recognition of community and the local area as its physical expression. By recognizing the notion of community, *ningeq* goes some way to perpetuate it. An individual hunt of large sea mammals (such as bearded seals, but excluding the beluga hunt) is complemented by communal consumption. However, it may be argued that sharing is an ecological requirement if the precarious situation of Arctic hunting is taken into consideration. Bad weather, storms, rotten ice and the absence of seals are all common. Sharing may then be seen as a form of insurance for unsuccessful hunters. Compared with Inuit, other hunter-gatherer societies such as the Hadza (Woodburn 1968) are the epitome of Sahlins' 'original affluent society' (Sahlins 1974). But, however strong the argument for the ecological perspective, factors that are culturally determined should certainly not be ignored. The emphasis on ritual as active ideology (Fienup-Riordan, ibid) and a humanistic approach to hunting (Riches 1982) are both necessary and pertinent. The latter is influenced in part by the sociology of knowledge, with its concern for understanding the definitions and meaning of reality as held by the members of a society that go to make up a 'universe of meaning' (Berger and Luckmann 1984). Being socially derived, this universe of meaning is a reification in that, being a product of society it turns back on itself and helps to create society.

This book does not seek to discuss community in terms of social structure, but holds that it is culturally constructed. While such reification may be criticized, the people of Kangersuatsiaq regard their community as a tangible entity, especially when viewed in relation to other places. Community as a cultural construct (or even a symbolic construct) is valid in the discourse of anthropology because it is valid in the discourse of a community's legitimate members (Cohen 1987).

As discussed above, the identity of Greenlanders as hunters and the significance of the 'genuine' Greenlander adds a further dimension to the ideology of subsistence in modern Greenland. The cultural value of sharing and giving meat takes on a new meaning in that it symbolizes the differences held to exist between the towns and villages. Identity is now threatened as a result of conflicts of interest between hunters and advocates of economic development within the Home Rule government, viewed from the hunting districts as internal colonialists. All this has a profound effect on sharing and the ideology of subsistence. This theme will be explored further in the next chapter.

10

Community and development

Hunting and development

This chapter discusses the conflict between political and economic ideals, as held by the Home Rule government and municipal authorities, and the values that persist in small northern communities such as Kangersuatsiaq. Today, in modern Greenland, the hunting districts are facing a ideological conflict as a result of Home Rule government policy and development strategy.

The structure of Greenlandic Home Rule is based along the lines of the former Danish administration, with the expressed intention of developing the country in terms of Greenlandic conditions, aspirations and available resources. But talk of development is something of a contradiction. Because of the enormous transitions and upheavals since the abolition of colonial status in 1953, Greenland occupies the enviable position of being an overdeveloped post-colonial country (Alavi 1972, Dahl 1986), especially when the lack of a strong internal social and economic foundation is taken into account.

Despite continued dependency on Denmark, the Home Rule authorities have begun to carve an impressive autonomous niche as they aspire to political and economic maturity. By the mid-1980s they had taken over control of the KGH (now the KNI, or Greenland Trade, see Chapter 2). In 1985, Greenland became the first country to leave the EEC, but negotiated and achieved Overseas Countries and Territories Association status which allows access to European markets. In taking over control of state-owned institutions (including, in 1988, the Greenland Technical Organization), the Home Rule authorities are strengthening their political power.

The ruling Siumut party favours the process of 'Greenlandization' as the way to achieve their goal of greater economic and political independence. The aims of Siumut allow an understanding of the politics of development, because there are others for whom a complete break from Denmark is not a desirable prerequisite for the future of self-government. Atassut, the opposition party, favours co-operative links with Denmark and it must be pointed out that the Home Rule referendum included the votes of the Danish minority (one fifth of the population), as well as the majority Greenlandic part of the franchise. Whatever the nationalistic origins of Home Rule, it was not defined in ethnic terms, but was concerned with the territory of Greenland. The Home Rule government is composed entirely of Greenlanders, however. While many key positions in public institutions continue to be held by Danes (partly because administrative organization has remained the same, the only difference being geographical as many institutions have moved from Denmark to Nuuk), government bureaucracy is the exclusive preserve of a Danish-speaking Greenlandic elite.

The expressed aim of Siumut, then, is increased political and economic independence from the former colonial power. It is beyond the scope of this study to evaluate and assess the viability and likelihood of this, except to say that the Home Rule authorities need, and desire, an increase in revenue from both renewable and non-renewable resource exploitation. At the same time the Home Rule government states that the protection of Greenlandic Inuit culture is also a priority. However, there are tensions and emerging conflicts of interest between the politics of development and customary subsistence based modes of livelihood.

Throughout the 1970s, Siumut claimed much of its support from the more peripheral areas of the country and from occupational groups such as the hunters and fishermen. Since 1979 they have stressed the importance of hunting, fishing and sheep farming as Greenland's main occupations and look favourably at development of the villages. As was shown in the previous chapter, the emphasis on a way of life characterized as traditionally Greenlandic is derived from ideas about 'true culture' now found only in remoter districts and villages. But while the Home Rule government demonstrates a commitment to hunting, for example through its subsidy of the trade in sealskins and training schemes for hunters and their wives, when the possibilities of economic benefits arise the hunting districts can become conveniently remote.

In the 1970s, for example, Siumut opposition to the proposed Arctic Pilot Project was based on the likely threat to sea mammals, as well as to the hunting population in the northwest, by the shipping of liquid gas from the Canadian High Arctic south through Davis Strait. However, in the early 1980s, attitudes changed in the case of Jameson Land on Greenland's east coast. In 1983, Siumut agreed to allow oil exploration to go ahead there. This decision was attacked by the Greenlandic press as 'naive' and was viewed generally as detrimental to the hunting population of Ittoqqortoormiit. In 1984, *Sermitsiaq*, one of the two main national newspapers, reported Siumut as continuing to regard oil development as vital to the future economy of Greenland. *Sermitsiaq* went on to accuse politicians of misleading people into thinking there were alternative possibilities of routing tanker traffic away from the hunting areas. Economic interest, rather that Inuit cultural interest was taken to be the Siumut line.

At the moment, oil exploitation is not going ahead on the east coast. However, it is a possibility for the future and, for many people, there is no doubt that it would be catastrophic for the local hunting way of life and for the environment.

Changing perceptions of landscape are a useful indicator of the extent of political and economic development in nation states. In Greenland, in the years since the introduction of Home Rule, there seems to be a growing divide in attitudes towards the physical environment. Hunting communities, such as Kangersuatsiaq, regard the environment as a place that provides them with their immediate needs. But as Chapter 4 outlined, it is also an expression of, and metaphor for, the community. Attachment to the environment is both sentimental and symbolic. There is a powerful feeling of belonging; naming and memory show how places have a far deeper meaning than is immediately apparent.

The differences in environmental orientation are marked most profoundly when local attitudes are compared to those of Home Rule. The small community area is lost in the larger map of Greenland. Local hunting grounds become Greenlandic territory and the environment is seen as something to develop in the national interest; the homogenization of the landscape is accompanying the homogenization of Greenlandic society. The political and economic fragility of Greenlandic Home Rule would be ameliorated with the meeting of economic needs ensured by profits from resource harvesting. Dependency on much foreign aid and knowledge would then be reduced.

Seen from this perspective, the environment becomes something with an explicit political and territorial meaning, invested with a degree of authority arrived at through legislation and agreement. In this way, the Home Rule authorities are viewed from the remoter villages as internal colonialists apparently no different from the Danish administration. Their standpoint corresponds to what Brower, in an Alaskan context, calls the White Orientation Mix (1988: 42). The development of the fishing industry, together with the extraction of non-renewable resources is seen 'as an avenue through which to achieve certain national and corporate goals' (ibid). Brower's view of north Alaska is equally valid in a Greenlandic context. His criticism of the White Orientation Mix is directed at southern environmentalist attitudes. Conservation seems to have a sincere concern for wildlife and nature, but the lifeways of people 'are regarded as expendable'. While hunters in Upernavik district may not be threatened with oil development, their way of life faces gradual erosion from a fisheries based five-year plan. It is consideration of this to which I now turn.

Local politics – the Upernavik district development plan

In the spring of 1987 the Upernavik municipal authorities unveiled the *Kommune og Erhervsplan*, a five-year plan to develop the entire district based on the inshore Greenland halibut fishery. I have previously mentioned that seal hunting in Upernavik has become marginal because of the modernization of the rest of Greenland. The present wish to integrate the hunting districts into the economy stems as much from the municipalities, at least in the case of Upernavik, as from the authorities in Nuuk. In Upernavik, Siumut controls the municipal council and continued success in the 1989 local election sealed the party's dominance of the 1980s.

During fieldwork, interviews with representatives of the municipality in Upernavik town, from the mayor downwards, revealed a consensus of opinion that the 'hunting days are over'. The attitude was one that placed the district alongside other hunting societies simply because 'they do not fit the image of the industrialized and increasingly urban world' (Müller-Wille 1987: 355). Instead, the development plan emphasized the huge stocks of fish to be found in the district and encouraged the hunters to travel out into the many inner fjords to exploit these rich areas. The plan concluded with the municipal authority's insistence that fishing was the future for both the town and the ten villages in the district.

In his New Year speech for 1990, broadcast on radio and published in the national newspapers, Prime Minister Jonathan Motzfeldt looked back on the first ten years of Home Rule and re-emphasized the importance of fishing for the country as a whole. The central role of a homogenized Greenlandic culture is often stressed by politicians in such reiteration of the necessity to step up development of the commercial fishing industry. But definitions of culture are broad when placed in the context of political rhetoric. Again, the emerging sense of nationalism implies an articulate, homogeneous Greenlandic community (see Chapter 2) thus obviating recognition of a wider social complexity.

From the perspective of industrial capitalism, given that fishing is a functional component of a modern industrial Greenlandic society, then hunting becomes somewhat anachronistic. This incompatibility is not regarded as a barrier of any particular concern, however. It is only temporary because the relative strength of modernization ensures that the demise of hunting is inexorable. This 'withering away paradigm' (Berge and Piore 1980: 88–9) results in a modern and homogeneous industrial state, when modernity has rendered tradition and local knowledge obsolete. In contemporary Greenland, the idea of an underdeveloped north, compared to a dynamic, modern developed south, is more of a rationale for change than claiming that halibut fishing is necessary in order to nullify the effects of the anti-sealing campaign.

If Upernavik district is regarded as the periphery (with industrial Greenland as the core) then, because of decisions taken at the local level, development and change may be seen as internal rather than intrusive. Such a view would ignore the very diversity within the district itself. The plan for the municipality is very much a part of 'Greenlandization', approved by the Home Rule government which also supports it financially. At the time of fieldwork there was substantial opposition to the plan, particularly from the northern villages of Kullorsuaq and Nuussuaq.

It is important to point out that the majority of people I talked with were not against the idea of development. New housing, a chance to earn money in the fish processing plants, improvements in telecommunications, and so on, are welcomed. But when their homelands are labelled as peripheral and having resources that could benefit others (who, from the villages, are seen to be just as remote as they themselves are seen from the south) then this gives rise to disagreement. The northern settlements have limited and inadequate freezing facilities for the fish they are encouraged to catch, while the municipal authorities are intent on developing more readily profitable areas such as Innaarsuit and Kangersuatsiaq. A question arises, in the mind of the hunter turned fisherman, as to who really benefits from developing the district. Above all, there is concern for the future of subsistence seal hunting.

As well as fish and shrimp processing plants, the plan outlined many other developments. Since 1987 there have been improvements in telecommunications and electricity and most villages have received television. The municipality also wishes to develop tourism, which will be made easier owing to the construction of an airport capable of taking fixed-wing aircraft. Tourism is seen as all the more attractive because of the profit incentive (Upernavik Kommune 1987: 53). However, the plan also stressed the importance of improving health care, particularly the problems of getting emergency cases from distant villages to hospital.

The village of Innaarsuit, however, is seeing the biggest development so far. Situated to the north of Upernavik town, Innaarsuit is growing in population (about 100 in 1988). Recent construction includes a store and warehouse, fuel and water tanks, a small fish processing plant and the store manager's residence. It is hoped that families will move in from the smaller nearby settlements of Naajaat and Tussaaq, attracted by the benefits of a store and the ready supply of drinking water. An important seal hunting area, Innaarsuit also has some of the best fishing grounds in the district. It is a successful model of how the municipal authorities view development of the villages during the early 1990s. By encouraging the depopulation of Naajaat and Tussaaq, however, there is something a little reminiscent of the Danish centralization policy of the 1960s. The euphoria surrounding the opening of the new store in Innaarsuit in 1989, however, ignored one very important fact: in order to develop Innaarsuit, the KNI closed down the store in Tussaaq.

Kangersuatsiaq – a changing village

In Chapter 1, I made an important distinction between 'village' (the physical and administrative place) and 'community' (a complexity of values, ideas, feelings, social relationships, locality and continuity) as used throughout this book. Both structurally and physically, Kangersuatsiaq is changing as a village.

During the period of fieldwork, several major changes took place. In the summer of 1987, the people of Kangersuatsiaq received a new generator, an extension to the pier in order to accommodate larger vessels, and a road was constructed to give access to a new rubbish dump on the far side of the island. There was also one new house built and, shortly before Christmas, an aerial was set up to allow the reception of television. During the autumn, the fish processing plant was constructed on the far side of the harbour. 1988 saw the building of six new houses and the arrival of a Honda All-Terrain Vehicle (ATV) to transport all household rubbish to the dump. The early 1990s are bringing more changes. A road is being built to allow pedestrian and dogsledge access to the fish processing plant, and there are plans to build considerably more houses. The latter will include a large new residence for the KNI store manager. Water needs will also be taken care of with the construction of a tank and treatment works.

In 1987, the arrival of the new KNI store manager (a local man who had been living in Upernavik town) saw an increase in the availability and type of goods. When I arrived in Kangersuatsiaq in the spring of 1987, the store contained basic food staples such as rice, margarine, tea, coffee, and sugar. There was a small selection of non-perishable tinned foodstuffs and very little else. One year later, the store contained the same basic food staples, but people began to experience great difficulty in moving around the aisles with their shopping baskets. Large, expensive bicycles were now propped up against the deep freezers, or were parked rather precariously near shelves upon which marmalade vied for space with CD players and sleek-looking stereo stacks.

Because of the inshore halibut fishery, some people now have surplus cash with which to buy video cassette recorders, televisions and modern music systems. The increasing appearance of such luxury goods reflects the astute and ambitious character of the KNI manager, who makes no secret of his determination to make his store the most profitable in the district outside of the town. Successful application to the KNI for an extension to the store, together with increased warehouse facilities, would be dependent on an expansion in demand for store-bought goods. It says something of the store manager's understanding of how much cash is available among those who are likely to want to spend it, that allows him to capitalize on the seasonal fishery.

Criticism of the KNI manager as 'thinking like a Dane' is not unknown. Although never forcefully expressed, it comes from hunting families still struggling to buy kerosene for heating and food staples to supplement their diet. Income from sealskins does not extend to the purchase of luxuries: the money is needed for items that are often in short supply. During winter, the store runs out of potatoes, margarine and UHT milk, but there is still the possibility of buying a stereo.

The construction of the fish processing plant, however, has had the most immediate impact. It is operated by KTU (Kalaallit Tunisassiorfiat – the processing division of the KNI) and managed by a local man. In addition it employs a total of ten people on a casual basis. Other employment opportunities, apart from full-time positions in the KNI (store, bank and post office), are provided by the municipal council. Such casual work involves the collection and disposal of household rubbish and sewage.

During summer many young people are engaged to maintain and repair footpaths, and to clean up the rubbish hidden for several months by the winter snow.

Increasingly, young people are also taking work away from the village during summer. This is mainly in the fishing industry, particularly on the factory ships operating along the west coast. For most people, summer is the only time when they can earn necessary cash. For many families who have relied on selling sealskins throughout the winter and spring, the summer halibut fishery presents an opportunity to earn a considerable amount of money. Most people move out to camps and the fish are taken back to Kangersuatsiaq for sale to the processing plant.

Hunters are also encouraged to fish for halibut during winter, but there are difficulties in travelling out to the fishing grounds owing to poor sea ice conditions. June and July have traditionally been 'dead' months when there are fewer ringed seals in coastal waters. When shot, those that are around tend to sink before the hunter has a chance to retrieve them. This is because the seals have yet to build up a thicker layer of blubber in preparation for the winter. Fishing takes place at a time of year when hunters need to turn to alternative activities. This is an important point that will be returned to later.

The developments outlined above are resulting in an increased institutionalization of roles. The new generators, to provide electricity for both the village and the processing plant, need to be maintained full time. This is done by a mechanic who originates from Nuuk, but has now settled in Kangersuatsiaq. In addition to the midwife, the catechist and the teacher (who is a Dane), the number of people in regular employment has grown, giving rise to a degree of social stratification.

This is not to suggest that Kangersuatsiaq was previously characterized by complete egalitarianism. There have always been the institutionalized roles of catechist and trade manager since the establishment of Kangersuatsiaq. In addition there are the publicly ascribed statuses of big hunter and *ilisimatooq*, which are based on the recognition of prowess, skill and 'wisdom', though such status is never flaunted by those who have achieved it. Other social categories are based on personal characteristics – jealousy, envy and personal rivalry certainly exist – and social interaction between certain people is minimal as a result. By far the greatest foundations for social polarization, however, are political party allegiance and attitudes towards drinking.

As far as the latter is concerned, about half of the adults in Kangersuatsiaq are members of the temperance movement. Most would argue that alcohol abuse is indicative of life in the towns, the influence of which threatens to affect severely the social fabric of the community. Some fifteen adults are regular drinkers, about five of whom are alcoholics. In the early 1970s, the Kangersuatsiarmiit voted against the sale of alcohol in the store. Since then the only way to acquire it has been through the KNI in Upernavik and individual orders arrive with the supply boat during the summer, or with the helicopter in winter.

A more regular supply of alcohol is favoured in the form of *immiaq*, a home brew beer made from water, yeast and raisins. The temperance movement holds regular meetings and social gatherings, such as bingo and feasts, to celebrate its aims and persistent opposition to drinking. Drinkers, by contrast, tend to drink alone or in small groups of three or four. Consumption of alcohol takes the form of binges and, while drinkers are often the subject of temperance society meetings, conversation is good humoured and loaded with reference to the much maligned position of drinkers in the community.

While this chapter is not concerned with a sociological interpretation of drinking, reference to it illustrates the existence of a polarization between social categories in Kangersuatsiaq. However, this must be contrasted with current developments in the village. As they exist, differences between good hunters and bad hunters, drinkers and non-drinkers, Siumut and Atassut party supporters, the successful and the envious and so on, stand in stark juxtaposition to the kind of social stratification emerging as a result of the institutionalization mentioned above. While present categories are based on differences between people as members of the community, and are in principle fluid, the economic development of the villages is creating categories of people based on authority and lifestyle, categories which are institutionalized and frozen.

Leadership and authority

With the exception of the catechist (and in pre-Christian days the *angakkoq*), the customary Greenlandic hunting society has had no tradition of institutionalized figures of authority. This has changed since the advent of Home Rule, at least in the wider society. But in the hunting districts there is still negative feeling and profound mistrust of the concept of leadership. A consideration of linguistic usage allows a greater understanding of why it holds such a negative position in community cognition.

The Greenlandic word for leader/person in authority/official is *naalagaq*. The word for a manager or foreman, such as those who run the store and the fish processing plant, is *naalagaasaq*. But both words convey a sense of superiority, because they refer to somebody who is of an imperious nature. Anyone felt to be asserting personal superiority is described as *naalagaaniartoq*; 'someone trying to be better than others'. A *naalagaq* is domineering and 'demands obedience' (*naalaqqutooq*), while others are reduced to subservience (*naalagarsiorneq*). Obedience is most often spoken about as a desired trait in children, and in a religious sense it is said to describe how people should react to God. The word for Christian worship is *naalagiarneq*, and when people go to church (*naalagiarpoq*) they are listening to and obeying the word of God. Furthermore, Danes are described as 'demanding obedience' and *naalagaq* was used to categorize colonial administrators and polar explorers who hired Greenlanders as sled drivers and hunters on expeditions. Immediately, it creates a relationship based on superiority–inferiority.

A feeling of egalitarianism is fostered by such central features of community life as illustrated throughout this book. The return of dead relatives as *atsiat*, the sharing of names and feelings of kinship ensure that a strong sense of difference is obviated at most times. The lack of regular interaction between members of the temperance movement and a family of drinkers does not mean gifts of meat will not pass between them, or that mutual aid will be denied to a name-sharer or an *atsiaq*. This is illustrated by Piitaaq's birthday in Chapter 8, for example.

Big hunters do not flaunt their success, but acknowledge the need for meat of those who are less prosperous. When new-born children receive names they are receiving something of the people for whom they are named. It is a matter of individual meaning as to what significance the name has. A person may believe an *atsiaq* is the reincarnation of a loved relative, while for others the *atsiaq* is important as a memory. Several people named after the same *aqqa* all share something of that person and of each other as name-sharers. In turn, they are connected to the family of their *aqqa* and to the families of one another. The name conveys a powerful awareness and feeling of sociability, warmth, security and mutual aid. The emphasis is on similarity and equality, rather than authority and inferiority.

The development of specialized roles in the village has the potential to cause conflict and intrude upon this cultural framework. Some people are now vested with a degree of authority and interact with others on a different level: as employer, KNI/KTU official, patron, broker. They join the catechist, midwife and school leader as representatives of the wider society. In addition, their association with the world beyond Kangersuatsiaq is consolidated by regular interaction with people of authority in Upernavik and other towns. They are set apart from other people in the village because they have a specialized knowledge of things other than hunting and fishing, and are themselves accountable to remote figures of authority.

The catechist is seen in relation to the priest, who is distant and powerful in matters of the spirit; the midwife provides access to the doctor, who as a stranger is both distant and feared; the Danish teacher, himself an outsider, is answerable to the school leader in Upernavik. The store and fish processing plant managers are involved with a wide network of people in the KNI/KTU, representatives of which often visit the village, and the elected members of the village council have a responsibility towards the municipality.

Moreover, all these people interact with Danes who occupy positions in the KNI, education, health services, the municipal council and in construction. They stand apart from most in the community because of their ability to communicate in Danish, which becomes a metaphor of sophistication and modernity. Although West Greenlandic is the official language of Greenland, the presence of Danish is no less obviously felt than in the days before Home Rule. It is a compulsory subject in school and is spoken widely in the large towns of the south, although mainly by young people. Teenagers who go to the boarding school in Upernavik have a chance of succeeding in education only if they have a reasonable knowledge of Danish. Access to the employment market also depends in part on linguistic competence. But a command of Danish cuts across the ethnic divide, which isolates those (both Greenlanders and Danes) who have no knowledge of each others' language.

In Kangersuatsiaq, fluency in Danish accentuates the development of social differentiation. It is also metonymic as it is accompanied by a set of values and norms, and behaviour and lifestyle that differs from those people who are not part of such a group. In comparison to most people, those mentioned above lead private lives, live in the newest and most comfortable houses and work from nine to five. They seldom visit people other than immediate kin and hunting is a weekend activity.

Other members of the community are seen most frequently as clients, customers, worshippers, patients, parents of schoolchildren and as employees. In light of the changes taking place, all this would seem to pose a threat to patterns of interaction and to the idea of community. Indeed, the situation sketched out in this chapter goes some way to contradict the themes of previous chapters. The question that needs to be considered is whether the 'total social person' is in fact incongruent with modernity. This will now be taken up in the next section.

Kangersuatsiaq – a continuing community

The decline of community – early approaches

Anthropological approaches to the study of community can trace a lineage that includes social theorists and thinkers from Adam Smith through to Durkheim and Weber. Seen in terms of industrialization and the division of labour, the small cohesive community is believed to be rendered obsolete by the inexorable path of progress. The influence of evolutionary perspectives led to the sociological analysis of society as an organism. Thus, Smith saw the division of labour as a progressive force necessary for the great improvement of production. However, he saw this progress as having a negative side in that it led to the erosion of social unity. In *The Theory of Moral Sentiments*, Smith presented a proto-Durkheimian view of social unity held together by moral sentiments and sympathy. Developments in the division of labour undermined this and led to a greater inequality.

For Marx, modernization produced a 'specialized man' mutilated by the division of labour which has caused him to become a stranger to himself (*entfremdung*). Instead of work defining and expressing humanity, it only dehumanizes to the point where people no longer recognize themselves in their activities and production. This progression from an non-industrialized society to an industrialized one was seen by social theorists as an elimination of the former by the latter. Tönnies termed this change as one from *Gemeinschaft* to *Gesellschaft*. The original German words are essentially untranslatable, but *Gemeinschaft* refers to a society based on close and harmonious social relations supported by morality, intimacy and sentiment. Juxtaposed to this is *Gesellschaft*, the society of specialized roles and individuality where the person interacts with a wider network of associates. Values, ideas and relationships are personal and distinct and opposed to those that are common to the society of *Gemeinschaft*.

Such nineteenth century theories placed society on a morphological and historical continuum where 'primitive' societies developed into 'higher' societies. The former were seen as internally differentiated into segments of a similar nature with an almost negligible division of labour. The latter were internally differentiated into complex and distinct social institutions with a marked division of labour. Durkheim termed these two stages of the continuum as mechanical and organic solidarity.

Mechanical solidarity is characterized by similarity and the collective conscience. Behaviour is not influenced by individual consciousness but is directed by common beliefs and sentiments that transcend the individual. This contributes to social cohesion and sustains a close-knit communal life. On the other hand, organic solidarity is not based on the similarities between individual members but on heterogeneity. It provides a classic foundation for the functionalist analogy of society as a physical organism. Durkheim, as opposed to Marx, did not see the division of labour and the fragmentation of homogeneity as necessarily disruptive. Instead, he stressed that specialization requires co-operation. The division of labour increases the interdependence of the members of a given society, which forms the basis for organic solidarity, thereby reinforcing social co-operation.

However, specialization entailed the risk of anomie because, being based on self-interest, it undermined the collective conscience and existing moral consensus. For Durkheim, nineteenth century industrial Europe showed disturbing signs of anomie evident in high rates of suicide, marital breakdown and industrial conflict. While Marx proposed the abolition of capitalism as the solution to alienation, Durkheim believed that anomie could be eliminated within the framework of the society that gave rise to it.

By establishing a code of ethics (a new form of moral consensus) to replace self-interest, individuals would be re-integrated into a social solidarity that imposed social controls to counter individualism. This would be achieved through the formation of occupational associations essential for a functional organic solidarity based on professional ethics.

Durkheim's optimistic theory differs from that of Tönnies, who saw the progressive development of individualism (*Gesellschaft*) as negating the original phenomenon of *Gemeinschaft*. For Durkheim, although mechanical solidarity was replaced by organic solidarity, modern industrial society still contained collective activity similar to many small non-industrial societies. Continuing the evolutionary trend, Weber saw contemporary Western society as disenchanted due to rationalization: the deliberate calculation of the means to attain a goal, which had replaced the traditional action (i.e. that based on custom) of small, close-knit, integrated communities. Through calculation, Weber argued, life becomes instrumentalized and loses sentiment and tradition to what is rational.

These theories and later sociological and anthropological works saw the homogeneous community as the natural form of human social association. Furthermore, in the face of modernity community is not given very much chance to survive (Gusfield 1975). The anti-urbanism of the Chicago School regarded the city as the epitome of social disorganization. The greater the move to urbanization, the greater the loss of community (e.g. Redfield 1947). With modern urban society seen as less meaningful the decline of community was necessarily mourned.

The persistence of community

While much work on urbanism as antithetical to the rural used Durkheim's dichotomy, several studies showed the continuation and persistence of communities within the urban setting (e.g. Whyte 1943, Liebow 1967). Recent studies of Britain have also done much to argue this (see Cohen 1986). Even when people migrate from rural areas to urban centres many features of behaviour are retained within a different institutional framework. For example, Lewis's study of migrants to Mexico City showed that family and *compadrazgo* ties were not weakened and found no evidence of a drift to anomie (1973: 125–38).

But while rural communities themselves are modernizing and undergoing profound change there is not necessarily the accompanying decline experienced in some areas (e.g. see Brody 1973). The recent changes in Kangersuatsiaq must not be seen from the perspective of structural determinism, thus implying a severe social fragmentation. The very notion of 'community' as I have used it in the preceding pages rejects an analysis of social structure and institutions in favour of a sense of community as held by its members.

Cohen argues that the persistence and assertion of community is evidence that it has not been rendered obsolete by modernization. By focusing on ways people express how they feel they belong to a community, in particular how they see themselves as differing from other places, he shows how community is a symbolic construct (Cohen 1985). Whatever form it takes, 'community . . . need not therefore be seen as an anachronism in urban-industrial society' (ibid: 117). Cohen's emphasis is on the resilience of community as a co-existing part of a modernizing and industrial society that need not be antithetical to its interests. Rather, it is one of a number of possible 'modalities of behaviour' that 'is simply an example of, what Dumont (1980) calls, "the encompassment of the contrary" in complementary opposition' (ibid). I shall return to the relevance of complementary opposition to the case of Kangersuatsiaq below. The collapse of the geographical boundaries which formerly isolated communities has now resulted in the erection of a symbolic boundary.

Despite its latitudinal position high above the Arctic Circle, Kangersuatsiaq is no longer as isolated as it was in the recent past. During summer and autumn a KNI supply boat calls once a week. In winter and spring, weather permitting, a helicopter arrives once a fortnight. Mail between Upernavik and the rest of the world takes an increasingly shorter time to arrive. The cost of air travel puts other places in Greenland out of the reach of most people, but it is possible to travel to Nuuk relatively easily if one desires. The helicopter means that emergency medical cases can be sent to Denmark quickly and safely.

The enforced isolation of the polar winter seems to be something of the past, as people can, if they have the financial means, leave to visit friends and relatives or return to Kangersuatsiaq for Christmas and Easter holidays. Telephones, TV and video bring the voices of friends and images of the outside world into the living room.

But this does not result in cultural homogeneity. People in Kangersuat-siaq still mock the dialect of Upernavik Kujalleq, and people in Kullor-suaq also tell jokes about 'southerners' (i.e. the Kangersuatsiarmiit). Whatever the sense of emerging nationalism and of a Greenlandic community, people in Kangersuatsiaq still perceive that there is a difference between them and people in other places.

When I was working as a teacher in Kangersuatsiaq, young people told me of their dislike of Upernavik because it was a 'lonely' place where 'every day you ask "who is this face?"'. Teenagers often drop out of the boarding school in the town because of homesickness. This seems to be common to villages in other parts of Greenland where they are not regarded as dropouts, but are welcomed home (Langgaard 1986: 304). Town life is seen as the opposite to the warmth of the community, where everyone has firmly established relationships. Heavy drinking, violence, marital breakdown and Danish values are used as symbols to define places such as Nuuk and Ilulissat, especially by those who have experience of them. While Kangersuatsiaq has its fair share of alcohol abuse it does not involve the violence associated with it in the towns.

Sometimes these negative aspects of urban life intrude in minor ways, but this does not mean they are any the less significant. When Eirik returned to Kangersuatsiaq (see the portrait in Chapter 9) he challenged the established ways of ascribing status to individuals. Following several frustrating months in attempting to live as a hunter, Eirik began to have success in shooting seals. He wasted no time in telling people of his adventures and even began to telephone friends in Nuuk when he returned home from expeditions. After some time, he found his audience at home anything but ready and attentive. The telephone calls to other people became more regular. This would have gone unnoticed if it were not for the fact that Eirik made his calls from the store.

In conversations with his children, friends and his ex-wife, he would describe in detail the routes taken and the number of seals killed. But above all else he took pride in describing himself as a 'big hunter' (*piniartorsuaq*). His father, Josepi, was also regarded as a *piniartorsuaq*, just as several other older men were. The crucial difference, however, is that Eirik was asserting an identity of self-imputed status in direct contravention to the community. As a result, he acquired a reputation as a *naalagaarniartoq* ('someone trying to be better than others').

People in authority, or those who perceive themselves to be different and assert it, pose a possible threat to community organization. In Alaskan Eskimo communities where the young became leaders, conflict arose between them and the older generation of traditional leaders whose positions were based on hunting skills (Hippler 1970). However, in some areas of north Alaska, change was facilitated by a whole set of complex interacting factors which allowed aboriginal patterns of behaviour to exist in a context of southern modernity. Here, the obligations of kinship provided a framework for the unemployed and the unemployable to be supported by the employed (Hippler ibid: 6).

Despite dramatic changes in administration and an increase in relations with the outside world, it is possible that the social patterns found in places such as Kangersuatsiaq can co-exist with those new ones now appearing. In fact, it is the very persistence of these existing social patterns that needs to be considered and understood in order to shed new light on culture change.

On a very general level, it is easy for studies of social change to fall back on empiricism. The changes that took place during my fieldwork, and which will continue to take place, may mean the face of the village is being re-shaped, but the building of a fish plant and the creation of jobs does not necessarily entail a corresponding change in Kangersuatsiaq as a community. Because they reside in the mind, values and beliefs do not disappear with the building of new houses or the execution of a plan to develop the district.

Indeed, this ethnography suggests that names, kinship, sharing and a feeling of community form part of a value system that cannot be underestimated in terms of both its strength and adaptability. While retaining a sense of continuity, their importance lies in their ability to absorb the impact of change and prevent community disorganization.

As far as naming is concerned, I hope to have shown that it conveys a sense of continuity and sociability and that names contain information about individuals and their relationships with others (Goodenough 1965: 275). Given that each person's name is a vital component of a complex pattern of relationships, then it is a vital link in an overall chain of social and psychological support. A change in the name severs the link that gives a sense of identity with others.

Discussing the psychological implications of changes in naming practices in the Canadian Arctic, Williamson says that Inuit lost 'names which were part of their source of integration with the traditional networks' (1988: 250). Contacts with whalers, fur traders and, more significantly, missionaries resulted in the adoption of European names and the rejection of Inuit personal names. For the missionaries, Inuit names were symbols of 'pagan' soul beliefs (Williamson ibid). The result of such changes was a narrow network of personal relationships that 'increasingly isolated the individual Eskimo within his own person' (ibid: 257).

Williamson argues there is little consideration of the damage done to naming patterns within an overall study of psychological problems experienced by Inuit. Integration into the wider society and the loss of identity it entails, together with the adoption of behaviour characteristic of that society, results in very little security and friendship. The loss of an important network of name relationships have implications for social fragmentation together with a damaging effect on the personality. Name change and network loss contribute to a state of anomie (Williamson ibid).

In Greenland there has been a long history of naming using Danish and other European names. The use of first names and patronymic names of non-Inuit origin is now seen as being traditionally Greenlandic. In addition, there is also an established social stratum of influential Greenlandic families that trace ancestry to Danish founding fathers in the eighteenth century.

As I mentioned in Chapter 5, Greenlandic naming also differs from that in Alaska and Canada because there the name is asexual. In the Greenlandic context, there is an institutionalized tradition of a gender-specific, non-Inuit network of names. However, this is not to suggest that names lack any spiritual foundation. They are Christian in the literal sense that missionary activity changed the Inuit names; but the missionaries did not secularize them. In Chapter 5 the contemporary conceptions of the soul were outlined and it was shown how pre-Christian notions were incorporated into the Lutheran context. This syncretism allowed for the continual return of dead people as *atsiat*.

Greenlanders, through their names, do not disappear from the social map at death. They remain part of the community and continue to extend their network of possible social alignments. Thus, a recently deceased person will continue his/her existing relationships through an *atsiaq* and will be linked to the name-sharers and kin of that *atsiaq*. This sense of continuity, together with kinship, provides a secure foundation for the persistence of community. Because both people and places are remembered, these memories carry clues as to the meaning of belonging to a particular community. Indeed, they are the defining components of that community.

Just as names, places, memories and kinship provide continuity, I showed in Chapter 9 how the giving and sharing of meat also stands for the continuity of personal relationships. Somebody who is unable to hunt, or who does not hunt and so has no meat to give or share 'lacks the social and spiritual bonds that make gift giving both necessary and possible' (Fienup-Riordan 1983: 346). So with the increase of wage labour possibilities these bonds may be threatened, not only because of jobs but because of a commercial fishery that brings money, rather than meat into the household.

If, as both Home Rule and the Upernavik municipal authorities hope, more hunters become fishermen, can social relationships and the sense of community continue to find expression and re-affirmation through sharing and gift giving? This question can find only a provisional answer, which is given in the next section. This looks at the nature of the inshore halibut fishery and how local attitudes differ from external developmental aspirations. As will be shown, these local attitudes find expression in, and indeed are founded upon, hunting.

Subsistence hunting, halibut fishing and sustaining community

Fishing communities differ in technological development and technical organization. Along the west coast of Greenland fishing is capital intensive and industrialized. In Upernavik district it is small-scale and lacks the sophisticated technology necessary to make it viable in a way that fits in with the five year development plan. However, fishing is not a new form of activity for the Kangersuatsiarmiit. As a subsistence activity it has always been an important supplement to seal hunting (e.g. Bryder *et al.* 1921). The main species of fish caught have been cod, tom cod, Atlantic salmon and Arctic char. These are all seasonal and, apart from tom cod, are caught for domestic consumption.

Fishing is similar to hunting, or rather it can be said that it is hunting. The fisherman, like the hunter, depends on catching non-domesticated prey. However, the selling of tom cod and Greenland halibut marks off fishing from seal hunting because of the commercial element. Unlike seals, fish became cash-convertible. The reaction to the tinned seal meat factory outlined in the previous chapter was negative precisely because seal hunting has not become secularized, and has not acquired as a rationale a mainly monetary incentive.

In Canada, for example, hunting became secularized because of the relationship with the fur trade. The process was one whereby the original soul belief was eroded and the propitiation of animals became less important. There was a 'commercial and material undermining of the traditional religion, and with it, inevitably, the undermining of the values and beliefs which gave coherence and meaning to the society' (Williamson 1974: 72). In addition, the missionaries aided the fur traders in their attack on the religious beliefs of the Inuit.

In Greenland, while there was intensive missionary activity throughout the eighteenth and nineteenth centuries, the preservation of Inuit culture was of importance to the Danish administration. While there remains respect for the souls of seals, other animals (such as the fox) and birds and fish do not have the same degree of prominence in Inuit thought, however. So, in Kangersuatsiaq, tom cod and Greenland halibut remain outside the sphere of gift giving and the distribution of catch shares. An exception to this is during the winter, when frozen halibut is valued as a source of fresh meat and makes a welcome change from seal. It is also something that is given away occasionally as a gift to those people who do not fish through the ice during February and March.

Because halibut are seen as 'money in the water', there is a difference between how important halibut are seen to be for the Greenlandic economy and for the local household economy. In 1988 the Home Rule authorities purchased 7,787 tons of halibut from inshore fishermen (Statsministeriet 1988). Of this figure, 2,576 tons came from Upernavik district which makes it a prime fishing area for integration into the national infrastructure. However, halibut fishing is more immediately remunerative for the Kangersuatsiarmiit.

The most striking feature of the halibut fishery is that it differs from more capital-intensive fishing, in that men work in pairs and there is minimal investment in equipment. Most use hand-operated lines sunk from fibreglass dinghies and fish for their immediate needs, thus becoming 'money-gatherers'. In the late 1980s, most men who were fishing did so because they needed money for a new house or boat, or a better outboard motor, or because they needed money for the household economy as a supplement to cash received for sealskins.

One hunter, for example, a man in his late thirties, fished for two summers (in 1986–7) and for three weeks in 1988 until he had enough money to build a new house. For the rest of the summer of 1988 he went out hunting only occasionally while he worked on building the house with his two brothers and his sister's husband. When they needed ready cash, his wife took casual work in the fish processing plant and the family lived off store-bought food.

When a man returns from a successful hunt, he gives the seal to his wife or, if unmarried, to his mother or sister. In the same way, women are given money from the inshore fishery. Apart from the purchase of such items as bullets, benzine and nets, it is women who look after household expenditure using cash to ensure the continuity of the household. It is women who take sealskins to the KNI, women who do the shopping at the store, and women who buy kerosene for heating. Seen in terms of the local sphere of consumption, money from the halibut fishery is more immediately important for reproducing the basic viability of the household, rather than the viability of the Greenlandic economy. It must be remembered that the Kangersuatsiarmiit are not experiencing the introduction of cash into a 'traditional' pre-capitalist economy. Since the establishment of Kangersuatsiaq the use of money has resulted in an interpenetration of cash and subsistence sectors in the local economy.

From a Western perspective, money is perceived as socially disruptive, which is why it is seen as an inappropriate gift. For the Kangersuatsiarmiit money is often regarded as an equivalent in kind and is given away regularly as a gift. This is most common on birthdays and is not restricted to a close network of kin. I had been in Kangersuatsiaq only a few weeks before I celebrated my birthday and received several small cash gifts. In turn, I chose to give money on birthdays, confirmations and at Christmas. Meat and fish is not given away on such occasions as gifts are store-bought goods, such as music cassettes, tinned fruit, cigarettes, chocolate, pairs of socks and other items of clothing. Money can be given as a substitute for such gifts.

Money can also be used as a substitute for another type of gift. In 1988, there were signs that some people were beginning to share out money as others would distribute catch shares. One man returned from his first summer working on a ship that processed halibut and held a party in the community hall to which everyone was invited. He spent most of his money on beer, soda pop, cakes, chickens, beef, lamb and cigarettes. All was given away freely and almost everyone attended. The party was similar in feel to a first catch celebration. When another man finished fishing for the summer, he bought presents for the four children who were his brother's *atsiat* and gave gifts of money to the two teenage girls who were named for his mother. Among other examples, people received money gifts from a woman whose husband had enjoyed a successful catch, while I received a gift of a pair of socks from an old man celebrating his son's fishing season.

When people are earning money because of permanent employment gift giving to these people does not stop. In October 1988, a young hunter gave a large share of seal meat to the manager of the fish processing plant, a man whose family enjoys expensive imported lamb and beef from the store. The young hunter gave the meat because the manager was his name-sharer. Another wage earner gives regular gifts of store-bought food to a twenty-three year old woman because she is his daughter's *angerlartoqut*. One of the men with a position in the municipality seldom has time to visit his two older brothers because of work commitments, but will often take seal meat to the house of a three year old named for his dead younger brother.

Gifts of money, like gifts of seal meat, express and cement bonds of kinship and close social association because sharing 'has had long emotional importance for the Eskimo as a vital element in the social organization upon which the survival and perpetuation of the group depends' (Williamson ibid: 30–1). Whatever the form sharing may take, the link between persons and things is, in a Maussian sense inseparable. Money is not necessarily alienable or separable, but because of its value as a gift it can contain an element of the giver. The meaning of money rests on a morality of earning money that informs its subsequent use.

To give money as a gift, or to see it as the equivalent in kind of some other item, contrasts with individual acquisitiveness that is threatening and disruptive. While cash gifts can express bonds of social relatedness, money in itself is essentially transient, that is, until it is made into a gift. Seal meat, whale meat, *mattak* and fish can all be prepared in various ways for storing. In summer meat can be dried; in winter frozen. Money, however, is harder to save. An episode from my fieldwork stands out as symbolic of the transient nature of money, together with the threat money poses to the secure network of kin.

In 1988 Juuna and Eirik decided to fish for the whole summer, instead of helping David to build his new house. Rather, it was Eirik who wanted to earn money, leaving his brother and myself to build the house. In total, Eirik and Juuna earned around 8,000 Dkr and Juuna kept the money in a drawer in his house. Whenever the men returned to Kangersuatsiaq for occasional breaks from fishing, Juuna would join us in building David's new home, while Eirik took the opportunity to travel to Upernavik to buy beer. As the summer went on, it became apparent to Juuna that Eirik was spending the money they were both earning. While David recognized that Juuna needed to earn money so that he could buy himself a boat and a new rifle, he failed to understand Eirik's unwillingness to help with the house. That he was spending the money on alcohol soon became an object of criticism within Kangersuatsiaq, particularly as several others who were building houses were doing so with the help of close male kin.

172

Once, when he returned from Upernavik sporting a black eye and severely bruised face, Eirik could not hide that he had been involved in a fight. By the end of the summer fishing season Eirik had spent all the money that he and Juuna had earned. Eirik's behaviour caused comment because it denied the values of the long-term cultural framework in favour of short-term individuality. While individuality is important, expressed in the return of a person through the name, it is tied to an enduring social order that lays claim to, and ultimately transcends, the individual. In Kangersuatsiaq, despite such isolated episodes threatening to displace collective sentiments, the money economy cannot be separated from the subsistence economy. Cash and subsistence are not juxtaposed but co-exist. The problem arises when there is a conflict over the meaning of money, or over the use to which it is put.

Rather than assuming new developments will transform community life, the focus should be on how the community transforms and absorbs outside influence into its traditional and symbolically constructed network of shared values. While the Kangersuatsiarmiit are increasingly involved in a wider economic system, the values and self-images that make Kangersuatsiaq a community do not easily lend themselves to the emergence of a class structure. They could not provide the basis for heterogeneous economic interests that, in fact, would intrude upon and erode a profound sense of community and cultural identity.

The development of a modern profit–oriented economic system and complex infrastructure can allow existing social patterns to survive. These patterns, founded as they are on a secure underlying framework of shared values, provide a stability that prevents the disorganization of community. This can only happen, however, if the changes now occurring in Upernavik district proceed at a pace that is not so dramatic as to harm relationships that provide this sense of continuity and allow community to persist. Because subsistence hunting is now seen as something that impedes development, a dichotomy is established between the old and the new, the primitive and the modern. But such an opposition is complementary in that each encompasses the other. If a person's son can be their grandfather, or if two non-genealogically related women can be sisters and use the reciprocal terms, then a hunter can also be a fisherman and the manager of a fish-processing plant can be the name-sharer (and equal) of an employee.

The assignment of different roles and kinship terms to the same person does not have to entail any degree of incompatibility. A person, as an *atsiaq*, has a complex range of relationships with which to contend and each is congruent rather than conflicting. A person who believes one thing about an *atsiaq* one day and another the next is likely to baffle the anthropologist who desires interpretation. But the logic of inconsistency is the problem of the ethnographer and the planner and of all those who would seek to understand and judge Inuit culture in terms of their own ethnocentricity.

As the Kangersuatsiarmiit find themselves part of an increasingly complex wider Greenlandic society, it is possible that a sense of community can be sustained through a process of adaptation and the transformation of new things, together with the retention of what already exists. In this way, each person can remain part of an enduring social order that maintains cultural integrity and guards against internal fragmentation.

11

An Arctic homeland in the modern world

As the first Inuit area to have achieved a degree of self-government, Greenland represents a significant opportunity to examine the social, economic and political processes of development and nationalist ideology in the Arctic, and in peripheral regions generally. But as I have tried to show in this book, the fundamental aspects of local organization deserve equal attention, especially as people work out distinctive meanings about Greenlandic identity based on attachment to local communities. The developments taking place in Greenland, however, have to be seen in a wider world context. Because of its colonial and post-colonial history, Greenland remains inextricably linked to Denmark. But, as a Fourth World people, Greenlanders are forging stronger cultural bonds with other Inuit groups in Siberia, Alaska and Canada. The increased emphasis on an export-oriented fishing economy will also tie Greenland to other countries as trade agreements are negotiated and signed.

Greenland's contemporary world profile is highlighted further because of its Arctic location. Throughout the circumpolar north industrial activity and the commercial exploitation of both renewable and non-renewable resources brings with it the real threat of severe environmental damage. This was most recently illustrated in the spring of 1989, when over 10 million gallons of crude oil spilled into Alaska's Prince William Sound from the tanker *Exxon Valdez*, which ran aground because of human error. In the light of the ecological, economic and cultural devastation caused to the area, no one can say that fears of a similar spill elsewhere in the Arctic are unfounded. Furthermore, attention is focused on atmospheric pollution and the effects of global warming because damage caused to the Arctic ozone layer by increased emissions of man-made greenhouse gases, such as methane and carbon dioxide, has a bearing on weather patterns and the environment worldwide.

Obviously, what happens in the Arctic in an economic and environmental sense is the concern of the global community, just as events in the wider world are of concern for the Arctic's indigenous peoples. Too often, however, external ideas of what is right and what is wrong for the Arctic and its people contravene basic human rights and intrude upon Inuit cultural values in negative ways. The designation of wildlife refuges and national parks to safeguard animals and the environment, for example, often restricts the rights of Inuit to hunt in those areas, and anti-sealing campaigns are yet another form of southern, urban-centred cultural imperialism. Because Euro-American multi-national corporations regard the Arctic as a frontier, or as a wilderness, claims can be made that its exploitation is justified. A cursory glance at a map of the Arctic gives an impression of empty spaces, with vast areas of territory named by early explorers who ignored the existence of indigenous names that bind the landscape with human imagination and experience. To name a place in a way that denies the past and present use of the land by indigenous peoples establishes a claim to possession by outside interests, and opens it up to the possibility of resource development.

The values of science and technology that underpin the process of industrialization are essentially distinct from nature. The ideology of progress derives its rationale from the belief that transcending the natural world and re-shaping the environment is for the benefit of humankind. Technological advancement and economic growth gives a false sense of mastery over the environment, separating us even further from the intuitive, spiritual and mythical aspects of human existence. In an increasingly commodity-oriented world, the Arctic, itself viewed as a commodity by those who do not live there, is coming under pressure from the economics of supply and demand, the global hunger for various forms of energy and the further spread of industrial capitalism.

Determined that protection of the Arctic environment and its resources should recognize customary rights and be in accordance with Inuit tradition, the Inuit Circumpolar Conference (ICC) has sought to establish its own Arctic policy for an Inuit homeland that reflects Inuit concerns about future development, together with ethical and practical guidelines for human activity throughout the Arctic. The ICC gives priority to the need to safeguard renewable and non-renewable resources, to preserve and ensure the future of Inuit languages, to develop efficient wildlife management systems, and points out the importance of integrating Inuit cultural values in aspects of economic policy. As indigenous people, Inuit continue to declare that they have a fundamental right to claim the Arctic as their homeland. The extent to which Inuit have utilized vast areas of territory in northern Canada, for example, was well documented in the 1970s by the Inuit Land Use and Occupancy Project. In Chapter 4 of this book, I have discussed the importance of the local environment as a resource base for Inuit in Greenland, and it is clear what an oil spill, or mining activity, or industrial development would mean to all northern indigenous people who have such an immediate and intricate relationship with their physical surroundings. Fears for what the future exploitation of resources on a commercial scale would mean to the environment also induced Inuit throughout the Arctic to establish strategies for self-determination. As has been noted, this resulted in the emergence of Inuit communities and the assertion of ethnic identity.

Dahl (1988) has argued that the shaping of an ethnic identity in Greenland was a consequence of colonialism, but while Canadian Inuit ethnic identity has been strengthened by the claims process, the situation in Greenland is now rather different. The social and economic changes that took place as a result of Danish development policy led to the image of a Greenlandic nation, an Inuit homeland: *Kalaallit Nunaat*, 'the Greenlanders' land'. This image was reinforced by the Danish-speaking Greenlandic elite, who represented all ethnic Greenlanders when demanding Home Rule. Since Home Rule, however, the initial ethnic identity has given way to a political identity informed by a nationalist ideology that no longer plays on ethnicity. Committed to a process of nation-building, Greenlandic Home Rule wishes to develop the economy in terms of Greenlandic conditions and aspirations. But how difficult is it for such development to proceed in accordance with the customary Inuit regulation of relations between the human and natural worlds? There is a danger that the current development strategy will create its own specific problems that are not too dissimilar to those of the post-colonial period in the 1950s, 1960s and 1970s, and which generated the initial antagonism towards the Danish administration. The ideological conflict between commercial fishing and subsistence hunting is one example of this, and it is bound to intensify as localized social economies are gradually integrated into the national infrastructure.

Because industrialized societies provide the model for both the structure of government and economic policies in developing countries, the course of modernization tends to follow that taken by former colonial powers. Furthermore, while developing countries are in their present state of economic disadvantage owing to a colonial history and exploitation by industrial nations, this often consigns them to a continuing situation of dependent development long after independence.

The continued dependence on Denmark and desire for greater autonomy has led Greenland to concentrate on substantial investment in the fishing industry, rather than attempt any broadening of the economy. Sheep farming remains marginal, confined to the southernmost districts, and high extraction costs and declining world prices do not make an expansion of mining for minerals such as lead and zinc viable, although this is not to exclude the possibility of an economic initiative that will encompass non-renewable resources in the future. For the time being, however, the fishing industry, based mainly on cod and shrimp, remains the only profitable economic activity. Furthermore, the current development strategy aims to increase exploitation of the waters in Greenland's 200 mile territorial zone that makes up its primary resource base. This involves the modernization of the fishing fleet, with larger offshore vessels capable of greater capacity, the further development of towns and larger villages, and the construction of modern fish-processing plants. However, there is a need to diversify the catch as the over-reliance on cod and shrimp leaves the fishing industry vulnerable to economic and environmental fluctuations (Poole 1990).

In Greenland, the process of nation-building demands some form of integrated economy and unified identity. But it is often forgotten that it is industrialization that provides the occasion for the growth and spread of nationalism, not the other way around. As Gellner has put it '. . . nationalism is not the awakening of nations to self-consciousness; it invents nations where they do not exist' (1983: 168). Writing on ethnic origins and nationalism, A.D. Smith (1986) regards the nation as a collectivity of shared values that have a mythic quality. In keeping with the idea of myth as a direct expression of its subject matter, myths come into play when rituals, ceremonies, or social and moral rule demands justification. It is the function of myth as charter (Malinowski 1974) that expresses, enhances and codifies belief. As a community with a shared history, culture and territory, the nation defines and reaffirms its own distinctiveness through myth and a variety of cultural symbols that also act to strengthen a feeling of political, economic and social cohesion. In this way, a belief that the nation is the 'natural' form of social organization obscures an understanding and general awareness that it is historically constructed.

Since Home Rule, there has been an emphasis on Greenlandic cultural symbols that are used in defining national identity. Some of these symbols are of shallow historical depth, such as the national flag and the national day, while others, taken from the hunting way of life, signify a cultural heritage that can trace its beginnings to the first human settlement in Greenland, and act to strengthen tradition by expressing common origin and future. The designation of 1987 as the 'Hunter's Year' (*Piniartut Ukiuat*) by the Home Rule authorities, for example, seemed an appraisal and celebration of the past carried through into the present. Yet, in the modern world, hunting is far from being economically lucrative as the Home Rule government has to subsidize the trade in sealskins. It will be difficult for hunting to remain a key value of contemporary Greenlandic society with the promise of untold riches from fishing and the possible future development of oil, minerals and gold.

In places such as Kangersuatsiaq, hunting does remain a definite cultural reality of which development can be a flagrant violation. While seal hunting has vital importance for nutritional and dietary requirements, it cannot be separated from its cultural and social aspects. This is why anti-sealing campaigns and policies of economic development are not so much an attack on the subsistence economy, but are an assault on Inuit culture. For Greenlanders there is a tension of interests as to how to proceed with the process of economic development. There seems no doubt that commercial fishing will continue to be developed in Upernavik district and that the villages will be characterized by a mixed subsistence and wage economy. However, as I have suggested, it is possible that the changes taking place can be incorporated into an existing cultural framework without the ideology of subsistence being replaced by a commodity-oriented economy. One of the most outstanding aspects of

Inuit culture, which I hope to have conveyed, is the emphasis on continuity rather than finality, especially where the person is concerned. Also, kinship is a supreme example of adaptation, allowing for the transformation and establishment of kin ties.

This capacity for adaptation and continuity has also been documented by anthropologists as a powerful feature of many other indigenous societies, particularly hunter-gatherers. It is the ability consciously to select, absorb and use new cultural items that is noteworthy, rather than any indiscriminate and passive acceptance of everything which is introduced from the outside. What is striking about Inuit is a willingness to see potential and possibility in all things; not only in commodities, but in people, kinship, animals and the environment, in imported belief systems and in modern technology. In being re-shaped and modified, new cultural items take on new meanings and, rather than being necessarily disruptive, can actually go some way to convey, express and strengthen fundamental tenets of local unity. Identity cannot be generalized and is not static, but is created and effectively managed through transformation and cultural adaptation in constantly shifting social environments.

In Kangersuatsiaq, individual experience, together with a sense of belonging to a specific locality, informs the idiosyncratic working out and subsequent definition of identity. During my fieldwork, there were signs that the assertion of the importance of community and local identity would be important in the future for a sense of cultural distinctiveness as Greenland strengthens its political and national identity. Indeed it is this assertion, together with ideas about being a 'genuine' Greenlander, that is emerging as a response to development and used in the persuasive maintenance of cultural boundaries. The self-image of village culture is informed by ideas of 'true' culture which, to a large extent, emanate from urban Greenland. But these ideas remain central for a community under threat from 'Greenlandization'. The complexity of different meanings and shared values that remain important at the local level are often ignored by politicians, planners and developers. Because of a tendency to compartmentalize and stereotype, together with the assertion of political and economic strength from the centre, cultural diversity in Greenland is obscured and misrepresented by a nationalist ideology.

In this book I have attempted to give something of a glimpse of life in a contemporary Greenlandic hunting community. During the process of ethnographic writing, anthropologists can never really hope to capture all aspects of another culture, or to even successfully translate a different way of seeing in terms of their own understanding. From the safe distance of scientific objectivity, ethnographic prose can all too often lack the sense of immediacy, the vividness and colour, the texture and the intricacy that is the human experience. In some ways, I regard this book as a progress report, conscious that there is much more to grasp and appreciate than I have written down. There is still so much to learn about how the Kangersuatsiarmiit conceptualize their environment, about how they regard animals, and about the relationships they share with one another.

Yet, on the basis of only a shallow understanding, it is possible to appreciate the value of these things and, on a wider level, to learn from such human knowledge and experience as we reassess our own relationships with the environment and with ourselves. As socio-economic, technological and material changes continue in Greenland and throughout the Arctic, it is my belief that Inuit knowledge about seal hunting and other forms of subsistence, together with what is meant by a sense of community, as described in this book, can inform debates about development. Seal hunting takes place in a specific environment; a seascape that forms part of a larger system of memory, thought and existence. Sealing not only uses this background, it continues to underpin this larger system and acts as a charter for community life. Any threat to seal hunting is a threat to community life, to the relationship of human beings to their environment, to animals and to each other. The continuity of subsistence hunting provides the foundation for a secure kin-based network, for sharing, and for the continuity of both person and community.

In many cases, development denies the rights of the individual, and of the small community caught up in a conflict with national politics or multi-national corporations committed to the pursuit of economic progress. Throughout human history, the colonial encounter, fuelled by the politics of domination and subjugation, has resulted in cultural genocide whenever indigenous peoples have been regarded as being in the way, or morally and culturally inferior, or simply different. It would not be too foolish or extreme to suggest that economic development in Greenland is a form of slow, cultural genocide for the remaining hunting settlements. A way of life is in danger of disappearing because it is perceived as anachronistic and inconsistent with the values of modernity. Again, I have argued that the subsistence culture is resilient enough to withstand the current process of change. Economic development is not wholly incompatible with subsistence in places such as Kangersuatsiaq, provided that government policy recognizes the importance of a sense of locality, and allows people the chance and time to absorb the changes into a customary mode of production and network of values. The experience of cultural innovation and involvement in other systems is overwhelming, however slight.

On a pessimistic note, it may well be that the pace of development will deny the existing social structures of the villages any possibility of adaptation. The future of Kangersuatsiaq and similar communities is even more uncertain owing to policies of centralization that are planned to be implemented throughout the 1990s. There are indications that industrial development and economic investment will be concentrated in the four major centres that are currently experiencing the biggest growth, namely Nuuk, Ilulissat, Sisimiut and Qaqortoq. It is anticipated that the population of these towns will continue to increase at the expense of some outlying settlements, where the population will be allowed to decline and stagnate.

This signals a return to the situation of the 1960s, although it has not yet been made explicitly obvious if certain villages will be starved of investment and social and economic opportunity. It remains, however, that the structure of industrial nations elsewhere is the model for the future development of Greenland. Committed to growth, the expansion of a market economy, and a higher standard of living, the Home Rule authorities now equate political autonomy and cultural survival with financial control, increased productivity, an export economy, urbanization, and the emergence of an entrepreneurial private sector and class structure. The scenario is a future free from grants, subsidies and loans from Denmark and other countries, and the vision is of a highly developed, viable economy run by a people with the organizational skills to look after their own financial interests.

With the current pattern of further urbanization and technological advancement, however, industrialization is redefining the Inuit relationship with the environment, and leaves open the possibility of further individual estrangement and loss of a sense of place, just as the disruptions of the 1960s alienated many people from their kin-based networks and from their relationship with the subsistence economy. As the various chapters of this book illustrate, the present political agenda, with its emphasis on growth and economic progress, is in moral and ideological opposition to the customary ideology of subsistence that characterizes the remaining hunting communities. Although the protection of Inuit culture is an expressed aim of the Home Rule government, there is little to indicate that Inuit cultural values are considered of any significance for guiding and informing the economic policies that are being put into practice.

The problem is one of political, cultural and ideological transitions. In Greenland, Canada and Alaska the self-determination claims process was unavoidably defined within the framework of Euro-American political and legal systems contrary to traditional Inuit systems of egalitarianism. In the modern world, the politics of community consensus have given way to more centralized forms of power that leave no room for previously important aspects of political and cultural organization at the local level. The future is inextricably bound up with this new centralized political structure, but at the cost of losing an intricacy of relationships and connections that define and sustain a unique form of human existence.

The situation in Greenland could have future parallels elsewhere in the Arctic where self-determination is high on the agenda for other indigenous peoples. The achievement of political autonomy carries the real threat that those who set out initially as leaders and representatives for a Native group may eventually distance themselves from wider cultural interests. Already in Alaska, following on from the Alaska Native Claims Settlement Act (ANCSA) of 1971, there are tensions between traditional values and the aspirations of profit-making regional corporations established by the Act. A situation of contested ethnic identities is played out within a context of overall political change and economic development, where kin-based subsistence lifestyles struggle for survival against the onslaught of the industrial world. The Inupiat of Alaska's North Slope are experiencing the cultural upheavals that accompany the multi-billion dollar world of oil, together with the radicalization of a Native elite, and the complexity of relations, values and ambitions that go to make up a stratified and fragmenting society.

Similarly, with the establishment of the Inuvialuit Final Settlement Region in the Mackenzie Delta region of the western Canadian Arctic, and the likelihood of a Nunavut Final Agreement in the eastern Arctic, Canadian Inuit are also finding themselves in a position of having more constitutionally protected rights, together with shares in the profits from resource development and membership in government agencies. However, self-government, multi-million dollar corporations, settlement regions, economic and political development, Native institutions, wildlife boards and policy planning committees, all require organizational and managerial skills, together with high and demanding levels of leadership and authority. Political and cultural autonomy cannot be realized and sustained without this. Moreover, the possibility for internal conflict increases as Native leaders involve themselves further with wider world systems of political organization, economics and jurisdiction.

In a world of commodities and human needs, the Arctic is regarded as a vast storehouse of energy and potential wealth. But one precious resource often overlooked by outside developers is indigenous human knowledge and experience, together with the sense of community people share with each other and with the environment. The cultural values of communities such as Kangersuatsiaq reaffirm the relationship people have with all aspects of existence. In claiming the right to autonomy, Inuit throughout the Arctic have stressed repeatedly the importance of preserving this relationshsip for both present and future generations. The political ideologies Native leaders now espouse, however, are not too dissimilar from the very features of Euro-American culture that brought about the fragmentation of Inuit society during the colonial encounter. As Inuit gain more control over their own lives and lands, it is to be hoped that they do not separate themselves even further from the fundamental cultural values they set out to defend and protect.

References

Alavi, H. 1972 'The State in Post-Colonial Societies: Pakistan and Bangladesh' *New Left Review* 74

Atuagagdliutit/Grønlandsposten Jan. 6th 1977 (from Press Clippings on Greenland, issue no. 21) Feb. 3rd 1977 (from Press Clippings on Greenland, issue no. 21) feature article, November 30th 1983, p34 supplement on Upernavik, March 8th 1989

Baglin, D. and D. Moore 1970 *People of the Dreamtime*. New York: Walker/Weatherhill

Balikci, A. 1970 *The Netsilik Eskimo*. New York: The Natural History Press

———— 1986 'Ethnography and theory in the Canadian Arctic' Paper presented at the annual meeting of the American Anthropological Association, Philadelphia

Basso, K.H. 1984 'Stalking with Stories: Names, Places and Moral Narratives among the Western Apache' in E. Bruner (ed.) *Text Play and Story*. 1983 Proceedings, American Ethnological Society, Washington D.C.

Ben-Dor, S. 1966 *Makkovik: Eskimos and Settlers in a Labrador Community*. St. John's: ISER

Berge, S. and M. Piore 1980 *Dualism and Discontinuity in Industrial Societies*. Cambridge: Cambridge University Press

Berger, P. and T. Luckmann 1984 *The Social Construction of Reality*. Harmondsworth: Penguin

Besson, J. 1979 'Symbolic Aspects of Land Tenure in the Caribbean' in M. Cross and A. Marks (eds) *Peasants, Plantations and Rural Communities in the Caribbean*. University of Surrey: Department of Sociology

Birket-Smith, K. 1924 'Ethnography of the Egedesminde District' *Meddelelser om Grønland* 66

———— 1936 *The Eskimos*. London: Methuen

Boas, F. 1901 'The Eskimo of Baffin Island and Hudson Bay' *American Museum of Natural History Bulletin* vol. 15 part 1

Born, E.W. 1987 'Aspects of Present-Day Maritime Subsistence Hunting in the Thule Area, Northwest Greenland' in L. Hacquebord and R. Vaughan (eds) *Between Greenland and America*. University of Groningen: Arctic Centre

Brice-Bennet, C. 1977 *Our Footprints are Everywhere*. Nain: Labrador Inuit Association

Briggs, J. 1970 *Never in Anger*. Cambridge: Harvard University Press

———— 1979 *Aspects of Inuit Value Socialization*. Ottawa: National Museum of Man

———— 1985 'In Search of Emotional Meaning' Paper presented at the American Anthropological Association Symposium on Psychoanalytic Anthropology, Denver, Colorado

———— 1986 'Expecting the Unexpected: Canadian Inuit training for an Experimental Lifestyle' Paper presented at the Fourth International Conference on Hunting and Gathering Societies, London

References

Brody, H. 1973 *Inishkillane: Change and Decline in the West of Ireland.*
Harmondsworth: Penguin
—— 1975 *The People's Land: Eskimos and Whites in the Eastern Arctic.*
Harmondsworth: Penguin
—— 1983 *Maps and Dreams*. Harmondsworth: Penguin
Brower, W. 1988 'The Conflict between Environmental Orientations in Arctic
Alaska' *Musk-Ox* 36: 40–3
Bryder, H. *et al.* 1921 'Upernavik Distrikt' in 'Grønland i Tohundredaaret for
Hans Egedes Landing' *Meddelelser om Grønland* 60: 430–516
Brøsted, J. 1986 'Territorial Rights in Greenland' *Arctic Anthropology* 23 (1&2),
325–38
Burch Jr, E.S. 1975 *Eskimo Kinsmen: Changing Family Relationships in
Northwest Alaska*. San Francisco: West Publishing Co.
Burghardt, A. 1973 'The Bases of Territorial Claims' *Geographical Review* 63:
225–45
Carmody, D.L. 1981 *The Oldest God: Archaic Religion Yesterday and Today.*
Nashville: Abingdon
Carrithers, M. *et al.* 1985 *The Category of the Person*. Cambridge: Cambridge
University Press
Chance, N. 1990 *The Inupiat and Arctic Alaska*. Fort Worth: Holt, Rinehart
Winston
Cohen, A.P. 1982 *Belonging: Identity and Social Organization in British Rural
Cultures*. Manchester: Manchester University Press
—— 1985 *The Symbolic Construction of Community*. London: Tavistock
—— 1986 *Symbolising Boundaries: Identity and Diversity in British Cultures.*
Manchester: Manchester University Press
—— 1987 *Whalsay: Symbol, Segment and Boundary in a Shetland Island
Community*. Manchester: Manchester University Press
—— 1990 'Rites of Identity, Rights of the Self' Mimeo, Department of Social
Anthropology, University of Edinburgh
Cohen, E. 1976 'Environmental Orientations: a Multi-dimensional approach to
social ecology' *Current Anthropology* 17 (1): 49–70
Cooke, A. 1981 'A Gift Outright: the Exploration of the Canadian Arctic Islands
after 1880' in M. Zaslow (ed.) *A Century of Canada's Arctic Islands 1880–
1980*. Ottawa: Royal Society of Canada
Crantz, D. 1820 *The History of Greenland*. London: Longman
Dahl, J. 1986 'Greenland: Political Structure of Self-Government' *Arctic
Anthropology* 23 (1 & 2): 315–24
—— 1988 'Self-Government, Land Claims and Imagined Inuit Communities'
Folk 30: 73–84
—— 1989 'The integrative and cultural role of hunting and subsistence in
Greenland' *Etudes Inuit Studies* 13 (1): 23–42
Damas, D. 1971 'The Problem of the Eskimo Family' in K. Ishiwaran (ed.) *The
Canadian Family*. Toronto: Holt, Rinehart and Winston
—— 1972 'Central Eskimo Systems of Food Sharing' *Ethnology* 5(2): 220–329
—— 1975 'Three Kinship Systems from the Canadian Arctic' *Arctic
Anthropology* 12 (1): 10–30
Debenham, F. 1942 'Place Names in Polar Regions' *Polar Record* 3 (24): 541–2
Dillard, A. 1974 *Pilgrim at Tinker Creek*. New York: Harper's Magazine Press
Douglas, M. 1963 *The Lele of Kasai*. Oxford: Oxford University Press
—— 1975 *Implicit Meanings*. London: Routledge and Kegan Paul
Dumont, L. 1980 *Homo Hierarchicus*. Chicago: Chicago University Press

Egede, H. 1818 *A Description of Greenland*. Copenhagen: Johan Christoph Groth

Epstein, A.L. 1978 *Ethos and Identity*. London: Tavistock

Evans-Pritchard, E. 1963 *Essays in Social Anthropology*. Glencoe, Illinois: The Free Press

———— 1965 *Theories of Primitive Religion*. New York: Oxford University Press

Faris, J.C. 1973 *Cat Harbour: A Newfoundland Fishing Settlement*. St. John's: ISER

Fienup-Riordan, A. 1983 *The Nelson Island Eskimo: Social Structure and Ritual Distribution*. Anchorage: Alaska Pacific University Press

Firth, R. 1951 *Elements of Social Organization*. London: Watts

Fortes, M. 1975 'Strangers' in Fortes, M. and S. Patterson (eds) *Studies in African Social Anthropology*. London: Academic Press

Freeman, M. (ed.) 1976 *Inuit Land Use and Occupancy Project*. Ottawa: Department of Indian and Northern Affairs

Gad, F. 1973 *The History of Greenland vol. 2*. London: Hurst

———— 1982 *The History of Greenland vol 3*. København: Nyt Nordisk Forlag

Gellner, E. 1983 *Nations and Nationalism*. Oxford: Basil Blackwood

Gessain, R. 1980 'Nom et Reincarnation chez les Ammassalimiut' *Boreales* 15–16

———— 1984 'Dance Masks of Ammassalik' *Arctic Anthropology* 21 (2): 81–107

Goffman, E. 1972 *Relations in Public*. Harmondsworth: Penguin

Goodenough, W. 1965 'Personal Names and Modes of Address in Two Oceanic Societies' in M.E. Spiro (ed.) *Context and Meaning in Cultural Anthropology*. New York: Free Press

Gregory, C. 1982 *Gifts and Commodities*. London: Academic Press

Guemple, D.L. 1965 'Saunik: Name Sharing as a factor governing Eskimo kinship terms' *Ethnology* 4 (3): 323–35

———— 1972 'Kinship and Alliance in Belcher Island Eskimo Society' in D.L. Guemple (ed.) *Alliance in Eskimo Society: Proceedings of the American Ethnological Society, 1971*. Seattle: University of Washington Press

———— 1979a 'Inuit Socialization: a study of children as social actors in an Eskimo community' in K. Ishwaran (ed.) *Childhood and Adolescence in Canada*. Toronto: McGraw-Hill Ryersen

———— 1979b *Inuit Adoption*. Ottawa: National Museum of Man

Gunn, N. 1969 *The Silver Darlings*. London: Faber and Faber

Gusfield, J.R. 1975 *Community*. New York: Harper and Row

Haller, A. 1986 *The Spatial Organization of the Marine Hunting Culture in the Upernavik District, Greenland*. Bamberg: Universitet Bamberg

Hansen, K.T. 1986 'The Tukaq Theatre: a cultural harpoon head' *Arctic Anthropology* 23 (1 & 2): 347–58

Hertz, R. 1960 *Death and the Right Hand*. London: Routledge and Kegan Paul

Hippler, A. 1970 *From Village to Town: an intermediate step in the acculturation of Alaskan Eskimos*. Minneapolis: University of Minnesota

Hobsbawm, E. and T. Ranger (eds) 1983 *The Invention of Tradition*. Cambridge: Cambridge University Press

Hocart, A. 1970 *The Life-Giving Myth and Other Essays*. London: Tavistock

Ingold, T. 1980 *Hunters, Pastoralists and Ranchers* Cambridge: Cambridge University Press

———— 1986 *The Appropriation of Nature*. Manchester: Manchester University Press

Jenness, D. 1967 *Eskimo Administration: IV Greenland*. Arctic Institute of North America Technical Paper 19

Jørgensen, A. *et al.* 1978 'Demographic Studies of Two Villages in the Upernavik

References

District' *Meddelelser om Grønland* 202: 1–20

Kennedy, J. 1982 *Holding the Line*. St. John's: ISER

Kleivan, H. 1969/70 'Culture and Ethnic Identity: on modernization and ethnicity in Greenland' *Folk* 11–12: 209–23

Kleivan, I. 1960 'Mitaartut: Vestiges of the Eskimo Sea-Woman Cult in West Greenland' *Meddelelser om Grønland* 161 (5)

—— 1979 'Studies in the Vocabulary of Greenlandic Translations of the Bible' in B. Basse and K. Jensen (eds) *Eskimo Languages: their Present Day Conditions*. Aarhus: Arkona

Kleivan, I. and B. Sonne 1985 *Eskimos: Greenland and Canada*. Leiden: E.J. Brill

Knuth, E. 1967 'Archaeology of the Musk-Ox Way' *Contributions du Centre d'Etudes Arctiques et Finno-Scandinaves* 5

La Fontaine, J. 1985 'Person and Individual: Some anthropological Reflections' in M. Carrithers *et al.* 1985

Langgaard, P. 1986 'Modernization and Traditional Interpersonal Relations in a small Greenlandic Community: a case study from South Greenland' *Arctic Anthropology* 23 (1 & 2): 299–314

Leach, E. 1961 *Rethinking Anthropology*. London: Athlone Press

LeMouel, J. 1978 '"Ceux des Mouettes". Eskimo Naujamiut' Museum National d'Histoire Naturelle. Institut d'Ethnologies Memoires

Lévi-Strauss, C. 1972 *The Savage Mind*. London: Weidenfeld and Nicholson

Lewis, O. 1973 'Some Perspectives on Urbanization with special reference to Mexico City' in A. Southall (ed.) *Cross-Cultural Studies of Urbanization*. New York: Oxford University Press

Liebow, E. 1967 *Tally's Corner*. Boston: Little, Brown

Lienhardt, G. 1985 'Self: Public, Private. Some Anthropological Representations' in M. Carrithers *et al.* 1985

Lopez, B. 1986 *Arctic Dreams*. London: Macmillan

Lyck, L. 1990 'International involvement, autonomy and sustainable development in the Arctic' *Polar Record* 26 (159): 309–12

Mair, L. 1963 *New Nations*. London: Weidenfeld and Nicholson

Malinowski, B. 1922 *Argonauts of the Western Pacific*. London: Routledge and Kegan Paul

—— 1974 *Magic, Science and Religion and Other Essays*. London Souvenir Press

Markham, A.L. 1894 *The Great Frozen Sea: a personal narrative of the voyage of the 'Alert' during the Arctic Expedition of 1875–6* London: Kegal Paul

Mauss, M. 1966 *The Gift*. London: Routledge and Kegan Paul

—— 1979 *Seasonal Variation of the Eskimo*. London: Routledge and Kegan Paul

—— 1985 'A Category of the Human Mind' in M. Carrithers *et al.* 1985

Mattox, W.G. 1973 'Fishing in West Greenland 1910–1966: the development of a new native industry' *Meddleleser om Grønland* 197 (1)

Muensterberger, W. 1989 'The False Face: Observations on the Reaction to Maskers and Strangers' in L. Bryce Boyer and S.A. Grolnich (eds) *The Psychoanalytic Study of Society 14*. Hillsdale: Analytic Press

Murdoch, G.P. 1949 *Social Structure* New York: Macmillan

Müller-Wille, L. 1987 'Indigenous Peoples, Land-Use Conflicts and Economic Developments in Circumpolar Lands' *Arctic and Alpine Research* 19 (4): 351–56

Nansen, F. 1894 *Eskimo Life*. London: Longmans

Needham, R. 1979 *Symbolic Classification*. Santa Monica: Goodyear

Nelleman, G. 1960 'Mitarneq: a West Greenland Winter Ceremony' *Folk* 2: 100–13

Nelson, R. 1969 *Hunters of the Northern Ice*. Chicago: Chicago University Press
—— 1983 *Make Prayers to the Raven*. Chicago: Chicago University Press

Nooter, G. 1975 'Mitartut: Winter Feast in West Greenland' *Objets et Mondes*, Etes: 159–68

Parry, J. and M. Bloch (eds) 1989 *Money and the Morality of Exchange*. Cambridge: Cambridge University Press

Petersen, R. 1963 'Family Ownership and Right of Disposition' *Folk* 5: 269–81
—— 1965 'Some Regulating Factors in the Hunting Life of Greenlanders' *Folk* 7: 107–24
—— 1989 'Traditional and Present Distribution Channels' in Greenland Subsistence Hunting. Report prepared by the Greenland Home Rule Authorities for the 41st meeting of the International Whaling Commission, San Diego, June, pp 107–116

Plaice, E. 1990 *The Native Game*. St. John's: ISER

Poole, G. 1990 'Fisheries policy and economic development in Greenland in the 1980's' *Polar Record* 26 (157): 109–18

Price, J.A. 1962 Washo Economy. Nevada State Museum Anthropological Papers No. 6

Radcliffe-Brown, A.R. 1940 'On Social Structure' in *Structure and Function in Primitive Society*. London: Cohen and West

Rasmussen, K. 1930 *Intellectual Culture of the Hudson Bay Eskimos*. København: Nordisk Forlag

Redfield, R. 1947 'The Folk Society' *American Journal of Sociology* 52 (4): 293–308

Riches, D. 1982 *Northern Nomadic Hunter Gatherers: a Humanistic Approach*. London: Academic Press

Rink, H.J. 1866 *Eskimoiske Eventyr og Sagn*. København: C.A. Reitzels Boghandel
—— 1875 *Tales and Traditions of the Eskimo*. London: Henry S. King and Co.

Robertson, M. 1984 *The Newfoundland Christmas Mummers' House Visit*. Ottawa: National Museum of Man

Robinson, B.S. 1973 'Elizabethan Society and its Named Places' *Geographical Review* 63: 322–33

Rosaldo, M. 1980 *Knowledge and Passion*. Cambridge: Cambridge University Press

Rosaldo, R. 1984 'Grief and a Headhunter's Rage: on the cultural force of emotions' in E. Bruner (ed.) *Text, Play and Story*. 1983 Proceedings American Ethnological Society, Washington D.C.

Sahlins, M. 1974 *Stone Age Economics*. London: Tavistock

Sandell, H. and B. Sandell 1986 'Kap Hope: a settlement and its resources' *Arctic Anthropology* 23 (1 & 2): 281–98

Schneider, D. 1968 *American Kinship: a Cultural Account*. Englewood Cliffs: Prentice Hall

Simmel, G. 1950 'The Stranger' in K. Wolff (ed.) *The Sociology of George Simmel*. New York: Free Press
—— 1979 *The Philosophy of Money*. London: Routledge and Kegan Paul

Smith, A.D. 1986 *The Ethnic Origin of Nations*. Oxford: Basil Blackwood

Sonne, B. 1986 'Toornaarsuk: an historical proteus' *Arctic Anthropology* 23 (1 & 2): 199: 220

Spencer, R.F. 1959 *The North Alaskan Eskimo: a study in Ecology and Society*.

References

Smithsonian Institution Bureau of American Ethnology Bulletin 171. Washington D.C.: U.S. Government Printing Office
Spier, L. 1925 *The Distribution of Kinship Systems in North America*. University of Washington Publications in Anthropology
Statsministeriet 1988 *Grønland 1987 Arbog*. København: Grønlandsdepartementet
Storr, A. 1988 *Solitude*. London: Flamingo
Søby, R. 1969/70 'The Eskimo Animal Cult' *Folk* 11–12: 43–78
———— 1986 'Angerdlartoqut: the child who has returned home' *Etudes Inuit Studies* 10 (1 & 2): 285–96
Tanner, A. 1979 *Bringing Home Animals*. St. John's: ISER
Tawney, R. 1972 *Religion and the Rise of Capitalism*. Harmondsworth: Penguin
Toelke, B. 1976 'Seeing with a Native Eye: How many sheep will it hold?' in W. Capps (ed.) *Seeing with a Native Eye*. New York: Harper
Tuan, Y.F. 1971 'Geography, Phenomenology and the Study of Human Nature' *Canadian Geographer* 15 (3): 181–92
Turner, V. 1969 *The Ritual Process*. Chicago: Aldine
Upernavik Kommune 1987 *Kommune og Erhervsplan*. Upernavik: Upernavik Kommune
Whyte, W.F. 1943 *Street Corner Society*. Chicago: Chicago University Press
Williamson, R.G. 1974 *Eskimo Underground*. Uppsala: Uppsala Universitet
———— 1988 'Some Aspects of the History of the Eskimo Naming System' *Folk* 30: 245–63
Wilson, G. 1939 *Nyakyusa Conventions of Burial*. Johannesburg: University of Witwatersrand Press
Wilson, G. and M. Wilson 1954 *The Analysis of Social Change*. Cambridge: Cambridge University Press
Woodburn, J. 1968 'Stability and Flexibility in Hadza Residential Groupings' in R. Lee and I. DeVore (eds) *Man the Hunter*. Chicago: Aldine

Select glossary

anersaaq	Breath; the breath soul
angerlartoqut	A child named after its dead sibling
aqqa	A deceased person after whom an atsiaq is named
ateq (pl. atiit)	The name and, in the sense used in this book, the name soul
ateqqaataa	The first new born child to be given a recently deceased person's name
atiik	Name-sharer
atiitsara	'My name-sharer'
atsiaq (pl. atsiat)	A person who is named after a dead person
eqqarleq	Relative (i.e. someone who is not defined as a member of the ilaqutariit)
ilaqutaq	Kinsman
ilaqutariit	Family comprising closely related households
ilisimatooq	Someone with much knowledge/wisdom
isuma	Mind/rationality
kalaaleq	Greenlander/Inuk
kalaallisut	The Greenlandic language
kalaallit	Greenlanders/Inuit
Kalaallit Nunaat	Greenland; The Greenlanders' Land
Kalaaliussuseq	Identity as a Greenlander
kalak	A 'genuine' Greenlander
kiinaq	Face
kiinarpak	Mask; lit. 'over-face'
kiserliorneq	Loneliness
kiserliortoq	Someone who lives in loneliness
mitaarneq	The act or state of being disguised
nalliuttuusaartoq	An atsiaq who celebrates his/her aqqa's birthday
ningeq	Distribution of catch-shares
nuna	Land
peqatigiit	People born the same year
piniarpoq	To hunt, to want
piniartoq	Hunter, 'he wants'
puisi	Seal
qallunaaq	Dane
qivittoq	Mountain wanderer
sila	Weather, the outside, intelligence, consciousness, the universal breath soul
tarneq	The personal soul

Index

adoption 81–2
Alaska 13, 15, 16, 101, 168, 175, 181–2
Alaska Federation of Natives (AFN) 16
Alaskan Native Claims Settlement Act (ANCSA) 16, 181
anger, negative attitudes to 151–2
angerlartoqut 132–4, 172
animal-rights movement 27, 176
animals
   in Inuit thought 25–7, 136–46
   in Western consciousness 25
Arctic, as economic frontier 12–23, 175–82
Arctic Pilot Project 156
Atassut 19, 156
atsiaq 10, 67–9, 71, 86–94, 118–35, 169, 173
authority 162–4
Avanersuaq 22, 24, 57

Balikci, Asen 64, 78
baptism 67–8
barter, with whalers 13
beluga hunting 30, 35, 144
Ben-Dor, Shmuel 8, 113
Berger Inquiry 14
Bering, Vitus 15
Besson, Jean 39
Birket-Smith, K. 63
birth 63–4
birthdays 92, 134–5
Briggs, Jean 74–5
Brower, W. 157
butchering seals 140–1

Canadian Arctic 13, 14, 16, 21, 176, 182
caribou hunting 40, 47, 56
cash gifts 171–2
centralization 19, 180–1

childrearing 69–75
Christianity 15, 17, 60–3
coffin making 107
Cohen, Anthony 8–9, 166
colonial status, abolition of 19
commercialization of hunting 26, 144–6
Committee of Original People's Entitlement (COPE) 16
Common Trading Company 17
community
   perspectives on 164–6
   symbolic construction of 8–10
consumer goods 18, 160
Copper Inuit 147
Crantz, David 62, 63

Dahl, Jens 22, 177
Danes as strangers 102–7, 116
death and outsiders 104–9
development in Greenland 18–20, 155–74, 175–82
diseases, introduced by Europeans 13
dispute, between households 84
doctors, as outsiders 104–7
Durkheim, Emile 28, 164–5
drinking 110, 161–2

ecology 152–4
economic isolation, of Greenland 17–19
education, in Kangersuatsiaq 32
Egede, Hans 17, 61, 62
employment 160–1
environment
   as locality 38–58
   as national territory 157
environmental damage 175, 176
environmental policy 176
ethnic conflicts 1, 19
Exxon Valdez 175

fictive kinship 81–6, 88–93
Fienup-Riordan, Ann 141
first catch celebrations 26, 124–5
fish processing plant 159–60
fishing industry 18–19, 157–9, 170–4,
    177–8
Fortes, M. 60
frontier ideology 12–15, 175–6
funerals 107–9, 120–3
fur trade 13, 14, 18

gas development 14
Gellner, Ernest 22, 178
Gemeinschaft 28, 164–5
'genuine' Greenlanders 146–52
Gesellschaft 164–5
global warming 175
Greenland
    Danish settlement in 17–19, 102–4
    first Inuit settlement in 24
    Home Rule in 1–2, 19–23, 155–7,
        175–82
Greenland Technical Organization
    (GTO) 103, 155
Greenlandic identity 1–2, 20–3,
    146–52, 178–9
Greenlandization 1, 155–7, 178
Guemple, Lee 64, 77, 83, 94

Hadza 153
halibut fishing 32–4, 157–9,
    170–4
Haller, Albert 40, 152, 153
Home Rule Commission 19
Home Rule government, composition
    of 1, 156
hospitality 114–15
Hudson's Bay Company 13, 14
hunting 24–37, 136–40, 144–5
    and new technology 26–7

icescape 41–2
ilisimatooq 7, 73, 161
Ilongot 91
incest taboos 92
industrialization 18–20, 177–82
inferiority, feelings of 105
Ingold, Tim 42, 43
inheritance 44–6, 92
Innaarsuit 159
institutionalization of roles 160, 161,
    162–4

Inuit
    contacts with whalers 13, 15, 17,
        168
    ethnic identity 1, 8, 15–17, 19–23
    self-government 15–23, 175–82
Inuit Ataqatigiit 19
Inuit Circumpolar Conference (ICC)
    20, 21, 176
Inuit languages 11, 176
Inuit Tapirisat of Canada (ITC) 16
Inupiat 15, 181–2
Inuvialuit 14, 16
Inuvialuit Final Agreement 16, 182
isuma 69, 70, 73
Ittoqqortoormiit 22, 24

Jameson Land 156–7
Jenness, Diamond 18
Johanssen, Lars Emil 20
joking with children 74–5

kalaaliussuseq 20
Kalaallisut 1, 11
Kalaallit 11, 21
Kalaallit Niuerfiat (KNI) 24, 26, 103,
    155
Kalaallit Tunisassiorfiat (KTU) 160
Kangersuatsiaq, brief description of
    30–2
Kangersuatsiarmiit 9
Kennedy, John 8
kinship
    and community 76–7, 93–4
    and personal choice 81–6
    Eskimo-type 77–9
    models 77–9
    terminology 79–81
Kongelige Grønlandsk
    Handelskompagni (KGH) 17, 155
Koyukon 38–9
Kullorsuaq 35, 57, 86, 129

land claims 15–17, 39
landscape 38–40
    changing perceptions of 157
    and community boundary 42–7
    Western attitudes to 38–9
Landsting 19
Leach, Edmund 126
leadership 162–4, 168
Leinhardt, G. 65
Levi-Strauss, Claude 79, 87

local politics 157–9
locality 9, 38
loneliness 39, 114, 119, 121, 126,
    127–9, 131
  in landscape 113–14
Lopez, Barry 39
Luther, Martin 61
Lutheranism 60–2

Mackenzie Delta 14
Mackenzie Valley Pipeline 14
maps 47–9
Markham, Albert 30
Marx, Karl 28, 164
marriage 85–6
materialism, negative attitudes
    towards 28
Mauss, Marcel 59–60, 61, 146
meat selling 35, 144–6
meat sharing 141–4, 146–8
mechanical solidarity 28, 165
Melville Bay 29, 57
memoryscape 10, 39
midwife, as intermediary 104–7
mining 14
missionaries 15, 17
Mistassini Cree 138
mitaarneq 110–17
money 26, 28–9, 170–3
Moravians 62, 102
Morgan, Lewis Henry 78
Motzfeldt, Jonathan 158
Muensterberger, W. 116
mumming 110
Murdoch, George 78

name avoidance 68, 81, 87
name sharing 90–3
name soul beliefs 1, 7, 60, 63–5,
    66–7, 81, 88–90
  in East Greenland 81
naming 67–9
  and emotional expression 118–20
Nansen, F. 63
national identity 1–2, 22–3
national symbols 178
nationalism 21, 22, 175, 177–82
Native elites 19, 181–2
Netsilik Inuit 64, 147
New Guinea highlands, kinship in 77
ningeq 143, 153
Norman Wells 14

Nunavut 16, 21, 182
Nuussuaq 30, 35, 86

oil development 14, 15, 16, 156–7
onomastics 49–50
organic solidarity 165
Overseas Countries and Territories
    association status 155

patronymic names 68
Petersen, Robert 54, 153
perceptions of physical environment
person – concept of 59–60, 63–7
personal kindred 82
photography, at graveside 109
place names 49–54
  and power 50
  in storytelling 54–8
play 70–3
political party allegiance 85
progress, ideology of 12, 176
Prudhoe Bay 14, 15, 16

qivittut 56, 112–14

Radcliffe-Brown, A.R. 60
reciprocity 146–8
Rink, H.J. 63
Robinson, B.S. 57
Rosaldo, Michelle 91
Rosaldo, Renato 118–19
Rousseau, J. 17
Russian Orthodox Church 15

Sahlins, Marshal 146
Savissivik 57, 129–30
Schneider, D. 77
sea, prominence of 32, 40–1
sea mammals in Inuit cosmology
    136–9
Sea-Woman 110, 137
seals 32, 139–41
sealskins, sales of 27
seascape 40–1
seasonal round 32–7
secularization of hunting 26, 170
Sermitsiaq 156
Severin, Jacob 17
sexual division of labour 73, 139–41
shamans (angakkut) 17, 54–5
shyness, feelings of
sila 40–1, 69–70, 75

Simmel, G. 105
Siumut 1, 19, 155
Smith, A.D. 178
Smith, Adam 164
Spier, Leslie 78
soul beliefs 62–3, 65–7
strangers 101–2
    as guests 114–17
subsistence 24–9, 32–7
subsistence ideology 25

Tallensi 101
Tasiilaq 22
tenure 42–7
territoriality 42–7
trading economy, in Greenland 18
Tonnies, F. 28, 164–5
Tussaaq 159

Tuan, Y.F. 57

Uummannaq 24, 142
Upernavik 24, 26, 29–30
    development plan 33, 157–9
urban life, attitudes to 151, 167

village life
    appraisal of 21
    self-image 148–52. 167
visiting 106, 108, 114–15

warming of coastal waters 18
Weber, Max 164, 165
whaling industry 13
Williamson, Robert 168

Yup'ik 15